Rethinking Irish History

Rethinking Irish History

Nationalism, Identity and Ideology

Patrick O'Mahony
Lecturer in Sociology, University College Cork, Ireland

and

Gerard Delanty
Professor of Sociology, University of Liverpool, UK

First published in hardcover 1998

First published in paperback 2001 by
PALGRAVE
Houndmills, Basingstoke, Hampshire RG21 6XS and
175 Fifth Avenue, New York, N.Y. 10010
Companies and representatives throughout the world

PALGRAVE is the new global academic imprint of
St. Martin's Press LLC Scholarly and Reference Division and
Palgrave Publishers Ltd (formerly Macmillan Press Ltd).

ISBN 0–333–62797–0 hardback (*outside North America*)
ISBN 0–312–21402–2 hardback (*in North America*)
ISBN 0–333–97110–8 paperback (*worldwide*)

This book is printed on paper suitable for recycling and made from fully managed and sustained forest sources.

A catalogue record for this book is available from the British Library.

The Library of Congress has cataloged the hardcover edition as follows:
O'Mahony, Patrick J.
    Rethinking Irish history: nationalism, identity, and ideology / Patrick O'Mahony and Gerard Delanty.
      p. cm.
    Includes bibliographical references and index.
    ISBN 0–312–21402–2 (cloth)
     1. Ireland—Historiography. 2. Nationalism—Ireland––Historiography. 3. Group Identity—Ireland––Historiography. 4. National characteristics, Irish––Historiography. I. Delanty, Gerard. II. Title.
DA908.O46 1998
305.8'009415—dc21
                                    97–52927

10 9 8 7 6 5 4 3 2 1
10 09 08 07 06 05 04 03 02 01

Printed in Great Britain by Antony Rowe Ltd, Chippenham, Wiltshire

Contents

Preface to the Paperback Edition

Since this book was originally written in 1995/96 much has happened in relation to its central theme of national identity. The Republic of Ireland has experienced an unprecedented wave of economic expansion and, with the resulting material prosperity, a certain cultural self-confidence. An influx of immigrants and asylum-seekers is rapidly changing the country from being predominantly mono-cultural to multi-cultural. The Northern Ireland peace process has continued to ask profound questions of all the major political traditions on the island. The Catholic Church has continued its downwards spiral, a casualty of belated secularisation and the actions of its own clerics.

Notwithstanding these changes, the conservative orientation and implications of Irish national identity, the object of the book's critique, remain in place but under new circumstances. The codes of national identity are becoming re-elaborated in the course of social change and are breeding new reactionary strains, materialist, individualist, xenophobic and racist. The problem of violent nationalism has not been solved. Large-scale emigration was once seen as the central problem of Irish modernity, but today, in a paradoxical reversal of the fortunes of history, immigration into Ireland by asylum-seekers and immigrants has become the focus for a re-nationalisation of identity.

Yet this is not the full story. Nationalism today has lost its monolithic status and will have to live in a plural and culturally uncertain world in which many identities compete with each other. The inter-relation of social change with the dissolution of tradition has also created space for reflection on social, cultural and political differences; a space in which to search for new collective identities. Ireland, for better or worse, is undoubtedly becoming more contemporary, more in line with mainstream European modernity. As it becomes more modern, it enters more and more into an overt phase of crisis and contradiction. In this key respect, the message of the book is as pertinent as ever: the future cannot properly be made until the past is better dealt with. This above all requires the kind of critical reflections that are opened up, with all acknowledgement of possible fallibility, in the pages that follow.

It remains only to remark that the occasion of a paperback has provided the authors with an opportunity to make minor corrections to the text, which otherwise remains unchanged.

Patrick O'Mahony and Gerard Delanty

Acknowledgements

The authors would like to acknowledge the shaping influence of many discussions held with a large variety of friends and colleagues over many years. This group of people are too numerous to mention by name, but they constituted a vibrant community of discussants and influenced many of the ideas contained in the current book.

Specific thanks are due to a group of people who read the current manuscript in draft form and made many helpful comments and suggestions. This group includes, George Boyce, Tracey Skillington, Diarmuid Ó'Catháin, Andy Bielenberg, Mary O'Mahony, Jim Livesey and John Hutchinson. Also specific thanks are due to Marie O'Shea for gathering reading material and drawing attention to critical points.

The authors also wish to express their gratitude to the Centre for European Social Research, University College, Cork, for its contribution of resources for travel and book purchase.

1 Introduction: National Identity and Cultural Contradiction in Twentieth-century Ireland

This book explores the genesis and institutionalisation of the Irish nationalist movement in the Republic of Ireland.[1] It is written with a critical attitude. Critical reflection is indispensable for examining the consequences of previous decisions and actions and for deliberating upon and establishing new goals for society. On the whole, a critical reflective attitude towards tradition has not been widespread in Ireland. Irish identity has appeared fragile, defensive and ultimately dismissive in the face of criticism, though a constant stream of dissatisfaction about Irish life permeates aesthetic, journalistic and everyday communication. This dissatisfaction until recently has failed to manifest itself as a concentrated critique of key aspects of identity and institutional practices. The society has felt afraid of finding problems with itself and of exposing contradictions. This fear is now lifting and this book arrives in a climate of greater openness and deeper reflection. Scandals and crises abound to advance critical tendencies. They arise in areas such as state and business corruption, the exposure of the sexual crimes of clerics and the cruel authoritarianism of church institutions, the revision of abortion law and attitudes under the pressure of events, marital breakdown and the introduction of divorce. Looking across the spectrum of these issues, it is not difficult to see evidence that the single-mindedness of the Irish path through the twentieth century is becoming lost in a moral maze. There is, however, little clarity over what value to attach to what has been lost and uncertainty over how far criticism should be extended. This book argues that criticism of the Irish twentieth century needs to be deeper and more extensive if the society is to establish a more mature basis for its self-understanding and functioning in the new century.

The focus of the book is on the construction and institutional realisation of national identity in the Irish Republic, formerly the

Irish Free State. On the whole it is not concerned with either British 'responsibility' for 'colonial exploitation' or Protestant and Unionist 'intransigence' towards Catholic and Nationalist aspirations or, indeed, with the contemporary conflict in Northern Ireland. While in a longer book the interplay of the different actors' responsibility for prejudice and myopia could be examined, it is assumed in this book that Irish nationalism was sufficiently successful in its goal of achieving national self-determination as to deserve responsibility, positively or negatively, for shaping this century in the southern part of Ireland, allowing of course for the nature of the resources it historically inherited and the continuing affect of events beyond its borders. The 'story line' of this book is therefore the narrative of this nationalism and the national identity it succeeded in institutionalising. It is on this national identity that the book concentrates as it reveals the central backbone of the choices that were made over and beyond those that were 'forced' by existing situations and the logic of events. Irish nationalism on the whole *did* choose the kind of society it wanted, albeit in a conflictual, constrained and uncertain way, and its choices are revealed in the fluctuating fortunes and evolution of its code of national identity.

DEFINING NATIONAL IDENTITY

National identity is the cultural outcome of a discourse of the nation. This identity serves many purposes. Firstly, it provides a sense of collective belonging to a group of people who perceive themselves bonded by common experience, and a reference system for distinguishing one group of people from another. Secondly, it is the basis for deciding who should be allowed to be full and acknowledged citizens of a nation-state. Thirdly, it influences the character and goals of this nation-state in a manner supposed to be in the collective interest of all the people. National identity is located in the space between the collective cultural identity of the nation's people – what they consider themselves to be and desire to become – and the political identity that transfers the substance of cultural identity into values that underpin political activity. It is, therefore, both a cultural and political phenomenon, endlessly translating changes in collective images of desirable ways of living into goals of political life.

No modern society, and still less a modern democracy, can survive with merely one all-encompassing identity. Along with national identity, there exists other collective identities such as class identities, identities held by protest groups, local and regional identities and many others. Yet, national identity claims a kind of universality since everyone in a given nation-state, whether they like to do so or not, is forced to take up a relation to it. Universality is bestowed on national identity through its association with the institutions of the nation-state, the framework of rights and obligations that predominantly decides the nature of modern citizenship. The original construction and constant reconstruction of national identity decides who has a right to be a citizen of the nation-state. Modern citizens of relatively stable states, on the whole, do not have a choice about which nation they belong to. Citizens are mostly through birth ascribed membership of a nation whose rules of membership will already have been historically constructed out of a motley of elements which may have grounds in fact or simply be invented.[2] Criteria for deciding membership include geography, political economy, race, ideas of justice, language, religion, hatred or embracing of modernity, sexuality, desirable political values. The compulsory nature of national identity consists in that citizens have enormous difficulty in opting out of membership of a particular nation when, through the still-dominant form of the nation-state, it continues to regulate their rights, responsibilities and opportunities.

National identity is reproduced in an unstable field situated between cultural discourses of common bonds and practices and political discourses of interests and rights. National *cultural* identity is constructed around values and rules of collective belonging that are embedded in a nation's social institutions, for example, family, religion, education. National *political* identity is built upon the values and rules that guide political practice and institutions. While the two identities cannot be categorically separated, the first is primarily embodied in the cultural traditions and value systems present in social life while the second is built upon civic traditions operating in the political domain. National identity, the product of both these identities yet distinctive in its own right as a set of beliefs and values, therefore has a double reference. On the one hand, it refers to a cultural identity which decides who has the right to belong to a nation, and what belonging means, and, on the other hand, to a political identity which decides what political rights of citizenship such belonging confers. If a given national identity is located within the framework of a democratic constitutional state, then it acquires a quasi-universalist character which is anchored in the, at least, formal constitutional equality of all citizens. This compels discourses of national identity to be discourses that include all citizens, or at least all citizens to whom constitutional equality is extended. Tensions may arise between cultural discourses of the nation and the broader civic values that underpin a shared political culture. If political identity is shaped by cultural discourses of the nation and not by other cultural sources of political values, the introduction or preservation of norms that guarantee the fairness and impartiality of democratic institutions may be threatened. This may arise if shifts in national cultural identity that follow the wishes of a majority are too rapidly institutionalised. In this scenario, the rights of minorities, for example, may be rapidly diminished if a racist and xenophobic cultural attitude becomes widely diffused and politically significant. Hence, though national identity inevitably has a political moment in, for example, setting a value framework for political institutions, the degree to which that moment allows political procedures and values a degree of autonomy from rapid shifts in cultural preferences marks the extent to which discourses of national identity can be distinguished from rights of citizenship (Delanty, 1996c). As we shall attempt to show below, Irish history in the twentieth century has been a witness to the conflict between cultural ideas of the nation and rights of citizenship.

IRISH NATIONAL IDENTITY TODAY

In post-war Western European democracies, where a certain stability existed in the definition of who belonged to the nation in a period of expanding prosperity, the cultural nation code of shared tradition and identification lost ground to the political nation code of citizenship (O'Mahony, 1996). In this context, shaped by the global conflict of the super-powers, national identity was increasingly related to the constitutional frameworks of states. The characteristics that defined common cultural belonging through identification with the nation appeared to fragment and political cultural cleavages within the nation, but not *per se about* the nation, multiplied. While belonging to a nation-state continued to have a cultural moment, this retreated to cultural expressions of everyday life and background premises of institutions. The memory of the Second World War, the rise of the welfare state and the Cold War undoubtedly led to an exhaustion of nationalism as a political force. This situation was different from the inter-war period that had preceded it. In that period, unitary cultural definitions of the nation were on the ascendant, especially in Catholic Europe, leading to increasing authoritarianism, the demise of democratic institutions in many European countries, and the fragmentation of the hitherto existing European state system (Hobsbawm, 1991). It is also different from the present post-Cold War period, characterised by a populist revival where increasing identifications with the nation challenge once more cleavages within the nation. This is manifested not just in the extreme neo-nationalism which has gained ground in Belgium, Germany, Austria and France but in the rise of both a defensive cultural nationalism and xenophobia of which Britain has become a prominent example.

Paradoxically, the emergence of the new nationalism owes a considerable amount to the threat experienced by European nation-states as various forces appear to weaken their dominance as the exclusive organisational model for modern societies. These forces include the emergence of cultural and economic internationalism and the supra-national institutions of the European Union. Their impact is intensified by the complementary difficulties of national welfare capitalism which has left the nation-state without a coherent institutional model. In these circumstances, not just elements on the right but sections of the left too are beginning to mount a politics of cultural defence in which the form of life, and associated rights, established in the nation-state are protected from supranational onslaught. This politics can be discerned over the issue of Europe in Denmark, Norway, France and Britain, and to a lesser, but still significant, extent in most countries of the European Union.

Irish national identity follows a chronology, roughly consistent with the above. In the first instance, the formation of a modern, mass national identity, and its institutionalisation in a nation-state, gained momentum in the late nineteenth century and continued until the late 1950s. In this period, Catholic southern Ireland shared in the cultural anti-modernism and political authoritarianism of much of the Catholic part of Western and Central Europe, including Italy, Spain, Portugal, Hungary and southern Germany though, unlike these other countries, democratic institutions were preserved.[3] In the second phase, which began later in Ireland, and which continues to the present, a gradual shedding of the more extreme versions of anti-modernism came with a slow acceptance of growing secularisation, state welfare provision, sexual liberation, more pronounced individualism. However, in a third phase, which begins somewhere in this second phase and runs alongside it, the international return to explicit themes of the nation is also occurring. This return to the nation has two strands: it has been both backward looking in the sense of seeking a return to the certainties of traditional, Catholic Ireland and also forward looking, accommodating itself somewhat uneasily to social change while seeking to create a new cultural nation-code extending beyond existing institutional frameworks. These two strands are on the whole distinct from one another, their proponents separated by age and worldview though sharing a sense of the worthiness of the nationalist heritage.

As elsewhere in Western Europe, the recent return to nationalist discourse in the Irish Republic has a distinct resonance amongst substantial sections of the population. While the homogeneity of the population, enhanced by strict immigration laws, has until recently excluded the anti-immigrant or anti-asylum sentiments that fuel discourses of the nation elsewhere, and prosperity deriving from European Union membership precludes strong anti-European sentiments, the situation in Northern Ireland, where the Irish government plays an increasing role, has re-opened issues of the membership and extent of the nation which joins with the general uncertainty over identity as the country experiences a painful liberalisation. Uncertainty over what kinds of people should belong and what belonging should mean fuels new cultural discourses of the nation. This is reflected in contemporary Ireland in the way in which a cultural discourse of the nation is ambivalently related to a political discourse of sovereignty. Richard Kearney, writing in *The Irish Times*,[4] claims that it is normal for a society emerging from what he describes as colonial dependence to relate its identity to questions of sovereignty, though obsessions with sovereignty pursued too far are exclusive and distracting. What is now needed, in Kearney's view, are inclusive symbols which could help solve issues of contested sovereignty such as Northern Ireland. What are these inclusive symbols? Kearney answers the question rhetorically: 'Who is not sure of being Irish when Mick Galwey [an Irish rugby player] powers his way over the English line; when Neil Jordan [an Irish film director] scratches his head when he receives an Academy award; when Friel and McGuinness take Broadway by storm; when U2 explodes on to the European stage; when Nuala ni Dhomnaill reads her poems; when Mary Robinson addresses us *as Gaeilge*?'[5]

This text was written as one of a series by various Irish writers in response to an article by Geoffrey Wheatcroft originally published in the *Guardian*, and later in *The Irish Times*,[6] which claimed that the Irish, distinguished only by a waning Catholicism, were becoming more and more similar to the other peoples of the British Isles. Kearney's text is peculiarly representative of the new Irish discourse of the nation which Neil Ascherson[7] describes as 're-inventing', following Kiberd's book, *Inventing Ireland* (1995), an account of the nation-forming cultural inventions of writers and intellectuals.

What is representative in Kearney's text? In the first instance, it stands on its own cultural ground, making statements on Irish identity, and not directly responding to Wheatcroft's original article. The reader is not told of whether Kearney agrees or disagrees with the view that Irish national identity depends on Irish Catholicism, Wheatcroft's main contention. On matters of identity, it might be concluded, 'rational' argumentation on social facts is not so important as creating a new mythos to transcend these facts. Secondly, at the very beginning of the article, Kearney refers to the Irish emerging from 'colonial' dependence' and being right to 'reckon with the plural identities history bestowed on them – Gaelic and Anglo-Irish, Catholic and Protestant, republican and unionist'. In this reading, it appears as if 'post-colonial' Ireland was a clearing-house for difference and what is needed now are symbols of inclusion as carriers of a shift from the politics of sovereignty, in which difference has been played out, to a new identity base for a new politics. Less important, once more, is whether the ideologically charged notion of 'colonial dependence' really does describe pre-Independence Ireland. Whether 'reckoning' with difference is adequate to describe Catholic or Protestant sectarianism, and whether national reflection should really move on so smoothly from consideration of past failures, which has hardly begun, to creating a new basis for symbolic inclusion, which 'transcends' difference is open to question. Thirdly, the items that Kearney instances as a basis for symbolic inclusion are all examples of 'national pride' at which the Irish, the most nationally proud nation in the EU according to recent surveys of European attitudes, excel. But should it be inferred that these symbols of inclusion are a basis for addressing certain concrete problems Kearney instances, such as the absence of participatory democracy at a local level, the problem of poverty, the still continuing problem of clerical dominance of social institutions such as education and health, or above all, the 'clash of sovereignties' in Northern Ireland? Or, instead, do they merely represent rhetorical postures that Irish political figures are all too adept at using to evade addressing just these problems and the Irish public are all too willing to believe (Skillington, 1997)? Finally, it is not clear what the end of the politics of national sovereignty could mean? Kearney suggests a Europe of the Regions but institutionally this is far distant and the territorial importance of the nation-state, while diminishing in certain respects, remains central even if it is correct to understand the Northern Irish case as offering new challenges to the question of sovereignty, though this has much more to do with the tangled politics and culture of Britain and Ireland than with the European Union. In any case the idea of the Europe of the Regions in Irish nationalist discourse is frequently a means of pursuing national sovereignty and is not a postnational position (Delanty, 1996b).

In summary, this text is, in many ways, representative of a new wave of inventing the nation around cultural discourses. What 'we' did about accommodating differences was a natural response given 'our' experience of 'dependent' colonialism. Catholicism is not considered as intrinsic to modern Irish identity.[8] National cultural achievements, such as in sport, music and literature, are taken to have political messages. National cultural identification transcends the state and territoriality. This new nation construction resonates well, especially among a significant section of the relatively young who could not be described as traditionalist conservatives or irredentists. As a discourse of the nation, its oblique form and direct appeal, beyond the apparatus of historical, sociological or political scholarship, to collective aesthetic representations makes it hard to pin down. However, in Ascherson's phrase, it is real enough in its effects, producing a new identifying mythos of collective belonging, bonding the nation with communal and personal horizons, and, in some formulations, attempting to re-mobilise the once powerful presence in collective memory of an heroic view of a national struggle against oppression.[9] In the view of Dunne (1992), this new discourse suggests the emergence of a new cultural nationalism.[10]

The new cultural nationalism is reacting to the decline of the older nationalist discourse that crystallised in the nationalist movement and was institutionalised in the new nation-state, called the

Irish Free State, in the 1920s. The older nationalism had, in its institutional phase, been an unambiguously Catholic-conservative project, as will be outlined in detail later, but one which fed off the residues of a still older republicanism. It has left an evaluative legacy in the form of ideas of the good 'Irish' life that still has a powerful effect on social and political institutions and on personal identity.[11] The new nationalism, operating with different cultural premises, does not wish to discard all of this legacy. Its energy is applied to re-elaborating the cultural code of 'Irishness' in a new way to address new problems. There are two perceived major problem complexes that such a new code should address. The first is that of personal identity. Many who adhere to elements of a new 'pride in being Irish' wish to overcome the distance between different experiences of living in Ireland, especially moral and evaluative differences between urban and rural living. The second is that of creating a new nation code that, in various formulations which are rarely clearly distinguished, either seeks to transcend divided Protestant and Catholic identities or consolidates the cultural-political identity of 'nationalist' Ireland, bridging the identities of the population of the Irish Republic with Northern Catholics.[12]

The intellectual enemy of the new and old nationalism is historical 'revisionism'. Intellectually, revisionism has dominated Irish historical writing since the 1970s. Its first emanation was in the 1930s in the work of the historians T. W. Moody and Robin Dudley Edwards. Their declared aim was to place Irish history-writing on a professional level by making it more research based and methodologically sensitive. Revisionism sought to abandon what were perceived as retrospective accounts of history where earlier events and structures were improperly explained in terms of an assumed inevitable progression to the founding of the nation. It launched an assault on what it saw as myth-making, in particular the nationalist heroic theory of history with its central motif of 'Ireland as victim'. The professionalisation of the writing of Irish history was very much in the same spirit of the early revision of the Whig version of British history. Just as the Whig myth – the idea that British history has been the progressive unfolding of liberty as manifested in parliamentary sovereignty – had been exposed as largely bogus history, Moody and Edwards sought to show that Irish history cannot solely be seen as the struggle of a historical Irish nation to realise itself in a nation-state. Their approach has been broadly reflected in much professional history-writing in subsequent decades.

A second phase of revision began in the 1970s and has continued until the present. Modern revisionism has been encapsulated in the writings of Conor Cruise O'Brien, in particular his *States of Ireland* (1972), in F. S. L. Lyons' *Culture and Anarchy in Ireland, 1890–1937* (1982) and Roy Foster's *Modern Ireland, 1600–1972* (1988). According to a critic of revisionism (Bradshaw, 1994), recent revisionism is characterised by an unjustified scepticism of the Irish 'national past' as the unfolding of an authentic Irish historical community. In his view, as in the opinion of most critics of revisionism, while granting the need to scrutinise unsubstantiated myths, there is some historical substance to the nationalist notion of an immemorial Irish nation struggle to resist foreign invaders. Revisionists, in contrast, prefer to paint a picture of cultural heterogeneity and political ambivalence, emphasising more cultural diversity and internal conflicts within Ireland as reasons for its turbulent history. What irritates those sympathetic to a nationalist interpretation is the revisionist relativisation of notions of 'colonial exploitation' and 'national emancipation'. In the view of Bradshaw (1994), recent revisionists have taken a critical approach to history too far by engaging in unnecessary and iconoclastic demythologisation of national sovereignty, which he argues is both unprofessional and insensitive. Bradshaw wishes to defend a 'holistic' interpretation of history as a counter-revolutionary and stabilising force as well as an important source of identity. Little room is allowed for ambiguity or debate in so far as historical work touches upon issues of national identity.

Irish historical revisionism is more than an intellectual movement. It is associated with those in the Irish Republic who wish to see a new nation code that would build on elements that reflect better what they perceive as the real unfolding of Irish history. Two political and intellectual values propel revisionism, enlightenment rationalism and liberal pluralism. Enlightenment rationalism in the Irish context signifies a respect for the official administrative and political structures and cultures that come from the British tradition and a distrust for what is perceived as a certain primordialism and irresponsibility in Irish nationalism associated with its culture of romantic will that, in revisionist eyes, is always in danger of falling into unnecessary and illegitimate episodes of violence.[13] The second value, liberal pluralism, involves a desire to recognise that the Irish nation-state, internally, must accept cultural heterogeneity and, externally, must understand itself as placed in a larger context and acquire more self-limiting conceptions, especially where the Protestant peoples of Northern Ireland are concerned. Liberal-pluralism also describes the political philosophy of mainstream revisionism, the philosophy of an enlightened and democratic elite seeking to constructively move Irish self-perceptions and practices in a more responsible and secular direction. The political practice of revisionism is therefore to accept constitutional realities and not to play around with the demons of culture. By contrast with revisionism, the new cultural nationalism, like revisionism a loose but identifiable 'discourse coalition', places more faith in symbolic creativity, imagining a new, at least spiritually united, Ireland in which cultural differences would no longer have political implications. The value on which it relies is a romantic notion of national will which attracts support from a wide range of political affiliations, conservatives, social democrats, Green elements and others.

THE FUTURE OF THE PAST IN IRELAND

The Irish past remains potent. The argument between revisionists and the new nationalists is not simply an intellectual controversy about interpretations of history; it is also anchored in everyday consciousness and in political parties. The dominant party, the populist and conservative Fianna Fáil, is mostly associated with the older nationalism. The major political alternative to Fianna Fáil, Fine Gael, which has conservative and liberal wings, is heavily associated with revisionism. The left, small by West European standards, is divided. The bigger party of the left, the Labour Party, which is currently undergoing a revival in its fortunes, contains both revisionist and new nationalist currents, while the other parliamentary party of the left, the Democratic Left, is solidly in the revisionist camp. The Green Party is ambivalent but with strong leanings towards a romantic nationalism. More generally, leftish sub-cultures tend to be strongly nationalist, fusing this with suspicion of the extension of the European Union.

The first phase of conservative Catholic nationalism had vast power in shaping the national institutional order, imposing prescriptive codes governing such spheres as family, public sphere, the economy, education, and art. An inclusive code of national identity, emphasising what the condition of 'being Irish' means and what the society should do to fulfil this condition, provided the symbolic basis for conservative practices. This national identity has dominated the twentieth century. Even in the current phase of de-institutionalisation, it is constantly being re-elaborated. Its continuing influence is related to its importance in legitimating the origins of the state, which occurred in conditions of division, and the persistence of many institutional practices first established at the outset of the state in the 1920s. In everyday and intellectual consciousness, in spite of decades of revisionist-inspired writing, the national movement, and the nation code which resulted from its triumph, is not subject to sustained critique.

This is not to deny that revisionist positions have been partly institutionalised in the cultural self-interpretations of national history. Hutchinson (1996, p. 100) points out how revisionism was spurred by inter-communal violence in Northern Ireland and by a growing disillusionment with the performance of the existing state. The population of the Irish Republic, attested in many opinion polls, on the whole do not regard nationalist political violence in Northern Ireland as legitimate, though a majority continue to hold an 'aspiration' towards an united Ireland. The aspiration is a weak one. In both popular conceptions and in state policies (O'Halloran, 1987) unconditional support for national unity has never been strong. But the rhetoric continues. One of the main political goals of the revision of Irish nationalism has been to demonstrate that nationalist rhetoric matters. It creates a climate inimical to needed cultural and constitutional changes.[14] In its critique of nationalist rhetoric, revisionism has been partly successful. It has contributed to the emergence of a more reflexive relation to national tradition and its claims both within the Irish Republic and towards Northern Ireland. Revisionism has accompanied a period of rapid social change that has, both culturally and politically, moved the country in a pluralist direction.

The new nationalism gains its institutional power from a revitalisation of the still important sense of nationalist identification. The revitalisation, as already examined, marks a new orientation to maintaining an Irish lifestyle and also to the perceived availability of an expanded institutional role for Irish nationalism in the context of events in Northern Ireland that place the problem in a larger British–Irish political context. The new nationalism is disparate and unlikely, by contrast with the older nationalism, to congeal around well-defined themes or a political programme. Yet, it has considerable influence both in promulgating new cultural attitudes and in opposing the revisionist and general cultural dissolution of some of the older themes of national identity.

In this book it is argued, in contrast to the new and old nationalist discourses, that further reflexive scrutiny of the origins and development of Irish nationalism is called for. Neither in revisionist or new nationalist writing, has the central question of the *responsibility* of Irish nationalism for the subsequent history of the Irish nation-state been directly addressed, although some revisionist writing has implicitly commenced the process. This seems curious given the profusion of critical stances on Irish reality emanating from many social democrats, feminists, secularists, liberals and environmentalists on the limitations and contradictions of the society which this nationalism created.[15] The absence of sustained critique can only be explained by the continuing institutional power of conservative-nationalist cultural constructions. National identity in Ireland remains highly dependent on interpretations of the historical necessity of an extreme, conservative nationalism, while the society, separately but ceaselessly, questions its consequences. The conclusion has rarely been drawn that many of the problems that have beset Irish society since the late nineteenth century are to be explained by reference to the goals and prescriptions for the 'good life' contained in a national identity shaped by a conservative nationalism that believed itself to have ultimately succeeded only through violence.

In this situation of contradiction, the time is opportune to re-examine the historical responsibility of Irish nationalism.[16] To achieve this, it is necessary to show how the intervention of the nationalist movement transformed the development path of the society, creating, firstly, new cultural and political identities and, secondly, establishing a nation-state on the basis of these identities. Understanding the identity-forming practices of the movement is critical to understanding in what ways it consciously shaped the development of the society. The formation of a powerful national identity, dominating other identities, determined what the society was able to reflect upon and practically attempt for most of the twentieth century. The national identity of post-Independence Ireland was highly inimical to innovation. Differences within the movement prior to the nation-state, and even more so prior to the second decade of the century, that, under certain circumstances, might have produced a more innovative society were 'resolved' into a Catholic-conservative national identity that incapacitated the search for alternatives and facilitated the evasion of uncomfortable contradictions.[17]

Modern Ireland is still grappling with the legacy of this national movement. One of the principal reasons for the continuing influence of the themes of national identity which it sponsored is the reluctance to critically examine tradition rather than merely live within its shadow. This is manifested in the pervasive anti-intellectualism of the civic culture and the relative absence of theoretically informed critical social science. This is where this book comes in. Drawing on an extensive body of empirical work, it attempts to chart the impact of nationalism on the society's development in order to show the relationship between this movement and the many difficulties of the twentieth century in Ireland. Its viewpoint and *raison d'être* is that so many in a society cannot continuously portray themselves as discontented with their society's institutions – church, educational experience, politics, intellectual life, family – without confronting the reason why these institutions took the form they did. The fact that the politics of identity on the island of Ireland is still so predominantly shaped by an identity cleavage that was instituted in its present form more than a century ago attests to the continuing need to reflect on the consequences of past choices. The logic of conciliation between different expressions of collective identity, within the Irish Republic as well as between Protestants and Catholics, demands that the claims of traditional identities must be continuously examined if the expressions and politics of 'sub-national' identities and interests, in dimensions such as development, social politics, gender, and environment is to move more confidently to centre stage.

2 Nationalism and the Construction of Identity

NATIONALISM AND IDEOLOGY

The introduction presented a picture of an Irish national identity, still strongly influenced by the values of the national movement, continuing to impede the critical reflective capacity of the society. The major intellectual movement, historical revisionism, to have begun the process of questioning the virtues of nationalism – mostly in a highly oblique fashion – has not extended into a reflective and critical social scientific analysis of the function of national identity. Reflection upon identity has been dominated by the humanities with a new 'soft' cultural nationalism inspired more by literature and literary criticism than by history or social science emerging to contest revisionist historical writing.[1] Social science in Ireland has, in the main, not probed beneath the surface of nationalism to examine its role in shaping social and cultural structures. Generally speaking, it has not engaged in the debate over the role of the Irish past in the identity constructs of the present nor in the emerging debate on the sufficiency of these constructs. Without reflection on the historical formation of the identity of the Irish Republic, social science finds itself without the basis for critical engagement with the form of national identity that currently exists or the capacity to argue for new identity orientations.

Critical social science in the Irish context has plenty of objects of criticism at its disposal. While social scientific and historical practitioners tend to disagree amongst themselves on the affects of nationalism on the society, various groups of scholars diagnose that it has been historically afflicted with many social problems that remain acute. These include the subordination of women and the relegation of their concerns to secondary status, risks from environment-threatening dependent development, socio-economic inequalities, low levels of political participation, the low importance attached to the value of individual autonomy in socialisation and education, and clerical domination of key social institutions such as the family, the voluntary sector, education and health. What is noticeable

15

about critical inputs into public debate in Ireland is the general perception that the problems are large and that their scale has something to do with refusing to recognise them. Deliberate non-recognition implies that those forces who do not wish to address problems have the capacity to suppress them.

Social science in Ireland has remained disabled by refusing to programmatically address the issue of ideological power though many kinds of critical commentary in the media and everyday life entail the implicit premise that the power of ideology explains why the subordinated do not address the causes of their subordination. Part of the problem is achieving cultural distance from identifying with the nation. Most social scientists in Ireland writing on issues of identity do not see national identity as a problem. However, willingness to problematise the existing nation-code is a precondition for ideology critique. This book marshals contemporary sociological theory to begin this task. It claims that the form taken by national identity suppressed social and cultural changes that would have historically improved the innovation chances of the society. Today, the lack of critical reflection on this identity continues to frustrate debate and action on issues of material equality, gender, personal autonomy, and democratic participation. Hence, a critique of national identity as ideology is a focal point of our concerns.

The critical theory of ideology has suffered from its use in some forms of Marxism to explain the alleged persistent universality of domination. The concept of ideology in this usage serves to explain already known, general causes of domination which merely require to be located in specific cases. Problems arise if the causes of domination are perceived to be not self-evident and if empirical investigations throw up a wide variety of forms of domination that do not belong on the same functional or moral continuum as, for example, domination of workers, women or animals. Recognition of a wide variety of causes of domination, and of an equally wide variety of symbolic mechanisms of dominating and of resistance to it, points the theory of ideology in a more fluid and open direction. Control over the interpretation of situations is a resource, subject to endless configurations, for establishing relations of domination. While truth still remains in the Marxist assumption that structural inequalities *are related to* cultural interpretation systems that defend these inequalities and that are accepted by the dominated, it is not sufficient to suppose that structural inequalities will *explain* cultural interpretations. In any given case, actors will not simply understand their structural position through cultural models, they will also attach value to these cultural models themselves. However, the stated or implied preferences of actors for the continuation of a given state of affairs which a commentator, animated by the perception of possible alternatives, may not believe to be in their ideal or material interests, does not mean that explaining the formation of these preferences as a product of ideology has to be abandoned. In the instance where structural change is believed to be feasible but does not occur, ideological constructs serve to prevent the crystallisation of alternative perceptions of situations by those who, if equipped with reliable knowledge on such alternatives, might do something to bring them about. In the instance where structural changes are perceived, at least in outline form, but not deemed desirable by subordinated actors, ideology can still be held to work if preferences can be shown to be products of structurally constrained deliberation processes as, for example, censorship, authoritarianism, denial of information, and unequal access to education. These two cases are, of course, only idealtypically separated as they are often present together. In the case of national identity they are constitutively bound up with one another.

A number of further theoretical points require to be kept in mind when considering ideology. Firstly, differentials of power are intrinsic to the role of ideology. Cultural projections that legitimate, dissimulate or naturalise domination depend on institutional power for their effectiveness (Thompson, 1984). Institutional power guarantees that the statements or actions that are consistent with institutionally embedded sets of material or ideal interests have greater impact than less embedded sets. In a society, like mid-century Ireland, that placed relatively low value on material progress as against spiritual purity, those who argued for giving greater priority to economic progress or to secularisation had a hard time, notwithstanding the fact that, from a broader standpoint, they represented perhaps the pivotal value of modern society, the desirability of rapid economic growth. Secondly, ideologies have to be understood in a temporal frame. They have to be shown to be functional over time for the maintenance of a state of affairs that consistently benefits clearly defined interests. They are not simply a short-run product of conflict; they have to be institutionally embedded in stable configurations of meaning and of interests. Thirdly, ideologies are not merely instances of the projection of one group's power over another. They can also be collective illusions shared by all or nearly all, such as a myth of power where a nation-state is presumed, against all odds, to be capable of something it manifestly is not, as, for example, military conquest. Finally, ideologies are mostly not a cynical ploy to dupe other interests. In whole, or in substantial part, they are believed by their proponents. The presence of an ideology cannot simply be deciphered from manifest statements. It has to be related to institutional arrangements that, over time, select one set of interests as valid and another as not. Ideologies are collective representations that produce certain outcomes even when the relationship between agency, representations and outcomes is indirect. For example, few today would consciously support poverty as a virtue but poverty can be a necessary outcome of material inequality and accepted by those who defend inequality while not desiring poverty.

IDEOLOGY AND ATTRIBUTING RESPONSIBILITY

The introduction outlined the need to address the central issue of the responsibility of nationalism for the establishment of a Catholic-conservative social order in twentieth century Ireland. To speak of 'responsibility' does not, in the first instance, imply a critical position. While this book is highly critical of the historical and continuing impact of the outcomes of the national movement, a 'first-order' concept of responsibility is required that establishes *how* the national movement produced a Catholic-conservatism institutional order in spite of the fact that other, more radical currents were implicated in the process at all phases from mobilisation, through institutionalisation up to the present phase of tentative de-institutionalisation. However, a 'second-order' concept of responsibility is also present in representing the actual outcomes of Irish nationalism in the Irish Republic as *inimical to certain values* adjudged by the authors, and many liberal and critical currents within the society, to be desirable, such as, equality, autonomy, participation, and secularism. The second-order responsibility of Irish nationalism was to deny these values in twentieth century Ireland in, on the whole, a conscious and articulated manner. A defence of the societal implications of Irish nationalism cannot therefore be based on these values.

The issue of the attribution of responsibility fuses with the need for ideology-critique. The institutional order in twentieth century

Ireland did not simply happen. It was produced and maintained by social and cultural interests who defended it resolutely in the period of its hegemony. Now, in the era of its institutional decline, a positive view of the importance for collective memory of the Irish nationalism that produced it, if not always the values that followed, continues to be put forward. The earlier form of defence was a form of ideology that was underpinned by clear, unashamed material and symbolic interests. The later defence associated with the new cultural nationalism, while in some forms a kind of explicit ideology, takes more the form of a shield against ideology-critique. In these circumstances, ideology perpetuates itself. The critique of a conservative institutional order is blocked by the continuing legitimacy of its model of the past.

To undo this ideological confinement, and to establish a new basis for societal self-reflection and social change, the historical genesis of Irish nationalist identity and its reconstruction of the institutional order in the nation-state must be addressed. In this reconstruction, the absorption of socially radical currents, present in the earlier part of the movement, by a conservative model of national identity, will be documented. This requires that the context of mobilisation of the national movement in the pre-Independence institutional order, the forms of mobilisation and the phases of mobilisation need to be analysed to show how, over nearly a fifty-year period, the most conservative forces came to be dominant. Their dominance was then translated into the institutionalisation of Catholic-conservative values across the whole of society with the formation of the nation-state.

The variant on nationalist ideology that evolved in Ireland can be described as a communitarian-populist interpretation of classical republicanism. Republicanism, as an Enlightenment doctrine of popular sovereignty, stood for a strong sense of civil and constitutional government, the separation of church and state, opposition to monarchical despotism, the separation of powers, and the autonomy of civil society against the intrusion of the state. The idea of the nation emanating from a republican political philosophy was one of popular sovereignty and the ideal of a shared political culture based on universal citizenship. The republican idea is that sovereignty resides in society and not in the state. It did not have a territorial or geo-political reference point. Its origin lies in the Rousseauean notion of the 'social contract' residing in the 'general will'. The republican heritage became the basis of French and

American concepts of the nation, which was in these cases codified in civil constitutions. Amongst Irish Catholics, by contrast, from the late eighteenth century, republicanism was codified in a cultural form. The political community was defined more by reference to an integrated, excluded culture – Irish Catholics – than by reference to notions of civil society. Popular sovereignty issued in a culturally diffuse legitimation politics rather than one clearly anchored in rights of citizenship.[2]

In the remainder of this chapter, with a view to establishing a set of tools to examine critically Irish nationalist ideology, theoretical relationships between ideology, nationalist mobilisation and the construction of national identity are explored. Our approach is based on the insight that national movements can be analysed as producers of identity. This identity in the mobilisation phase is not a single identity but is differently articulated across various currents within the movement. In the subsequent section, we will also address how the symbolic outcomes of mobilisation are institutionalised as national identity if a separate nation-state is established and how, in this process, national identity acquires an ideological function.

NATIONALISM AS SYMBOLIC MOBILISATION

A sociologist of the new social movements, Karl-Werner Brand (1992), in a short but useful essay, addresses the task of showing how a constructivist mode of analysis may be built into theoretical frameworks for researching nationalism. The challenge, as taken up by Brand, is the development of a new theoretical perspective on the social construction of nationalist collective identities. The social construction of an identity involves the recognition that identities do not simply happen but are consciously created in communication processes. Phenomena constructed through communication may be real. For example, the social construction of injustice may reflect real injustice. On the other hand, they may be largely imaginary. Perceptions of injustice may not correspond with real injustice. The point is, however, whether they describe actual states of affairs or otherwise, social constructions have real consequences. People believe constructed phenomena when they acquire social legitimacy.

According to Brand, constructed concepts are used by social actors to make sense of collective interests. For example, nationalism is often used to develop an argument that some are economically exploited on ethnic grounds and those who are exploited have an interest in changing the social order. However, Brand is of the view that the analysis of such symbolic constructions of interests cannot by themselves indicate under *which conditions* collective interests come to be 'successfully' addressed through specifically nationalist constructions. For this task, structuralist or social interest approaches remain useful. Such approaches relate nationalist mobilisation variously to the consequences of industrialisation and modernisation, to processes of uneven modernisation, or to correlations between inequality and ethnic-cultural differentiation (Gellner, 1983; Rokowski, 1985). Social groups struggle to defend or improve resources, mechanisms of power and life-chances for their own against real or perceived threats and *sometimes* have recourse to nationalist constructions to illustrate problems they experience and to set new goals. Conversely, the social interest approach cannot provide a satisfactory explanation for nationalist mobilisation on its own either since interest conflicts have *to be interpreted through cultural models.*[3]

The decisive question, combining social interest and constructivist approaches, is under which conditions nationalist interpretation models, attempting to 'make sense' of given situations, acquire societal validity? Brand answers this question by a supply–demand account of the semantics used by various actors during mobilisation. Actors strive to make sense of the play of interests and values in their messages and over time these messages 'resonate' amongst interested audiences to a greater or lesser extent. The degree of resonance depends upon the success of the message in capturing and creating realities. More successful messages build a rapport between cultural producers and their audiences that over time acquires stability. The acquisition of stability is the precondition for establishing a collective identity through which actors categorise their 'true' interests and according plan for the future.

Applying this approach in the analysis conducted in the remainder of the book leads to the examination of the identities projected by various elements within the national movement against the background of their distinctive interests and the societal resonance of their messages. These projected identities, 'identity projects' are constructed in a 'relational field' which is created when groups with complementary or opposing projects mobilise to win support for their view of the world. The relational field of Irish nationalism is the space in which different elements of the movement play out their complementarities and differences before a participating mass audience. In this space, the elements of the movement influence one another's symbolic goals and strategies. Identities become re-shaped when proponents are forced to address new cultural circumstances such as the popularity of another actor's messages or structural circumstances such as increased or decreased prosperity or the outbreak of war. Identity is less a resource that is already there than a product of the dynamics of political mobilisation. The most important identity formulations of Irish nationalism did not precede the mass mobilisation of the late nineteenth century, they were created during the long mobilisation itself.

In the remainder of this section, prefiguring the analysis to follow in Chapters 3 to 5, structural and constructivist approaches are combined to propose a strategy for the analysis of nationalist mobilisation unfolding in three steps. The first step is to provide a contextual account of the long-run structures that condition certain kinds of mobilisation. The second step introduces a differentiated account of mobilisation actors showing how mobilisation 'wings' build from situations and construct identity projects and mobilisation strategies. The third step shows how mobilisation wings experience alignment or disalignment depending on their own actions and on the political and cultural opportunities for their policies and messages.

(1) The Context of National Mobilisation

A contemporary account of the contexts of peripheral nationalist movements is provided by Hooghe (1992). Like Gellner, Hooghe claims that modernisation is at the origins of nationalism. She defines modernisation as processes of social mobilisation, cultural standardisation and growing political participation. Modernisation causes social dislocation in the state which a social category, with a distinctive peripheral culture and resources, will perceive as unfair.[4] They will then express their grievances in a manner which leads the aggrieved community to blame the existing state and to mobilise against it in favour of greater autonomy. A nationalist movement thus takes off in the periphery.

Actors on the periphery are conditioned in their mobilisation by the level of modernisation in which they find themselves though they may deliberately or unconsciously refuse to recognise it. Such refusal is typical of what Tiryakian and Nevitte (1985) describe in their typology of nationalisms as anti-modern nationalisms of the periphery that retreat from modernity and of which Irish nationalism is a prime example.

In charting the contextual conditions that determine a transformative episode of action such as a nationalist mobilisation, an adequate understanding of both structural conditions and the contingent-historical societal situation through which structures are changed is necessary. The analysis of structural conditions as they have historically evolved has a threefold function. Firstly, it embeds the movement analysis in longer run variables clarifying basic questions about the nature of the mobilisation. Secondly, structural analysis provides a benchmark for assessing what a movement is reacting against and therefore trying to achieve. Thirdly, in assessing the outcomes of a movement it allows comparison between the state of society after the mobilisation with that before.

Contingent-historical factors such as wars, demographic shifts, international economic shifts, international cultural movements bring out contradictions in societal development that sometimes release the immanent, but hitherto unformulated, resolve of actors to take control of the modernisation process in their own interest. Not alone the will and the capacity to mobilise but the actual character of mobilisation may substantially depend on the logic of events. As we shall see later, the effect of the First World War on Irish nationalist mobilisation was profound, leading to the formulation of more radical goals than those that had been hitherto formulated and changing the balance of power between the nationalist actors.

(2) The Character of Nationalist Mobilisations

Nationalist mobilisations are very rarely unitary. They are characterised by a range of actor wings that take up distinctive positions within the overall mobilisation and, depending on a variety of factors, succeed or fail to gain a dominant position. In his study of European smaller-country nationalisms Hroch (1985 and 1993) identifies three vertical time periods and four typical fractions in nationalist mobilisations. The temporal distinctions are, firstly, the initial scholarly interest in the nation's history and culture towards the end of the eighteenth century; secondly, an active avant-garde with considerable societal impact by the middle of the nineteenth century; and, thirdly, the mass movement proper which tended to take off towards the end of the nineteenth century. In the mass movement phase, nationalist mobilisations can be sub-divided into various wings; clerical-conservative, liberal democratic, socialist and revolutionary. Each of these wings spring from recognisably different social situations, are the bearers of distinctive identity projects, and develop political strategies to realise their aims. The rise to political prominence of a range of nationalist actors, who adopt rapidly shifting positions towards one another in an often volatile situation, has a transformative effect on the 'relational field' of politics. The nationalist mobilisation may develop either or both antagonistic and accommodating relationships to the existing state whose legitimation it is, more or less fundamentally, seeking to erode or destroy. The mobilisation is often opposed by a counter-movement which, for a large variety of possible reasons, is diametrically opposed to its aims. The interplay between the mobilisation 'fractions' which we equate with Hroch's 'wings', the counter-movement which may also be broken into fractions, and the state authorities, constitutes the relational field of nationalist identity politics which, depending on the degree of success of the mobilisation and its principal objective, may work to create a crisis of legitimation that might ultimately lead to a regime crisis and regime transformation.[5]

Each of the wings of the movement needs to be understood within their *situation* which is the provided by the framework of social interests that animates the wing's mobilisation. Charting the situation of each of the movement wings places it in relation to processes of social change such as growing complexity following differentiation of social spheres and the stratification of social classes and the emergence of new kinds of social interest. In Greenfeld's (1992) Durkheimian term, structural factors such as differentiation and stratification lead to the production of 'anomie', a situation characterised by the absence of integrating, consensual norms in society as a whole. The existence of anomie is a precipitating condition for the emergence of a mobilisation goal of sufficient magnitude amongst a distinctive class of agents. In response, these agents may employ nationalist categories to make sense of their situation. They develop an *identity project* consistent with their situation which they project as an idea of the future nation. In this project, they seek to generalise their situation and endow it with appeal to a large section of the population. This requires that concepts of *identification*, based on the real or imagined values of the 'national' community to whom they appeal, and of *distinction*, the ways in which this national community is different from existing elites or other groups, need to be developed. In order to gain legitimacy for their identity projects *mobilisation strategies* are required that plant this project in the public sphere of cultural and political communication. It is therefore expressed as themes which have 'public resonance' in an emerging nationalist public culture and which draw their motive force from the social-psychological feelings of common experience (Brand, 1992).

The relational field of nationalist identity politics is constructed within an institutional framework established by the existing state. Domination of the state is the ultimate goal of radical nationalist mobilisations. Secessionist nationalist mobilisations presuppose that the existing state is unsatisfactory in that it acts against the cultural, economic, or social interests of groups in the society. It is represented as an instrument of domination against a specifically defined nationalist 'people' who are seen as 'the bearer of sovereignty, the central object of loyalty, and the basis of collective solidarity' (Greenfeld, 1992, p. 3). The state is thus embroiled in a continuous legitimation politics and tries to develop assimilative and containing strategies that keep protest within the bounds of convention both in terms of issues and strategies. The state attempts to keep politics within the spectrum of reform rather than revolution.

(3) Opportunity Structures and Identity Politics

The concept of opportunity structures, following Kitschelt's (1986) seminal article, has become very influential and has been used in three different dimensions; as political opportunity structures in the sense introduced by Kitschelt, as cultural opportunity structures for nationalist identity mobilisation in Brand (1992), and social opportunity structures as described by Eder (1993) when describing class as an opportunity structure for collective action. In our approach, social opportunity structures appear as input conditions to mobilisation and are part of a given wing's situation, while a combination of political and cultural opportunity structures appear as contextual conditions that determines a wing's identity project and political strategy. The idea of political, cultural and social opportunity structures, explicitly or implicitly, is becoming commonplace in literature on nationalism (Hooghe, 1992; Brand 1992). The concept is used to describe the institutional conditions that offer opportunities or barriers to the realisation of movements' goals. The concept is used in this book in two ways; firstly, it is used to show how different wings of the movement were assisted or inhibited by the institutional framework of the state in the mobilisation phase and, secondly, it is used to show how the wings of the movement ultimately sought to change the institutional framework to provide long-run, favourable opportunity structures for themselves.

Nationalism is above all a cultural mobilisation in the sense of a social group or groups envisaging a new ethical code consistent with their cultural identity. A movement identity becomes a societal ethical code if the movement gains institutional power and is in a position to transform its identity code into an ethical code binding on other actors. Movement wings in the mobilisation phase carry prospective ethical codes within their identity projects. Their goal is the institutionalisation of a national identity project spanning culture and politics which is consistent with the preferences of their constituency.

The cultural and political opportunity structures which appears in our view to be most relevant to analysing the mobilisation of the varied wings of nationalist movements are as follows:

(a) *Institutional access to state and public sphere*: this deals, on the one hand, following Kitschelt (1986) with the relations that a movement wing has with the state authorities (whether the door of public authority was open to its influence, whether it had a direct political role) and, on the other hand, whether it has influence on key agencies in the public sphere such as intellectuals or the media.

(b) *Openness of public sphere to its messages*: this opportunity structure assesses the conditions of reception in the society for actors' messages and identity mobilising strategies.

(c) *Receptivity of other movement wings to a wing's message*: this opportunity structure is generated by the capacity of movement wings to have their identity project absorbed by other wings or by the power of other movement wings to oppose their identity project. The existence of overlapping projects and common strategies may lead to the formation of 'discourse coalitions' where movement wings unite behind common programmes leading to the formation of a consensus movement and a master frame of identity.

The analysis of the mobilisation phase of Irish nationalism to be found in this book begins by outlining the general historical and long-run societal context. It then identifies the key wings of the late nineteenth century movement and sets them in this long-run context. It then proceeds to describe the identity project developed by these wings within the given opportunity structures in which they found themselves and how they developed programmes to improve these opportunities in their own interest. Finally, it considers how the wings of the movement progressed over time to a consensus position unified by the goal of national self-determination which relatively quickly issued in the foundation of a nation-state.

FROM MOVEMENT IDENTITY TO NATION-STATE: THE INSTITUTIONALISATION OF NATIONAL IDENTITY

A successful separatist nationalist mobilisation leads to the establishment of a nation-state and a new institutional framework. This institutional framework is heavily influenced by the manner in which a consensus identity across the wings of the national movement that takes place over the life span of the mobilisation. The establishment of state institutions places the movement in a position of dominance. Eder (1985) points to the central significance of the institutional framework for modern society as it offers the capacity to regulate the mobilisation of interests within an institutional order. The establishment of the nation-state involves the construction of a new institutional order responding to a new canon of interests associated with the nationalist movement. Institutional frameworks have to be made recognisable, operative, and legitimate to those who are affected by them. They are therefore embedded in a cultural order that provides sufficiently abstract points of reference for guiding action. Whoever defines this order also gets the chance to specify the institutional rules that should be followed.

National identity represents a major component of the cultural order used in regulating the institutional framework. National identity is especially powerful after a successful mobilisation. It functions as a kind of general will and it points the institutional framework in a more or less populistic direction, depending on the nature and strength of the claim to an identity of interests and of shared moral sensitivity, the collective perception of insecurity and threat, the type of leadership, the type of mobilisation of patriotic, anti-elitist and anti-intellectual dispositions (Rucht 1982).[6] The revolutionary implications of nationalist movements from the late nineteenth century tended towards right-wing, populist authoritarianism and an aestheticised politics. National identity provided the basis of an authoritarian political identity that represented a specific variation on a republican-romantic political philosophy. Such a political philosophy represented a bridge between a romantic, cultural identification, shared between elites and masses, and its translation into a political philosophy where democratic will-formation draws its legitimating force from settled, ethical convictions rooted in a romantic cultural identity. The tendency of this kind of moralisation process is to withdraw the primordial and civic bases of identity from reflexive scrutiny and to create a legitimation framework which, in its fundamentals, is transcendental and immune from testing.

National identity becomes socially effective through its effect on the institutional rules that govern social spheres, such as intimacy, education, and professional ethics. When institutionalised, national identity circumscribes which rules should determine social relations of different kinds. Social rules would be random and chaotic if they were not organised into hierarchical forms of social rule systems. The latter are social institutions which can be divided into formal and informal institutions (Burns and Dietz, 1992) such as, in the former case, the family and community which are produced and maintained by informal mechanisms, and, in the latter, state, enterprises, modern markets and democratic associations which are produced and maintained by formal mechanisms. According to Burns and Dietz, formal institutions typically reflect the division of power in a society. They tend to bring the results of social interaction into agreement with the social distribution of power. Institutions represent structures of social power and permit the mobilisation of human and material resources. This signifies that institutional regimes limit possibilities of interaction and selection.

Burns and Dietz claim that those who occupy a privileged position within an institutional order can effectively limit the opportunities for influence and decision-making of others and design institutional arrangements that help their interest to change those that do not. Institutional power is maintained by both normative and material means. Our theoretical assumption is that on the threshold of a nationalist revolutionary transformation, normative power though the legitimation of the ethical code contained in a particular version of national identity is the key to control over resources.

The actual or perceived exclusion of elites from the pre-nation-state hierarchy provides the impulse to persuade them to replace the hierarchy altogether with one of their own choosing and under their own control. They form alliances with the masses on the political, and, mostly, geographical periphery against the elites of the centre. The exact constitution of the post-independence elite and the precise balance between elite-maintenance and inclusion of subordinated groups still depends on the outcomes of the nation-forming and *nation-instituting* processes. The utilisation of national identity codes to construct social institutions that reflect the distribution of social power in favour of the elite is the mechanism whereby the imaginary of the elite is transformed into power over society. The national identity construct that is developed and utilised by an elite depends on their position within the social structure of a given society and on the nature of their ideological programme.

The national identity to be institutionalised will reflect the social and culture structures that bind the elite together. It will therefore reflect their social experience in communication networks, in holding institutional power, in material interests, and in conscious cultural practices. It makes a considerable difference if the elite is urban or rural, economic or cultural in orientation, conservative or radical. The impulse given to an elite's role in the shaping of a national institutional order is decided in the structures and outcomes of nationalist mobilisation and in the role of the elite in the institutional order that preceded the nation-state. Institutional continuity or discontinuity may decide the continuation of a democratic order, the low priority given to formal institutional spheres such as the economy, or the importance of the socialisation system. More generally, existing institutional experience will have an important bearing on what technologies and strategies of power are available and on whether the elite has the capacity to exercise them.

Nationality is organically connected to social mobilisation. Specifically, nationalist movements spring from a local cultural-political identity and its desire to control the expanding power of the state. In the late nineteenth and early twentieth century this power was expanding as the state became decisive for citizens' welfare. The nineteenth century had seen the emergence of the world market, the industrial production system and the bureaucratic state with its network of institutional powers. The massive increase in contingency created by the one required the other as a principle of stability and of order. But the state represented more than order. It also represented a huge structure of power whose interventions could be used to transform civil society. This transformation was further enhanced by the growth of professionals with whom the power of the state became more and more intricately related in the twentieth century. The state depended on professionals to run the growing number of institutional spheres directly or indirectly under its control.

Politics in the twentieth century increasingly came to reflect the 'interpenetration' of the institutional culture and powers of the state with other social spheres, especially the economy. Control over the state's interventionist powers, or the capacity to block others from access to that power, became the defining stake of the political. Further, through the agency of the state's powers, national identity was no longer a product of the definition of solidarities and meanings in civil society but a consciously reproduced project for which the educational system was the key socialising institution. Hence, the prize of state power was the great motive for nationalist mobilisations. If they could define and construct an ethical code for the nation reflecting their own identity, and gain control of the new power of the state, they could control the levers of social change in their own interest. They were encouraged in the belief that this was a feasible ambition by another nineteenth century phenomenon, the growth of powerful meso-level organisations, springing directly from civil society and organised on a national footing, of which political, religious, economic, trade, and cultural associations are the dominant examples.

This process of the expansion of meso-level associations was a base of learning in civil society which provided elites with confidence and competence in seeking and maintaining state power. But if the power of the state was to be maintained in conditions which required symbolic and reflexive legitimation a cultural order had first to be stabilised that had the double function of specifically interpreting the society to itself in a way which led to the routine reproduction of social order and also had the function of maintaining the power and purposive integration of an elite who had been central to the instituted state form in the first place. National identity has a symbolic function in guiding social rule systems. The manner in which it is specified produces an ethical code which is related both to maintenance of the distribution of social power and to general adherence to the value basis of social order.

However, it would be wrong to conclude from the above that elites in any sense have a free hand. There are two types of constraint on elite power which are connected to the blending of culture, interests and agency in given nationalist situations. The first constraint is that elites are not necessarily unified either culturally or socially and may therefore be either unable to organise towards long-term goals or to grasp the moment when it arrives. Divisions between urban and rural elites or between elites who wish to continue within a metropolitan context versus those who wish to mobilise the periphery may in some circumstances weaken the role of elites in nationalist mobilisation. The second constraint is that elites in the case of nationalism are riding a tiger. Nationalism from the late nineteenth century was closely related to the diffusion of mass, industrial society – which does not mean that societies had to industrialise to embrace nationalism – and was therefore bound up with cultural interpretation systems that could either maintain social integration or be 'functional' to mobilisations against it. It was also bound up with a re-shaping of the material basis of social interests in conditions where the volatility of structures and the mobility chances, upwards or downwards, of categories of individuals was much enhanced. The relationship of elites to mass society was therefore unstable as cultural ideologies spread with extraordinary speed or as coalitions of interests, in a deeper sense connected with class logics, constantly changed.

In these circumstances of volatility, the integrating power of the nation acquired great importance. In order to understand why this was so it is necessary to see national identity as a pivotal part of the cultural order of the nation-state. In general, the cultural system – to draw from both Habermas (1984) and Archer (1988) – is a symbolic repository of the explicit and implicit codes that bind cultural knowledge, social solidarities and personal competencies together into a framework that represents the symbolic basis for acting in a society, permeating all spheres of action. Members of a society share implicit and explicit knowledge of culture without which they could neither recognise the rules for acting in *this* society or in *this* sphere of action in *this* society. By means of what Habermas (1984), following Weber, describes as processes of rationalisation, the experiences of members of a society are symbolically abstracted and codified so that action does not begin from nothing but begins instead from an understanding of what counts as meaningful and appropriate in given circumstances. This understanding is not learned anew each new time by individual or group actors but is based on rationalisation processes that precede their constitution as individuals as groups. The cultural system will always contain more content than the members of a society utilise at a given time. What they do use depends upon the contexts of relevance in which, intentionally or unintentionally, they are located. Contexts of relevance depend upon the perceived needs of a society and especially on those groups who have the capacity to specify which needs are most important and in what ways they should be considered. What aspects of the cultural system are mobilised in a given society depends upon its cognitive schemata, belief systems, structures of reciprocity and expressive models of individual identity. It also depends on the society's capacity to act in, adapt or change these cultural structures in the context of the prevailing distribution of symbolic and material power resources. Upon the institution of a nation-state, dominant elites, depending on a range of institutional constraints outlined at the end of the last section, attempt to use their social power in an attempt to institute a cultural order which prescribes the range of valid knowledge, action co-ordinating social rules, the types of social solidarity and corresponding societal norms, and the competencies and dispositions that individuals are expected to possess as members of a national community. They therefore convert the imaginary identity projects of the nation, which build upon foundations initially provided by the intelligentsia, into an institutional project that works from already established inclusive and exclusive boundaries and conditions of national membership but, in the phase of state power, turns it into an operational code that specifies the institutional functioning of society. This process is the institutionalisation of a national identity and it defines in cultural, social and affective terms the conditions of the addition of the real to the imaginary nation.

3 Origins and Context of Irish National Identities

HOW NEW IS THE NATION?

This chapter presents the first facet of a three-phase analysis of nineteenth century Irish nationalist mobilisation by focusing on the historical origins of the movement and the contextual conditions that precipitated large-scale mobilisation. In the next two chapters the actual mobilisation itself is examined as a process of constituting a new national collective identity while in chapters six and seven the institutionalisation of this identity is addressed. The historical shaping of Irish nationalism and its various opposing movements has been a subject of much historical dispute. Old-style nationalist views, still repeated in everyday life and in the media, such as the view that the 'British' inflicted on the 'Irish' 700 years of conquest and colonisation, are no longer given much credence in historical writing, not least because many of the 'Irish' in fact originated in Britain and most of the British ruling elite originated from the French conquerors of England. The historical evidence does not support the idea of long-run and clearly defined separatist national consciousness existing in Ireland throughout the second millennium, though support can be found for a more subtle thesis that situates the political-cultural antagonisms of the late nineteenth century in a longer historical context. It is the purpose of this chapter to outline this context and to relate it to more immediate starting conditions of late nineteenth century nationalism.

The chapter, moving progressively forward in time, outlines the emergence of three identities in the early modern period, associated roughly with the confessional identities of the three major religious groupings, Catholic, Anglican and dissenters, and follows their transformation by the early nineteenth century into two contending confessional identities, Protestant and Catholic, with opposing republican and liberal political philosophies. Secondly, the institutional context of the Union will be outlined showing how the confessional divide exposed structural contradictions of the Act of Union that was expressed in delayed and partial democratisation from 'above'. Contradiction and delayed reform led to the emergence of a Catholic nationalism from 'below' and provided this nationalism with a range of opportunities for a form of mobilisation which tied the struggle for social and political rights to a confessional axis. Thirdly, moving from an historical to a contemporary nineteenth century plane, the relationship between socio-economic conflict and confessional identity in late nineteenth century Ireland is traced. This relationship gives rise to new forms of mass nationalist agency which adopted an increasingly radical attitude towards combined social and political change.

UNITY AND DIVERSITY IN IRISH HISTORY

Following Pocock's (1982) thesis that the historical context of Irish national development is the British Isles as a whole, we argue the formation of conflicting Irish national identities – the conflicting group affiliations – cannot be explained in purely endogenous terms.[1] Irish history can only be meaningfully understood in the broader context of the history of the British and Irish archipelago.[2] This is particularly apparent in the early modern period when Ireland's ruling classes backed what were effectively lost causes in England. Four times in the early modern period the Catholic traditionalist magnates in Ireland gave their support to failed causes in England: the Kildare support of the Yorkish cause during the Wars of the Roses, the Geraldine and O'Neill revolts which were part of the wider feudal-traditional rebellions of the north and west in the mid-sixteenth centuries, the royalist cause during the civil war period and the Jacobite cause in the late 1680s.[3] What has become known as 'general crisis of the seventeenth century' was crucial in shaping the future course of history since it established structural differences between Ireland and Britain.[4] These structural differences were reflected in political culture as well as in state-building and socio-economic processes.

It is best to begin with state-building because the key to understanding early modern Irish history was failed state-building linked to colonialism. In the sixteenth and seventeenth centuries, Ireland experienced a rapid transition with a major influx of commercially-minded colonists in the south and north of the island.[5] Thus, to follow Barlett's (1993, p. 313) pioneering analysis of the making of medieval Europe: 'Lithuania, Ireland, the Mudejars: the extremities of Europe experienced the process of homogenisation as a process of polarisation. The very same forces that drew the English, the Pomerians or the Danes into a more uniform cultural world could, in these outlying areas, actually erect starker cultural boundaries'.[6] Failed state-building was closely linked to incomplete colonisation on the periphery. The displaced native communities never accepted the legitimacy of their dispossession or of the colonial state which followed it. Bartlett's thesis is that modern Europe stems from processes of colonisation in the Middle Ages and that cultural fissures in its border or peripheral regions are to be explained by incomplete colonisation.[7] This is the context in which the extension of the English state to Ireland in Middle Ages should be viewed.

In relation to socio-economic processes, capitalism in England emerged from social change resulting in the commercialisation of agriculture over several centuries, a process that was stabilised by the mercantilist state (Macfarlane, 1978).[8] In Ireland, the development of a commercial agricultural capitalism was advanced by the settler community. What was particularly significant about this settler population was not the fact of settlers peopling a land that in fact was relatively under-inhabited, but that in those parts where the settlers established themselves as a majority, as in Ulster, they never succeeded in becoming a dominant ruling class.[9] This was in contrast, for example, to the Norman conquest of England when the indigenous Anglo-Saxon ruling class was entirely replaced by a new dominant ruling class from Normandy. Consequently in Ireland an enduring tension developed between the natives and settlers, a tension that was moulded by the Reformation, which expressed the competition for the land as a struggle between rival confessions (Brady and Gillespie, 1986). This point has been best stated by Lyons (1982, p. 134) in a well-known lecture:

> The seventeenth century derives from those two constants in the Ulster kaleidoscope – land and religion. Because the conquest was gradual, piecemeal, and often precarious, the settlers who struck their roots in the region did so under the conditions of maximum insecurity. This insecurity became a permanent part of their psychology. That it would express itself originally in religious terms need not surprise us, when we recall that their physical insecurity was at its most dangerous at the moment when the Reformation and Counter-Reformation were locked in combat on a European scale.

The permanent insecurity left by the colonial settlement led to the intensification of the differences between the two islands' already existing geopolitical differences. In England social conditions facilitated the emergence of capitalism, greatly assisted by the tremendous amounts of capital and cultural energy released in the Reformation (Hill, 1967, 1969). In Ireland, the British trend towards commercialisation and urbanisation tended to have less impact as the economy continued to be dominated by internal warfare between the great magnates. In the cultural sphere, the Reformation – which functioned as a cultural pacemaker of change in triggering off a series of succession struggles, new royal demands and religious innovation – linked society and the state in England, while in Ireland it began a process of cleavage between the state and the Catholic population.[10] This cleavage was never fully overcome. The extension of state power took on a confessional caste. The fact that the Irish magnates backed the Royalist cause in the Civil War and suffered the consequences in Cromwell's conquest and subsequent colonisation exacerbated the situation.

The incomplete extension of the Tudor and Stuart state to Ireland goes back to the failure of the medieval state to engage in full-scale conquest. When the Anglo-Norman elite extended their rule over Ireland they had to rely on making allies in Ireland and on papal support. Ever since Pope Adrian granted Henry II a bull giving him the Lordship of Ireland the papacy was an ally of monarchical supremacism. By relying on alliances with magnate power, the English state paradoxically strengthened the Gaelic order. The determined Tudor attempt to extend the centralised English state led to an impasse as the Gaelic magnates rejected a form of government that was incompatible with the liberties they had been granted under the polity of the medieval Lordship of Ireland (Brady, 1991). This was in contrast, for instance, to the situation in Wales where the power of the Marcher lords was eroded after they had been incorporated into the English state.[11] In Ireland, Tudor policy fatally oscillated between attempts to destroy the power of the magnates and to deploy them to extend the mercantilist state (Ellis, 1985; Lennon, 1994).

The enduring legacy of the conflict between state and society was the collision of three political-cultural groups in Ireland: firstly, the Catholic Gaels and the Catholic Old English (after 1642 increasingly synonymous), secondly, the predominantly Anglican New English and future ruling class, and, thirdly, Presbyterian-Scottish

dominated Ulster. The subsequent history of Ireland was determined by the complicated relationships and constantly shifting allegiances between these groups and their complex relationships with
the British state.[12]

The political-cultural diversity of Ireland is very largely to be
explained by processes of identification that extend beyond Ireland
and encompass the British and Irish archipelago as a whole. Cultural conflict in Ireland has resulted less from a simple dualism of
Britain and Ireland than from the fact that the dominant groups in
Ireland have been linked to opposing groups in Britain itself. At a
crucial stage in British history, when the Reformation had entered
a new phase in England and had precipitated a civil war, the numerically dominant Gaelic group in Ireland, along with the Catholic Old English settlers, attached themselves to the doomed Royalist
cause in England and opposed the Puritan parliamentary forces.[13]
The defeat of the Stuarts and the establishment of the English
Republic was inevitably a defeat for the Irish Gaels and Old
English, who with the other supporters of James were persecuted
by the triumphant parliamentary regime under the leadership of
Cromwell.

The English Civil War – in effect a war of the three kingdoms –
was then central to the formation of divergent traditions in Ireland: while uniting Gael and Old English into a Catholic Confederation, a new fissure became apparent between this confederation
and a culturally resilient Protestant settler population, the latter in
turn divided between its Anglican and Puritan parts. This already
complicated situation was further confused by developments in
England and on the continent when the restored Stuarts[14] – who
were in effect the Catholic puppets in Britain of the French – sought
to compromise the Reformation by making alliances with Catholic
elites, thus bringing about a crisis of identity in particular for the
more vulnerable Irish Protestants (Banard, 1990). This culminated
in the Glorious Revolution of 1688 when James II was de-throned
by a Whig dominated parliament which flouted primogeniture and
offered the Dutch Calvinist Prince, William of Orange, the crown.
James II, exiled at the French court, sought to regain his crown
with the aid of the Catholics of Ireland and a large French army
with which he sailed to Ireland where the Catholic elites had enjoyed a comeback since the Restoration. The rest of Europe was
thus put on the alert, for a victory for James would have been a
victory for France and a threat to the balance of power which

consisted of containing Louis IX, who also posed a threat to papal
supremacism. A major European battle, the Battle of the Boyne,
was fought in 1690 in Ireland when a pan-European – and in fact
largely Catholic international army, created by the Treaty of Augsberg
(1686) and consisting of the armies of the Pope, the King of Spain
and the German Emperor, under the leadership of William of Orange,
now King of England – defeated James and his French army, thus
putting an end to the last great Catholic and French backed bid
for the throne of England.[15] As with the defeat and execution of
Charles I in 1649, this was a defeat for the supporters of the Stuarts
in Ireland, the Catholic magnates. The Boyne represented the last
stand of the Catholic magnates and the royalist cause was finally
abandoned with the Hanoverian Succession.[16]

With the defeat of its ruling class, many of whom fled to the
continent, and the imposition of the Penal Laws, which discriminated against Catholics, the society gradually embraced the Catholic church, which provided a surrogate aristocracy. Gaelic identity,
undermined by the Penal Laws, was slowly absorbed into a folk
Catholicism which was not rationalised until the nineteenth century. From the late seventeenth century, and extending well into
the eighteenth century, Gaelic culture had been an important trans-
mitter of Enlightenment ideas between Ireland and Scotland where
Enlightenment culture had been particularly strong. This Gaelic
world, moreover, had strong military, cultural and economic links
with the continent, especially Catholic Europe extending over several centuries. While there is no evidence that Gaelic Ireland was
moving *politically* in the direction of a territorial nation-state (Richter,
1988), there is considerable evidence to suggest that there had been
a strong Gaelic *cultural* identity based on language. The maturation of this cultural identity was shaped by the anti-Catholic thrust
of the Penal Laws and the 'civilising process', to use a term of
Nobert Elias, of modern Catholicism.

In the aftermath of the 1690s Ireland lost its Catholic ruling class
and was left with an Anglican elite, isolated from the masses by
the great gulf of its religion, and in Ulster a large Presbyterian
population, entrepreneurial in spirit and equally resentful of Anglican
supremacism. In this extraordinary constellation of social forces,
cultural conflict cut across deep socio-economic fissures. The ruling elite, the Protestant Ascendancy, was Anglican and culturally
alien not only to the majority Catholic population but distinct too
from the northern dissenters who were also discriminated against.

The Anglican Ascendancy was in effect a prematurely restored *ancien régime*. In England itself the restored Old Order had to adapt itself to the demands of an emerging bourgeoisie but in Ireland the Protestant Ascendancy enjoyed near total hegemony in a society where the institutions of civil society developed within a confessional cleavage. Thus the 'patriot' tradition that eighteenth century Irish Anglicans appealed to was not that of Enlightenment republicanism but that of the Glorious Revolution of 1688 (which was in effect a restoration) the Anglo-Saxon racial myth of the Norman Yoke and the doctrine of the Ancient Constitution.[17] In this way new cultural identities became bound up with different interpretations of the past (Hill, 1988). The Protestant Ascendancy regarded themselves as the Irish 'Nation' on the basis of birth and residence (MacDonagh, 1983, p. 17). The Catholic tradition, on the other hand, appealed not to residence but to a communitarian ideology of descent from a dispossessed Gaelic civilisational order.

The largely Presbyterian Scottish settlers who dominated the north east of Ulster from the early seventeenth century supported first the crown, which had aided them in the establishment of the plantation, and then the parliamentary regime and later the Orange cause. Though closer than the Anglicans to the Gaelic Irish in cultural tradition and social status, the Ulster Scots, were as a result of the Reformation, hostile to Catholicism. However, as they had embraced the Reformation in its Calvinist version of Presbyterianism, they were also opposed to the Anglican Reformation which Charles had attempted to impose on Scotland. While radical Puritanism was always discriminated against, the Union of the two crowns in 1607 did bring about a partial reconciliation of Scotland and England, united by the Protestant Reformation and common gestation of an autonomous civil society.

The 'general crisis of the seventeenth century' – as a crisis in the relationship between state and society – remained unresolved in Ireland where the largest group, the Catholic Confederation, was never defeated in the way that its equivalent in Scotland and England had been (Devine and Dickson, 1983). In this way, three political-cultural identities had been shaped in Ireland. It was not so much the extension of the English central state to Ireland that was decisive – it had after all been extended to the rest of Britain (Ellis, 1991, p. 304; Ellis, 1994, p. 165; Hechter, 1975) – but that it was accompanied by the fault lines of the Reformation which shaped the three confessional identities: the divide between Catholicism

and Protestantism and the split within Protestantism of Presbyterianism and Anglicanism.[18] The three-fold nature of this divide had the inevitable consequence that processes of state-building
would be entangled in cultural-confessional conflicts. Ireland thus,
it may be suggested, had the character more of a European frontier
society than of a colony.

The genealogies of national identities that were to emerge out
of these struggles in the sixteenth and seventeenth centuries were
expressed primarily in different and opposing conceptions of political authority and in myths of property. The Protestant Ascendancy reflected the world-view of the eighteenth-century Whigs, who
drew on an autocratic version of Locke's argument that it is the
proper function of the state to protect property which is a natural
right. The state exists to protect civil society and if the state proves
itself to be disloyal and breaks the social contract, as the Stuart
state had, it may be removed. In this way British national identity,
constructed around civic codes of identity, became focused on the
sovereignty of parliament, which had removed, consigned to execution and later restored a monarchy that was perceived to be a
foreign puppet. But the danger of Franco-Catholic despotism since
the Act of Settlement of 1710, which bound the succession to the
House of Hanover, was gradually replaced by a new threat: the
spectre of revolution in the form of Jacobin and the new ideas of
popular sovereignty. British modernity was in fact built on the ground
of restoration. English liberalism developed under the aegis of the
restored old order – crystallised in the great Reformation ideology
of the absolute sovereignty of Westminster – in which aristocracy
and a nascent bourgeoisie formed an enduring alliance. This en-
gendered an ethno-cultural nationalism of its own: a racialised doctrine
of Anglo-Saxon supremacism and a political culture of institutionalised
anti-Catholicism.

On the other side, the Gaelic order, which had disappeared with
the final extension of the English state to Ireland from the 1690s,
had bequeathed the myth of dispossession, the enduring theme of
the 'Hidden Ireland' which became the basis of a retrospective notion
of the Irish nation from the eighteenth century onwards (Canny,
1987; Cullen, 1988). Central to this was the notion that sovereignty
is vested in a feudalistic genealogical bond between the ruler and
the ruled. The Enlightenment notion of a social contract between
state and society did not exist in the Gaelic world-view: the state
was not seen as the protector of civil society but as a foreign yoke

while society was seen as residing in a feudalist-traditionalist bond of peasant and ruler. Moreover, the consciousness of the Gaels was also formed by their absorption of the ideas of the Counter-Reformation (Canny, 1987). The political tradition of counter-reformation Catholicism, and not that of the Enlightenment whose diffusion was stifled by the Penal Laws, became dominant amongst Irish Catholics. The Gaelic order in Ireland, unlike in Scotland, did not have an opportunity to undergo immanent modernisation as a consequence of state repression in the aftermath of the Wars of Religion. Thus the two traditions, the Protestant Ascendancy – with its Whig ideology of parliamentary absolutism – and the Catholic Jacobite tradition – which slowly transferred its political philosophy from monarchy to republicanism – both claimed to represent the Irish nation in their appeal to different concepts of political authority: autocratic liberalism versus communitarian republicanism. Both were primarily civic codes of political identification, but were attached to excluding ideologies from the wars of religion. Deriving from these codes were two cosmologies of history: for the Catholic mind, one that saw history as a process of disenchantment and loss; for the Protestant mind, a belief in the march of progress and the absolute sovereignty of the state as represented by the British parliament.[19] Underlying both were strong undercurrents of millenarianism.

Alongside these political traditions was the Ulster Presbyterian tradition, which rooted in Puritan dissent and in its cultural tradition more Scottish than English, had more affinity with classical liberal ideology than with Whig parliamentary absolutism. Presbyterians, whose identity was shaped through the Scottish Enlightenment could be described as the representatives of classical republicanism and civic humanism (McBride, 1993; McFarland, 1994). Thus Ulster Presbyterians generally supported the liberals until the First Home Rule Bill of 1886, when they turned *en masse* to the Tories. It was this radical tradition of dissent – which must be sharply distinguished from the two dominant traditions – that for a time brought Presbyterians and Catholics together under the banner of revolutionary nationalism in the 1790s and which also inspired Presbyterian support for the Land League before its association with Catholic nationalism (Boyce, 1990; Curtin, 1985; McMinn, 1981; Stewart, 1977). As with the other traditions, it was pervaded by strong civic codes, with primordial exclusion, represented by Orangism, occasionally appearing.

Looking back over the formative centuries of cultural and political development in Ireland, it can be seen how it was the complex entanglement of the social question concerning the land with the religious question as posed by the Reformation that was really decisive in shaping the divergent identities of modern Ireland into the excluding codes of 'natives' and 'settlers'. It was along these cultural fault-lines that the question of state sovereignty was to run aground. In general, the Reformation rather than the Enlightenment was more important in Ireland for identity formation. Unlike Scotland, where the Enlightenment was able to strike roots in a society revolutionised by the Calvinist Reformation, in Ireland the politics of the Reformation had created a deeply divided society.[20] Therefore the Enlightenment was in general received in Ireland under conditions more or less established by the Wars of Religion. That in itself was not so much the problem, since the Enlightenment was also received in Holland and Scotland by religious traditions which were important for diffusing Enlightenment ideas. The problem was that the Reformation had led to opposing identities, one of which was able to gain control of the apparatus of state to dispossess the other.

While the state in modern political theory has generally been seen as a solution to the problem of society – the problem of the nature of legitimate authority – it never quite succeeded in this role in Ireland where a dominant tradition sought to reject the state in favour of a new notion of the 'nation' that was emerging with the Enlightenment. In taking over the republican notion of national sovereignty, Irish revolutionary nationalists from the United Irishmen to the Young Irelanders were primarily opposing the Old Order of the parliamentary Whig regime.[21] But the sectarian traditions and their primordial codes of identification inherited from the Reformation were not so easily overcome with the result that the modern notion of the Republic tended to express the communitarian idea of a society defined by the unity of tradition along confessional lines: a civic idea thus became transformed into a culturally specific identity, with perpetually latent primordial elements, emphasising that only certain categories of the population could belong, being added later. Thus both the liberal notion of the state – as expressed in the Whig ideology of the Ascendancy – and the revolutionary notion of the modern republic – as expressed in the Enlightenment notion of popular sovereignty – were rejected in favour of a cultural notion of the Republic defined by reference to a communitarian sense of nationhood. Ireland under the Union never quite resolved this basic tension in the interpretation of the state and its relationship to society. Anti-statist popular national-ism developed under the shadows of the Wars of Religion and the confessional identities they fostered. The anti-clerical strain in modern nationalism was relatively absent in the Irish case. Combined with the remnants of a premodern tradition contained in the memory of a Gaelic civilisation, nationalism could appeal to an ethnic con-sciousness which could constantly be re-invented and re-elaborated.

THE INSTITUTIONAL CONTEXT OF THE UNION: DEMOCRATISATION AND THE PROBLEM OF FEDERALISM

Conventional accounts of Ireland under the Act of Union of 1800, introduced as a response to massive disorder and communal strife in the 1790s, generally emphasise the problems it generated, thus painting a picture of state repression in contrast to an occasionally rosy picture of the patrician Grattan's Parliament. The reality was a society that had by the standards of the day achieved a relatively high degree of democratisation. But the crucial issue is that democratisation was fatally delayed and was confessionally unfairly distributed.[22] The result was the collision of two kinds of democ-ratisation: from 'above', democratisation of the state stemming from British liberal civic patriotism, and from 'below', the popular democratisation associated with modern nationalism.

Under the Union Ireland was represented at Westminster by 100 MPs from a total of 658, a ratio of 1 to 5.5 Irish to British seats or about 15 per cent of seats, increased to 105 after 1832. This num-ber was temporally reduced to 103 from 1870 but raised to 105 again in 1918. This made post-famine Ireland relative to its popu-lation over-represented in parliament (Ward, 1994, p. 39). Ireland was represented by 32 lords in the House of Lords and the Churches of Ireland and England were united into one 'United Church of England and Ireland'. The kind of union that had been achieved was largely constitutional and legislative. While the power to legis-late was transferred to Westminster, the actual administration of government and the judiciary still remained at Dublin Castle, which was the centre of the Irish executive. A complex machinery of govern-ment developed around a modern bureaucracy which formally separated the exercise of power from personal and traditional authority. Responsibility for government lay in the hands of the Vice-Regent and Lord Lieutenant, and his Chief Secretary, who often delegated a considerable amount of responsibility to his Undersecretary. The Union eliminated some of the notoriously undemocratic and oligarchic features of the Grattan's Parliament, such as the rotten boroughs and sinecures, and made possible the election to Parliament of Catholics who made up 50 per cent of Irish MPs by 1880. Constitutionally, Ireland was to be an integral part of the United Kingdom, although a uniform electoral law was not adopted until 1884 and the Irish franchise did not always match the British pattern (Walker, 1972/3). Changes in the Irish franchise law of 1850 led to significant increases in the numbers who could vote in the general elections of 1852, 1885 and 1913, though one of the principal electoral discrepancies between Ireland and Britain in the nineteenth century was that there were far more uncontested seats in Ireland (Carty, 1981, p. 27; Hoppen, 1984).[23] As far as trade and commerce was concerned, an Irish county was to occupy the same status as any of the English counties. The Union created a free-trading block between the two islands, though many discrepancies, such as the existence of two separate exchequers until 1817 when full monetary union was achieved remained.

The institutional structure of the later Irish Free State, established in 1922, owed much to the Union. The institutional framework of democracy and government, elections, the civil service, the role of law emerged from the Union. The British legacy provided for political stability in Ireland, particularly when compared with Habsburg, Tsarist and Hohenzollern legacies in eastern and central Europe (Lee, 1989b, p. 87). The Union provided structures for universal suffrage and the rule of law, thus preventing military authoritarianism, as in Germany, from gaining a foothold in the society. As in Britain itself, the rule of law remained formally separate from the state itself. Nineteenth-century Ireland also underwent relative secularisation, part of the general trend towards secularisation – the separation of church from state – that characterised much of Europe in the nineteenth century (Chadwick, 1985). Despite the existence of an Established Church until its disestablishment in 1869, the official Anglican church had relatively little political power.

By the early nineteenth century, Ireland had reached a relatively advanced stage of democratisation which limited state repression.

Along with Britain, the Low Countries, Scandinavia and Switzerland the emancipation of the peasantry had been achieved relatively early in history. Serfdom had disappeared in the Low Countries by 1300 and in England and France feudal services had been replaced before 1500 by money rents (Barraclough, 1992, p. 82). The abolition of the Gaelic order and incorporation of Ireland into the jurisdiction of the British state involved the progressive establishment of modern law and democracy. Since the Norman conquest the complex machinery of royal government – the administration of the shires, liberties, county courts, sheriffs of justice, written law and taxation – were all established in Ireland. By the time of the Union, Ireland had an advanced system of local government, a functioning judicial system based on common law, and a banking system, all essential for the working of a modern democracy. These facts must be measured against the myth of extensive political repression under the Union. Political repression was much more pervasive in nineteenth-century Russia, Spain, France, Germany, the Habsburg Empire and the rest of eastern and south eastern Europe than it was in the United Kingdom, the Low Countries, Scandinavia and Switzerland (Goldstein, 1983). The political institutions of nineteenth century British democracy allowed for relative freedom of political expression and established the conditions under which modern citizenship developed (Marshall, 1992). The rights of association, assembly, the right to form trade unions and to strike, freedom of the press were much stronger in the United Kingdom, including Ireland, than in most European countries, with the exception, again, of the north west of Europe and Switzerland.[24] If political systems are compared in relation to the establishment of clear rights and obligations of citizens which cover a large share of persons under the state's jurisdiction and in relation to the absence of arbitrary power, then by relative standards of the time Britain and Ireland had democratised fairly successfully between the 1750s and 1830s with the broadening of suffrage and the institutionalisation of modern citizenship (Tilly, 1993/94, pp. 19/20).

The comparative incidence of repression is important in that, as we shall argue in more depth in the following chapters, Irish nationalist mobilisation cannot be entirely explained by grievances and suffering. Identities are not pre-existing and mobilisation does not automatically follow from grievances (Tarrow, 1994). Nor can the emergence of a separatist national identity be explained by the memory of an ancient Gaelic civilisation. The survival of pre-modern ethnic traditions may be important to explain the rise of modern national consciousness, but it is insufficient as an explanation for nationalist mobilisation. Nor can it be mechanically assumed that the existence of long-run Catholic collective identity, emerging as a national consciousness in the nineteenth century, fused with the contradictions and problems of the Union to inspire mass mobilisation. In fact, democratisation was institutionalised to a relatively advanced degree from 'above' and it provided opportunities for democratisation from 'below' to gain strength. The manner in which the Union settlement became unpopular and was ultimately undone was in substantial part due to the *opportunities* it offered for a nationalist solution. What was crucial was that Catholics gained more and more power both socially and politically, and as they did so they began to perceive their situation differently: relative deprivation was perceived as absolute deprivation. The struggle for social and political rights was expressed along a confessional axis.

The structural contradictions of the society to which the Union was a response, together with the manner in which the Union was introduced, made its long-run endurance in Ireland improbable from the outset. The Union was a product of authoritarianism and counter-revolution, designed as it was to prevent the consequences of the American and French Revolutions from striking root in Ireland, and thus endangering Britain's restored ancien régime. Though it did prolong the Whig's ancien régime (Anderson, 1974; Mayer, 1981), the Union could not stop the tide of democratisation. However, democratisation was accomplished not through social revolution, but through the incorporation of the middle classes into the state (Clark, 1985). Thus one of the unique features of British democracy was that democratisation proceeded in two directions. On the one hand, it was primarily institutionalised via the institutions of the state through the progressive enfranchisement of the middle classes in order to diminish the possibility of social revolution. On the other hand, the tradition of popular democracy, which extended back to the Levellers and which was revived in the aftermath of the French Revolution, becoming much later a cultural component of the labour movement, represented a notion of democracy very different from that of parliamentary liberalism as it was focused more on society than on the state (Thompson, 1991). While in Britain the social question determined that these two concepts of democracy – the state tradition of liberal parliamentarism and the radical tradition of popular sovereignty – would shape modern politics along class lines in the formation of a Right and a Left, in Ireland, where the social question was tied to confessional conflicts, the two traditions of democracy expressed themselves in a conflict between defenders of the Union and champions of, variously, Home Rule or independence. Probably the greatest failure of the Union was that while it did facilitate democratisation, it was an uneven democratisation and had the effect of taking responsibility out of the society and concentrating political decision-making at Westminster. This vacuum was filled by a nascent nationalism from below.

The Union of Britain and Ireland was less an experiment in federalism than the political absorption of the latter into the former. Soon after the creation of the Union, its most vociferous opponents, the Protestant Ascendancy, quickly decided to support it realising that it was their best guarantee to continue to dominate politics. It meant little constitutional change for Britain and was far from a perfect solution to the problems of the two islands. Many Irish members of Parliament, from Butt to O'Connell, initiated debates on federalism as a model for the ideal relationship between the two countries (Boyce, 1991a; Jay, 1989; Kendle, 1989). Unfortunately there was little consensus on what federalism implied and how it could be institutionalised with the result that many of these federalist designs collapsed into confused demands, sometimes for the reform of the Union, other times for its repeal. The reason for the failure of federalism to become a coherent policy was that Britain was clearly uninterested in undergoing major constitutional change simply to neutralise the threat of revolution in Ireland. In short, federalism, as opposed to devolution or home rule, threatened the structural basis of the British constitution too deeply – for federalism would also have to be considered for Scotland, Wales and possibly for England itself.[25] This was something that Westminster was not going to seriously consider. While there was widespread interest in federalism for the colonies, it was considered inappropriate for the United Kingdom itself and Ireland, though often treated with ambivalence, was not generally regarded as a colony but as an integral part of the United Kingdom (Boyce, 1991a, p. 126). Federalism faded as a solution to the internal problems of the Union by the 1870s when nationalism was gaining in power and never became a serious policy of any of the major parties. While the British establishment, which clung to the absolute sovereignty of Westminster, was clearly not in favour of federalism, Irish nationalists for their part, perhaps due to the wider institutional climate, showed little enthusiasm for it as a means of finding solutions to the problem of cultural diversity though they could accept devolved Home Rule to include the entire island. They increasingly went in a nationalist direction, drawing their cultural resources from a potent form of Catholicism, conceptions of rural justice, and civilisational models of a 'restored' Gaelic order. It may be suggested that federalism was the great missed opportunity in Anglo-Irish relations.

The turn to a state-seeking ethno-nationalism in Ireland can be seen in the context of the international context when nationalism can be divided into three forms: state patriotism, the nationalism of unification and the new secessionism. In the first instance, state patriotism was reflected in the nationalism of the longer established states, such as France and Britain, which tried to foster a cult of the nation around empire building. In the second instance, the two unified states of Germany and Italy, established in the middle of the nineteenth century, serve as examples of nationalisms of unification, to which can be added nationalisms of reconstruction such as modern Turkish nationalism. Of these the foundation of the Italian state in 1850s was the most consequential, leaving a legacy of irredentist nationalism in its wake and inspiring revolutionary nationalism after the establishment of Young Italy by Mazzini. Thirdly, there was the rise of secessionist nationalism, which had its origins in the emancipation of Greece from the Ottoman Empire in the 1820s, a struggle which inspired romantic revolutionary nationalism all over Europe ever since Byron died at Mesolonghi in the name of the emerging Greek nation. The British liberals supported many of the continental nationalist movements, particularly the Italian, the Greek and the Bulgarian causes. While secessionist nationalism also inspired the separation of Belgium from The Netherlands in the 1830s, it was generally less prevalent in the nineteenth century when national identity was principally associated with the established states, though it was a powerful force in the foundation of modern Serbia and Romania in 1878 after the Congress of Berlin, the independence of Norway from Sweden in 1905, the independence of Iceland from Denmark in 1874. The Irish case was a clear example of such a secessionist nationalism that for a time in the nineteenth century led to the exploration of less than completely separated institutional arrangements.

Political Catholicism – represented primarily by Daniel O'Connell's

Catholic Association, which had spear-headed the movement for the enfranchisement of the Catholic gentry, and his Repeal Movement – mediated between the two kinds of democracy mentioned above, democratisation from 'above' and popular democracy. O'Connell mobilised large segments of the population behind a campaign for electoral reform. He was able to transform the original radical concept of democratic sovereignty – which had been articulated against the *ancien régime* – into the populist demands of political Catholicism. He simultaneously worked within the institutions of parliamentary democracy to serve the interests of his own peers, the increasingly numerous Catholic gentry and commercial class. Through the particular form that political Catholicism took in Ireland, Catholic Emancipation, democracy as legal-constitutional opposition slowly became a resource of nationalism. Social questions became overshadowed by the national question with which democracy was associated.[26] This was somewhat in contrast to Britain where the movement for social reform was closely linked with radical notions of democracy, a linkage which resulted in the imposition of a national patriotism from 'above' to contain social revolution (Colley, 1992).[27] In Ireland, the heritage of democracy was appropriated by nationalism, which also defined the social question in its own terms. Nationalism also capitalised on delayed Catholic Emancipation which was not introduced for nearly three decades after the union. Nationalism thus became associated with the principal source of indigenous social mobilisation in nineteenth century Ireland.

RESHAPING THE CONTEXT OF NATIONALIST
MOBILISATION: SOCIAL CHANGE AND MODERNISATION
IN THE LATE NINETEENTH CENTURY

The fallout of the 1790s, including the establishment of the Union and the protracted campaign for Catholic Emancipation followed by a long and unsuccessful campaign for the Repeal of the Union, led to the establishment of a definite national consciousness in Catholic Ireland. This was compounded by the seminal significance of the Famine, the last great natural calamity in Western Europe in which millions died, became impoverished or were forced to leave. While there has been much debate on responsibility for the famine, nothing could alter the fact that for later generations amongst the huge Irish diaspora in Britain and America, as well as for those remaining in Ireland, the famine appeared as a symbolic watershed. It also marked a material watershed, whether through its own immediate consequences or associated with long-run structural changes, in marking the end of a predominantly tillage agriculture and the emergence of livestock production for the expanding British market (Crotty, 1966). The switch to livestock led to a consolidation of agricultural holdings in the second half of the nineteenth century and the emergence of a self-confident class of tenant farmers within a transformed landlord system.

By the middle of the nineteenth century, the pattern of Irish politics for the subsequent seventy years was substantially shaped. A national consciousness had emerged that fused Catholic religious identity, democratic rights and social justice. This process of symbolic identification had been shaped by a long series of historical influences, the experience of dispossession, confessional discrimination and unequal citizenship in the eighteenth century, the republican cross-class culture of the United Irishmen which acquired strong sectarian connotations in the course of mobilisation, the memory of an independent parliament, the struggle for Catholic Emancipation, the Repeal Movement against the Union, and the Famine. It is true that this national consciousness still had a relatively limited constituency after 1850 but the symbolic mould of Irish nationalism emphasising deprivation and institutionally feasible alternatives to the status quo were in place and had already taken strong hold amongst educated Catholics.

The existence of an alternative consciousness, while not always consciously expressed or feasible to express, gave social change in nineteenth century Ireland the features of a paradoxical modernisation. Ireland was part of the most advanced national economy in the world and the most stable liberal democratic polity. Its location within the United Kingdom therefore implied participation in the most significant progressive aspects of the period; in communications, in reform-oriented government, in economic opportunity, in cultural competence, in professional advancement, in scientific and legal innovation. The initiation in, or extension to, Ireland of these features of modern society, in which even if the United Kingdom was not always the most enlightened it was never far from the forefront, happened more or less automatically. True, Irish politics in the second half of the nineteenth century gives the appearance of a constant struggle for nationally-denied rights but at the core of the major political movement of late nineteenth-century Ireland, the Home Rule movement, was the supposition that rational and not primordial criteria were the basis, and could in the future continue to be the basis, of the imperial treatment of Irish affairs up to and including an Home Rule settlement.

Yet by the late nineteenth century, and progressively more as the old century closed and the new century began, the Catholic Irish were less than happy with the nature of their citizenship within the United Kingdom. No major calamities intervened in this period in the form of war, disease, or barbarity that could exogenously explain why the graph of Irish national consciousness was so progressively rising and why the need for a nationalist, as opposed to national, identity became so important for so many of the Catholic Irish. An earlier nationalist historiography was able to explain it all by interpreting the events of the late nineteenth and early twentieth centuries as the inevitable working out of a powerful and long-run nationalist consciousness that finally and irrevocably succeeded in working out what was the problem, English rule, and, more significantly, how to go about getting rid of it. But few today are inclined to give much credence to the strong version of this thesis. Primordial, ethnic constructs were, as we have seen, certainly there as part of the mix in both a rationalised and a folk sense but the Irish national movement was shaped by an immediate context of the politics of progress and distribution, enlightened and dogmatic political institutions, volatile political cultures, the rapid transformation of social structures, as much as by any long-run inclination towards nationalism.

The paradoxically of the modernisation consists of the fact that the relatively advanced level of progress achieved by Irish society, as part of a larger political unit, by the end of the nineteenth century did not satisfy a new elite that had emerged with the Home Rule movement. Wherever one looks in the forty or so years from the beginning of the modern Home Rule movement under Parnell to the gaining of Independence the political, social and cultural orders, sometimes separately, sometimes together, sometimes with the involvement of lower social strata and sometimes not, is being unravelled by the Irish elite. And the direction in which this elite was moving, or more accurately elites, for they ranged across different social spheres and changed in composition over time, involved a profound assault on modernisation itself.[28] The society, and the collectivity can be spoken of with more confidence as time went on, had become dissatisfied with its own institutions, identity and situation. It is tempting and partly true to say that it had become tired of its own modernity.

The indicators of comparative Irish modernity by the end of the century, even more so than its beginning, were extensive. Ireland was one of the wealthiest countries per capita in Europe by the turn of the century (Bielenberg and O'Mahony, 1998) and enjoyed access to the world's most advanced labour market. Its primary and secondary educational systems were far better than average, though its tertiary system was underdeveloped due to denominational wrangling (Paseta, 1994). The level of formal 'constitutional' rights enjoyed were outstanding by the standards of the time and extend to a long list, freedom of thought, press, speech and communication, of association and assembly, rights for the protection of privacy, intimacy, and the inviolability of the person, rights of property, contract and labour and political rights of citizens. Literacy was relatively advanced by the end of the century and this supported an extensive press. The bureaucratic administration of the society was efficient and thorough. The communication system was advanced by most standards, remarkable by the standards of an isolated, predominantly rural society though one that was well integrated into international society as a consequence of its association with the empire.

Behind the back of this apparently impressive development lay a flip-side that was less sanguine. True, by world standards the Irish economy was doing quite well, and certainly much better than the impoverishment thesis that had prevailed up to the recent revisionist arguments inspired by Cullen (Cullen 1976, 1983; Gillespie, 1991) but it was doing relatively less well than the more prosperous, metropolitan regions of the UK that had enjoyed the benefits of industrialisation and lagged well behind the UK average (Bielenberg and O'Mahony, 1995) and, more importantly, it was developing in a different direction. As Hechter's (1975) analysis makes clear, in the UK division of labour Ireland's role was primarily that of supplier of agricultural primary produce and, apart from the North East, it never developed an industrial base to compare with the other Celtic peripheries, let alone England itself. Furthermore, due to the denominational split which, in southern Ireland, left a relatively small Protestant upper middle-class in a privileged, if increasingly contested position, social and economic power was disproportionately related to religious affiliation. Denomination-based power had major democratic and social implications. Democratically, the selection system for right of suffrage and, by extension, other participatory rights was conditional on socio-economic status. This meant that democratic rights and participation were dominated by Protestants until quite late in the century when suffrage reform and social change rapidly changed the balance (Alter, 1971). Socially, due to the necessary results of the interwoven circuits of socio-economic and political power, historical proprietorial advantages, possession of capital, placement in networks and probably cultural aptitude in certain dimensions of economic activity, Protestants, and this applies especially to the South where they were a relatively small minority, disproportionately dominated the upper reaches of social stratification. The flip-side of modernisation was also revealed culturally in the experientially conditioned shift amongst Catholics from deference to resentment which expressed itself in oscillation between a sense of inferiority and spiritual superiority based on the innocence of the victim. Both were thoroughly modern in the sense of requiring a conception of the equality with all others of the dignified self. Administratively, while the society nominally enjoyed the virtues of a legally and constitutionally responsible bureaucracy, the governance of Ireland was a curious, quasi-colonial hybrid with a distinct Irish executive which enjoyed a relatively significant degree of operational autonomy from the control of the legislature, a situation that could be tolerated given the United Kingdom's monarchical constitutional order.

But while Protestant hegemony, and opposition to it, was immensely significant as a factor in the rise of nationalism, offering a ready target for perceptions of injustice, there were also significant changes in socio-demographic composition and the distribution of power and resources within Catholic Ireland itself. Socio-demographically, and the most salient social fact of all in post-famine Ireland was the dramatic reduction of numbers. Population levels plummeted as Irish labour became centrally absorbed into the vast economic expansion accompanying intensified industrialisation in both Britain and the United States. The 'immiseration' thesis that once explained this phenomenon is now less popular as Irish emigration is increasingly being perceived to have responded to a large variety of push and pull factors and as Irish emigrants more rapidly reached higher levels of social status in their host countries. But it counts as a flip-side to the society's modernisation because it led to the consolidation of power and resources in the construction of a Catholic rural or small-town proprietorship whose social and economic power was applied to the socio-demographic programming of the society.[29] The chief instruments of the latter was a proprietoral class that enforced high levels of emigration due to farm consolidation and the non-utilisation of capital in industrial pursuits, and that gave considerable impetus to later rather than earlier marriages.

Nineteenth century Ireland was not immobile and rigid, but was a society exhibiting high propensity for social change. The Irish village, a key element in its predominantly rural social structure, was not an unchanged product of the past but a recent product of agrarian modernisation. The Union had extended political rights to the middle-class in 1829 and 1832, with enfranchisement being subsequently extended through the various electoral reform acts. The result of the progressive enfranchisement was that the Ascendancy lost control of government by 1886 and with the Land Acts they lost control over the material foundations of the society, which passed into the hands of the tenant farmers. Thus in Ireland, unlike in Britain, the native aristocracy were not the agents of change from 'above'; and also unlike Britain and much of Western Europe the working classes were not the agents of change from 'below.' The Irish path to modernity was undertaken neither by the ruling elites nor by the working class but by a rural bourgeoisie in alliance with a nationalist intelligentsia and Church that in time established a new elite and new principles of social stratification.

The relative wealth of this new elite was advanced by the improvements in the situation of the agricultural classes which took place in the second half of the nineteenth century. The annual average of agriculture output (excluding potatoes) rose by 40 per cent between 1851 and 1871 and farmers' incomes increased by 77 per cent in the same period (Winstanley, 1984, p. 8). The landlord class was also in the process of transformation: by 1870 nearly 40 per cent were Catholics and the number of absentee landlords had declined considerably. As early as 1854, 74 per cent of farmers farmed less than 30 acres and those who had 50 acres or more owned 60 per cent of the entire land of the country.[30] Most of the large land-holders were large estate-owners who sub-let their land to a variety of tenants of whom larger, and more prosperous tenants were becoming more numerous. In this process, Catholics gained in economic power and in social self-confidence. The relative wealth of post-famine peasants, when they started to accumulate capital, was partly due to the fact that rents were low in relation to the value of the land. This, together with extraordinarily propitious market conditions due to an exponential rise in British demand and modest industrial growth, led to major rises in incomes and living standards without significant growth in output. In these circumstances of improving productivity and market opportunity, Irish landlordism lacked the leadership, knowledge, entrepreneurial skill and drive to maintain its cultural, social and economic dominance (Vaughan, 1994, p. 222).

The paradoxical modernisation we have outlined was expressed within Ireland in the dimensions of, on the one hand, confessional cleavages linked to both social and democratic questions and, on the other, class divisions between propertied and non-propertied that created a remarkable diaspora and also impeded the articulation of adequate principles of justice.[31] But they were also expressed in the relationship between Ireland and the UK in diverging experiences of societal modernisation. These divergences gave impetus over time in the course of national mobilisation to the transfer of suspicion of British state-led modernisation to modernity *per se*. The main divergences were as follows.

(1) Division within the middle-classes ran along denominational lines between Protestant industrialists, largely in the North-East, and a Catholic middle-class which was mainly rural. Protestants, assisted by their religiously-based networks, remained in a proportionately privileged position until late in the century. The denominational divide was sharpened by the growth in sectarian tensions in the North-East with increasing tension between Catholics coming into urban industrial occupations from rural hinterlands and Protestants who already held them. This produced on both sides legitimating mythologies of origin and identity – Protestant Orangeism and Catholic neo-Gaelicism. The denominational divide also led to retarded secularisation due to the impetus given to religiously-based cosmologies of exploitation and domination. In southern Ireland, these cosmologies reflected the existing cultural power of the church and its growing social and political power.

(2) The society underwent massive socio-demographic decline rather than its opposite in the rest of the UK. Furthermore, a very high proportion of the population lived in rural locations. This produced, especially in southern Ireland, a structure of social roles that were based upon quite different cultural models to the British experience.

(3) The dominance of possession of or exclusion from property

as a principle of social stratification of which landed and small-commercial property was decisively important. The predominance of small-holding property also created a dominant petit-bourgeois stratum, rural small-holders and associated service-providers, which was different to the UK experience. The difference was copper fastened by the low development of urbanisation in much of Ireland.

(4) The continuation of a quasi-colonial executive with extensive powers led to a system of divided governance. This was remedied to some degree by the Local Government Reform of 1898 which created an elected system of local governance.

(5) The existence of an extraordinarily high capacity for political mobilisation by a wide range of actors.

(6) The continuation of a rural-based social structure and the noticeable absence of a large urban working-class.

Notwithstanding these structural contradictions the modernisation process in Ireland proceeded rapidly in economic, social, cultural and political dimensions. This was impelled by both political integration in the UK and also by geographical proximity to Britain which led to rapid economic and cultural integration. Economic integration consisted not of an alignment of productive capacities, southern Ireland remained a rural society in an economic sense, but in the capacity to produce for UK market conditions which overwhelmingly favoured livestock production in Irish agrarian conditions. Cultural integration proceeded by means of the anglicisation of Ireland, the target of the Gaelic cultural revival, and evidenced in the spread of the English language and in the penetration of English popular culture and mores.

But given the fundamental structural and cultural differences of the southern Irish population to the overall UK context instability was endemic. The very rapidity of social change impacting on a conservative social structure led both to enhanced social change and reaction against it.[32] The logic of this instability can, to a certain degree, be explained, from within the concept of differentiation itself. Functional differentiation, in the sense of a growing difference between social spheres associated with phenomena such as professionalisation and specialisation, arising from wider UK modernisation and shaped by locational contingencies had a profound affect on Irish society but it was constantly checked by a form of social stratification, in the sense of occupational and role distribution, that was not commensurate with it. Throughout the nineteenth century the society constantly reproduced marginal groups and excess individuals who were not relevant to the prevailing pattern of social power and opportunity and who chose, or were circumstantially forced, to emigrate.[33] Dysfunctional social stratification did not simply issue in massive emigration and landlord/tenant conflict but also in conflict between larger farmers and smaller farmers and landless labourers (Bew, 1978, 1987; Fitzpatrick, 1987) over wages and ownership of the scarce resource of land.

But dysfunctional social stratification was not simply confined to the land and emigration it also affected professional and urban Ireland and the working-class. Nineteenth-century Ireland was characterised by a relatively large service sector for a predominantly agrarian society. This was due to enhanced prosperity resulting from favourable price trends for agricultural produce. But the society was tending to progressively produce more trained professionals and lower-middle class candidates than it internally needed, leading to what has been characterised as 'blocked mobility' (Hutchinson, 1987). This became very significant for the rise of the new cultural nationalism of the 1890s. Finally, as elsewhere in Western Europe, the demands of the labour movement were a volatile factor. In a local study but with national implications, Lahiff has demonstrated that the new unionism had a significant impact in Ireland and led to a rising level of labour radicalism (Lahiff, 1988; O'Connor, 1992).

The consequences of mainly exogenously generated modernisation resulted in developments that caused large-scale structural contradictions on the social level. Some of these contradictions were ameliorated by the extremely rapid elite turnover that took place in the last two decades of the nineteenth century but some others gained new acuity. This elite transformation replaced the socio-economic and political power of a Protestant propertied and professional elite with a Catholic one. Socio-economically, the winners of the Land War were neither the Protestant landlords who were swept away, nor the landless labourers or very small farmers whose farming activities were always marginal, but the middle-to-large farmers who acquired landed property in very favourable conditions.[34] This laid the basis for a new Catholic elite comprising of these farmers, the small town self-employed, and urban professionals. By the end of the nineteenth century there were fewer people in rural Ireland, but they were better off, and the tenant farmers, Vaughan (1984, p. 4) points out, accounted for a significantly larger proportion of the whole. Carty (1981) adds that the victory of rural anti-Parnellism over largely urban Parnellism consolidated the establishment of a local and parochial political culture. Politically, change in the suffrage laws in the 1880s which meant that by 1890 16 per cent of the population had the vote consolidated a revolution in political representation and political power that had been begun by Parnell in 1880. Combined with the formation of a socioeconomic elite, this political transformation described by Alter (1971, p. 41) as the political emancipation of the bourgeoisie was, as in some other European countries, tightly bound up with the creation of a national party.

Irish nationalism was underpinned by related processes of elite transformation and class change. These two phenomena were manifested in the increased structural power and self-confidence of the rural and urban petit-bourgeoisie. This newly consolidated class produced a social and political elite within its ranks. Substantially in position by the end of the century, this elite turned to an immediate and ambitious imperative, to take control of the process of modernisation so that the formal and substantive rights and resources they had so recently and so rapidly gained could not be destroyed either by modernisation itself or by the actions of competing social groups. On the contrary, they should be extended to greater social, cultural and political domination. In true petty-bourgeois fashion they sought to stop historical processes which they could no longer dominate. This meant that any further differentiating and rationalising consequences of modernity, other than those that had produced them or furthered their interests, needed to be opposed. This was the essence of their idea of the Irish nation. The outstanding issue was whether in given social conditions they would be able to articulate it plausibly and subsequently realise it.

This petit-bourgeois class of medium-to-large farmers, rural, small-town and urban service providers including clerics, shopkeepers, publicans, doctors, solicitors, clerks, accountants, were the dominant class of twentieth century Ireland. Structural change along with their own conviction and organisational accomplishments led to the realisation of their values as the dominant values in the society. They were triumphant in defining what constituted Irish national identity and what goals the new nation-state should serve. In the next three chapters, which follow the composition and symbolic articulation of the mobilisation phase of Irish nationalism and the institutionalisation of a particular national identity, the presence of this class will never be far away. They absorbed and carried forward the version of the republican general will that was the political creed of Irish nationalism but ensured that this general will would reflect their interests above all. They carried forward, too, the sense of history as victimisation and gave it a subjective slant, history was their victimisation and they would set that to rights now. It is the insistent presence of this class and the consistency with which they pursued their interests, along with their symbolic domination of the society, that allows the term 'ideology' to have true meaning in twentieth century Ireland.[35] Irish national identity was not only their achievement but it was shaped above all by their preferences and values. Without them a national movement would not have taken off; the Irish labour movement only switched to nationalism relatively late on, the disproportionately Protestant middle-class remained Unionist. It will become apparent in the following pages how the national identity that was the institutional blueprint for twentieth century Ireland was shaped ultimately by the Catholic lower middle-class whose relatively powerful position in the social structure of the society became abundantly translated into symbolic power.

4 Nationalist Mobilisation and the Cultural Construction of the Irish Nation

THE IDEA OF AN IDENTITY PROJECT

This chapter outlines the conceptions of nationalist collective identity articulated by the main wings of the nationalist movement from the nineteenth century origins of the Home Rule Movement to Independence. The analysis starts from the structural and historical-cultural conditions that helped give the Irish national movement its particular character. Irish society was experiencing a form of modernisation that nationalists perceived as not under their control and on the whole moving in a direction that compounded their perceptions of historical disadvantage. Articulating with these structural factors and perceptions was another cultural discourse, a narrative of what it meant to be 'Irish'. This discourse could be differentiated according to the degree of exclusiveness and purity that was imputed to being Irish. As the nationalist movement progressed the discourse of 'being Irish' began to take on ever more exclusive and pure connotations. When the point of greatest consensus and extremism was reached it was fateful that the separatist programme was capable of being institutionalised in a separate state.

The discourse of national identity was expressed with variations in different wings[1] of the nationalist movement. Wings are sections of the overall nationalist movement that produced diagnostic evaluations of the problems of the existing United Kingdom institutional order and projected 'identity projects' for what they conceived as a new institutional order in the nation-to-be. These identify projects are imaginary constructs that are consistent with their own social and cultural interests. In an extremely fluid situation represented by nationalist mobilisation, the relationship between social interests and cultural projections of the common good is far from stable. Nevertheless, the movement wings examined here do exhibit a logic

in the way they connect symbolic representations of what they consider the problem to be and how that relates to their distinctive
social situations. The influence of each of them matters because
they are political actors who have attained a certain measure of
institutionally stabilised power manifested, for example, in the growing
centrality of the Church to the provision of social services, the
emergence of the Parliamentary Party as the only significant political
party in southern Ireland, the reconstruction of political culture by
the revolutionary nationalists, and the growing social influence of
labour radicalism.

The institutional environment of the wings of the nationalist
movement was characterised by the rise of a cultural politics of
identity which became more pronounced over time. Social interests were increasingly redefined on the basis of this identity politics. The wings are, in the phrase of Wuthnow (1992, p. 274),
culture-producing organisations that operate within the field of
nationalist politics. They therefore absorb, implement and re-shape
new cultural codes as they emanate from institutionalised cultural
producers in the public sphere such as intellectuals, cultural associations or currents of public opinion. The primary 'cultures' produced by the intelligentsia and their mass diffusion as secondary
'cultures' by the meso-level actors described in these pages are
diagnostic accounts of the problems of the present institutional
arrangements and prognostic visions of how they could be altered
for the better. It is the characteristic of focusing on 'becoming'
rather than the actual issues of current politics, which in their own
way gained ever more significance for everyday life in the era of
capital and of institutional reform, that shows the obsession with
identity that grabs hold of southern Irish public culture. But within
the deep heartbeat of this concern with the becoming of the nation
the insistent rhythm of the play of social advantage and disadvantage *within* the nation can still be discerned.

The identity projects produced by these actors are neither unified
nor uncontested from the outset. A contingent unification emerged
over time based on agreement across the wings over the form if
not the substance of self-determination. And the nationalist identity
code promoted in various ways in the pre-Independence period was
constested by the functional code of the 'British' model of societal
development with its older imperial and liberal codes being increasingly joined by the secular and social justice codes which many
Irish nationalists so hated and by an active British identity supported

mostly by a Protestant minority who were a majority in the North-East. It was for a time also internally contested within the nation by a labour movement code that associated itself with the concerns of British labour radicalism. The codes produced by nationalism together with these alternative codes make up what can be described as the 'relational field' of nationalist politics. However, since this book focuses on the later institutionalisation of national identity in the independent southern Irish state, its primary analytical focus is on the wings of the nationalist movement itself with analysis of other cultural or social forces being brought in as needed. The relational field that characterises the internal relations of nationalist identity politics is examined in the next chapter.

The four wings of the nationalist movement examined here follows Hroch's (1993) model, discussed in Chapter 2, which we adapt for use in the Irish case. The four wings are: 1) the clerical conservative wing, 2) the liberal democratic wing, 3) the revolutionary separatist wing, and 4) the socially radical wing composed chiefly of agrarian, labour and suffragist radicals. These will be examined from two standpoints, their *social location* which may be quite diffuse but still exhibits a discernible relationship to social interests and the *identity projects* they consciously promulgate. The previous chapter provided a picture of a socially modernising and increasingly more prosperous society that nonetheless manifested deep discontents. These wings reflect this development path. Their identity projects are conditioned further by the historical-cultural and institutional implications of Irish history which bequeathed 're-inventable' memories of confessional divide and injustice, the sundering of state and society, dissatisfaction with institutional arrangements and a rudimentary national consciousness, characterised by a republican political philosophy that could powerfully ignite into a mass politics. These divisions and sentiments had powerful mobilisatory potential when reconstructed by later nationalist representational practices. Cultural cleavages that first arose with the Plantations and the wars of religion in the sixteenth and seventeenth century, that were never resolved in the eighteenth century, erupting at its end into outright confessional conflict that compromised the Act of Union from the outset were now re-opened, albeit in a new form that paradoxically owed much to democratisation and material advances.

In the following sections of this chapter, each of the actor wings of the nationalist movement are described in turn beginning with

the church, before dealing with the liberal-democratic wing represented by the Irish Parliamentary Party, the cultural radicals and
separatist revolutionaries, and the social radicals. A few comments
are needed in each of these cases. In the case of the Church, our
focus is on the actual clerics themselves, who were extraordinarily
numerous in Ireland and who reflected a strongly religious worldview
held by a large section of the population. However, the Church
was itself highly organised and reflected a coherent expression of
preferred cultural arrangements though it was itself sufficiently large
to have significant material interests also. The parliamentary party
was the dominant, and for much of the pre-Independence period,
only political party in southern Ireland. As such, it was inevitably a
populist coalition containing many disparate elements. The third
wing, the revolutionary separatists incorporates both the cultural
nationalists and Republican separatist strands as one. While in more
fine-grained analyses distinctions could be drawn between these two
elements within the movement, our focus is on the history of the
cultural idea of self-determination which originated with the new
cultural nationalism and later found expression in the separatist
programme. This programme had, of course, long antedated the
cultural nationalism of the 1890s in the form of the Irish Republican
Brotherhood who had conducted armed rebellion against British
rule as long before as the 1860s but it acquired mass cultural momentum for the first time after the turn of the century. A combination of elements is also present, somewhat more uneasily, in the
case of the fourth wing under consideration, the socialist or radical
wing combined agrarian and labour movement radicalism. While
these two elements on the whole followed very different goals, and
had very different organisational expressions, they had a similar
structure of grievances in the marginalisation of their social interests
within the nationalist consensus hardening around them. The suffragist movement is also briefly addressed.

THE CLERICAL WING OF THE NATIONALIST MOVEMENT

(1) The Social Location of the Church

One of the most singular features of post-famine Ireland was
the rising fortunes of the Catholic church. At the most basic level,

the numbers of clergy rapidly rose as the general population declined increasing the proportion of clerics of all types in the population. In 1800 there was a priest for every 2,100 of the Catholic
laity, by 1870 there was one for every 1,250. The change with respect to nuns is even more dramatic. In 1800 there was one nun
for every 32,000, in 1870 there was one for 1,100 (Larkin, 1972;
Newsinger, 1995). On the demand side, the Church had no difficulty in attracting recruits, chiefly from amongst the lower middle-
class and the larger than average farmers for whom it had a decided
preference over recruits from lower down the social scale. This
owed something to considerations of maintaining middle-class respectability but also to practical considerations of the nature of
recruitment networks, levels of education and capacity to make a
financial contribution to the Church. On the supply side, a career
in the Church was a significant career outlet for many amongst the
lower middle class who did not stand to inherit property. The flow
of recruits to the Church was enhanced by the perceived need for
later marriage in the post-famine economic climate. It was enhanced
too by the accompanying moral climate which brought the Victorian repressive moralisation of sexuality to an extreme.

The Church therefore had no shortage of recruits. Its success in
gaining effective control of much of the nascent health and educational social services in the late nineteenth century allowed it to
expand its organisation scale and provide opportunities for these
new recruits (Inglis, 1987). The construction of the modern Catholic
Church, which had consolidated its organisation machinery by the
1860s, was one of the primary organisational achievements of the
Irish nineteenth century (Larkin, 1987). The construction of an
organisation in which financial flows, authority relations, technical
activities, coherence of structure and internal and external
communication were relatively smoothly integrated gave the Church
significant powers of intervention in defence of its material or moral
objectives. While it would be mistaken to ignore the moral conviction
that integrated the Church's activities and that gave its many clerics
a sufficient degree of ideological integration and communicative
guidance, perhaps too little has been made of its associated material
objectives. The Catholic Church in nineteenth and twentieth century
Ireland was a significantly sized enterprise employing many people,
engaged in vast building and property management projects, and
running a relatively large number of organisations (Inglis, 1987).

The nineteenth century clergy may be understood as part of the expansion of the professional class and also as part of the intelligentsia. The growth in the number of clergy is therefore related to these two major social phenomena following the categories provided by Perkin (1989). This proposition may be defended on a number of grounds. Firstly, the expansion of the Church in its core domain of religion and its acquired domains of teaching and health was part of the expansion of social services that characterised the period. Secondly, the clergy underwent a long and rigorous training producing a specialised and differentiated labour force. Thirdly, clerical activity was governed by professional rules of procedure and ethical codes. Fourthly, its recruitment base went lower down the social hierarchy than other occupations enjoying similar status. Fifthly, it controlled and regulated the conditions of its own labour market. Sixthly, its income did not depend on the market but in persuading society to attach a value for its services. Finally, clerics count as members of the intelligentsia for they take on, or have delegated to them, the symbolic function of constructing, maintaining and re-interpreting a societal ethical code, a key function fulfilled by the religious or secular intelligentsia.

The social and cultural world of the Irish cleric was a study in conservatism. The monastic and service orders lived communally in celibate co-existence while the priests, the key players, lived in private houses with housekeepers. The priestly cultural world was a paradoxical one. He belonged to the small-town, urban, or rural middle-class but differed from them in life experience in that he was celibate and imbued by his office with supreme moral authority, employing the interpretation and adjudication of sin as a technology of social control. His social networks were overwhelmingly middle-class and, correspondingly, the clerical vision for nationalist Ireland was of enlightened middle-class leadership.[2] Garvin (1987, p. 94) even claims that the priests were a substitute middle-class and, with the schoolteachers, represented the only intelligentsia in remote areas.

Irish Catholicism was not an intellectually rationalised religion. On the contrary, the Church prided itself on its identity as a folk church and it contributed to the pronounced strain of anti-intellectualism in twentieth century Irish civic culture (Whyte, 1980). In this the Irish church differed from its continental counterparts which were more closely associated with the conservative sections of the middle and upper classes (Connolly, 1987, p. 9) and helped to shape the major conservative, authoritarian and, later, Christian democratic ideologies of the twentieth century.

Overall, the priest was a patriarchal figure in his community who existed within a highly hierarchical, bureaucratic organisation. His technical activity was tightly prescribed by rules and his entire activity had an authoritarian caste. An expanding organisation oriented to moral control won nothing for being equivocal. This authoritarianism was well-adapted to survive in late nineteenth-century conditions in Ireland. As Rumph and Hepburn (1977, p. 15) point out, the Irish church was a peasant church and not associated with the *ancien régime* (Leighton, 1994). It therefore did not inspire any significant anti-clericalism and assiduously built up an institution-supporting collective memory in the minds of the populace. This constructed memory told of repression and of the Church siding with the under-privileged and of the complete identification of their moral identity and Catholicism.[3]

For much of the second half of the nineteenth century it persisted in an ambivalent position as a church within a state with another established church. This meant that the separation of church and state, resisted by the international church throughout the period (Whyte, 1980), was acceptable to the Irish Church.[4] But with the rise of the national movement the Church revealed itself progressively to have a communitarian ideology summed up in the twentieth century maxim 'a Catholic church for a Catholic people'. As in France in the period, the Church believed that the organised 'Catholicisation' of culture which it was assiduously affecting in the period should lead to the construction of a state that would enshrine a Catholic ethical code in its laws and practices (Birnbaum, 1991). Irish Catholicism was therefore markedly hostile to liberal pluralist ideas or practices in any form and was in general respectful of royal institutions and lawfully constituted authority, at least up to the last two decades of the nineteenth century (MacDonagh, 1983, p. 93).

In line with the international church, but to an unparalleled degree, the Catholic church sought to retain control of socialisation. It did so by establishing a firm grip on education as well as by the doctrine of familism (Cairns and Richards, 1988, pp. 59–62) with its chief tenet, the subordination of women and control over their sexuality through the doctrine of 'the home'. The University Question in nineteenth and early twentieth century Ireland revealed the extent of the Church's ambition in the educational sphere. Unparalleled in international comparison, it insisted on a Catholic university education for Irish Catholics (Whyte, 1980). It also revealed the limited and unthreatening intellectual role it envisaged for educated lay Catholics by supporting a vocational rather than a liberal educational philosophy (Paseta, 1994).[5] Familism in Ireland was the Catholic adaptation of the Victorian patriarchalism which sought to confine women to the home and introduced a new moralisation of sexuality. The Catholic church took this doctrine to extreme and rigidly proscribed the expression of sexuality and opposed the entry of women into public life, symbolically constructing them instead as defenders of faith and family life.

(2) The Identity Project of the Church

The identification of a Catholic identity project oriented towards the nation can be aligned with the rise of the new nationalism in the 1890s. By this time, the range of cultural interpretation models on which the Church drew makes a long list: Catholic corporatism and conservatism, Catholic communitarian identification, Catholic and general romantic anti-modernism, Catholic anti-collectivism and anti-materialism, identification with respectable middle-class, Victorian ideas of sexual repression and familism, nostalgia for a stable social order against the ravages of modernisation, hostility to liberalism and suspicion of democracy, hatred of urban, industrial life and the embracing of a rural idyll, hostility to emerging forms of popular culture which were dramatically upping the pace of cultural change, hostility to modern forms of artistic expression, and distrust of secular intellectuals. These cultural models, interpreted in relation to the Irish context by the 1890s, tended to suggest an interest of the Church in breaking the link with the United Kingdom state and tended to support the Church's perception, flushed with its political success against Parnellism, of the opportunity and necessity of defining the identity of the future nation in which it would play a dominant moral role.[6]

The collective identity of the Irish Catholic Church in the late nineteenth century and early twentieth century, which was so powerfully to influence the national identity of the future state, was one based chiefly on negativity towards cultural and social modernisation and positively on primordial and conventional codes. Primordial, in the sense that it became increasingly clear that the Church desired to exercise its moral supremacy within a Catholic nation and that Catholicism became a necessary characteristic to be considered a fully-fledged citizen of that nation. Others could enjoy

formal rights of citizenship but to participate fully in the codes of
collective belonging within the new state one had to be Catholic.
Irish Catholic identity regulated citizenship by means of a primordial communitarianism. Conventional, in the sense that participation in this life-world required fundamental agreement on values
and, even more potent and discriminating, the inexplicit foundations of habitual behaviour which separate appropriate and inappropriate behaviour in many social situations and, consequently,
those who truly belong and those who do not (Bourdieu, 1991).
The prevalence of primordialism was also, undoubtedly related to
the spirit of millenarianism that existed in the church's self-image,
which as Garvin (1986, p. 76) argues, was characterised by a sense
of self-righteousness and the notion that it was a persecuted group
(Keenan, 1983).

The identity project of the Church was above all to convention-
alise the Irish life-world, to render it unreflective, and to naturalise its moral code giving the impression of a timeless adherence to
dogma while in fact conducting a very contemporary moralisation.
The psycho-social technology of sin, and the doctrine of eternal
punishment, was precisely designed for the purpose (Inglis, 1987).
The posited presence and adjudication of sin rested on extra-mundane criteria which could not be subjected to the test of the social
and therefore created the possibility of unconscious power. The
Church specialised in mobilising a social psychology that emphasised the dark side of human nature, a nature disposed to evil,
imperfectible and continuously fallible, and always in need of external correction from an omniscient external body. The Church
by means of the technology of sin worked to prevent a concretisation
of ego-strength and individuation. The assertion of the self was
treated with suspicion, suppressed as a sin of pride. It succeeded
in institutionalising a moral code extending across the whole of
the Catholic life-world that penetrated even to the foundations of
the thinkable. Certain things were not thinkable, unconsciously
suppressed, a suppression that was social-psychologically sustained,
and that above all suppressed ideas of personal autonomy. The
Church succeeded in mobilising through modern organised means
the self-denial and collective identifications of the traditional habitus,
under assault from modernisation by the end of the nineteenth
century, and preserving it through organised cultural domination.

The Church therefore codified what it held in a morally relevant
sense as being Irish. It also similarly codified its standpoint on what

Irishness was not. Above all, it contributed to national identity a sense of belonging that did not depend on consciously held beliefs but rather drew its power from the taken-for-granted pre-critical identification with community. This community the Church increasingly defined as a Catholic community with an ancient pedigree dating back to before the Norman invasion. In this sense the Irish Catholic church contributed the code of modern, anti-modernism to Irish national identity. Above all, it powerfully reinforced the idea that the national identity of the new state-nation should be preserved from reflexive scrutiny and critique. This gave Irish national identity its pronounced uncritical, exclusive and anti-intellectual disposition.

THE LIBERAL DEMOCRATIC WING OF THE NATIONALIST MOVEMENT

(1) The Social Location of the Liberal Democrats

The emerging Catholic lower-middle class elite gave coherence to the Irish Parliamentary Party and provided its largely national-populist political programme a definite social and cultural orientation. Alter (1971, pp. 33–43) chronicles the change in the social composition of the representatives of the party from a predominantly Protestant, landlord caste to a predominately Catholic *'bildungs-bürgertum'*[8] – the educated middle class – under Parnell. The educated middle and lower-middle class, along with a relatively small cadre of farmers became the dominant political representatives of the party which sought its electoral mandate from an expanding but still narrow and exclusively male electorate drawn from the more prosperous rural and urban sections of the population.

The social identity, organisational basis and programme of the Party was forged in the 1880s from two key elements:[9] the desire of the new nationalist elite to localise political opportunity, power and influence, a desire politically projected at the new urban and rural electorate, and the incorporation of an emerging rural propertied elite whose drive for ownership of the land fuelled Home Rule politics throughout the period of the first two phases of Home Rule agitation in 1886 and 1893.[10] The social identity of the party reflected an elite that was to remain a mixed bag throughout the period. The party housed clerics, farmers, and the educated urban lower-middle class but appealed to a broader nationalist tending electorate. Its cultural identity was correspondingly mixed. Bew (1987, p. 6) describes the party as being 'affected by diverse, liberal influences as well as those of a more unsophisticated, elemental sort'. Fitzpatrick (1977, p. 92) gives an account of the populism of the Irish Parliamentary Party as embracing 'farmers and labourers, Protestants and Catholics, city and country, elements which could be expected, under Home Rule, to find their interests mutually at odds'.

The Irish Parliamentary Party was certainly populist. Its ideology stressed at different times and places the need for accommodation with the Unionist tradition in Ireland, the consistency of Irish Home Rule and an imperial identity, and the exclusivity of what was now becoming known as 'Irish Ireland'. Its historical origins lay not only in primordial sentiments of Catholic deprivation and identity but also in the cultivated memory of the previous episode of institutional independence represented by Grattan's parliament which had been dissolved in the Act of Union. Its nationalism was therefore tempered by a rational belief in the possibility and necessity of finding an institutionally satisfactory solution that would keep Ireland within the empire, which had distinct advantages in terms of middle-class careers, and which would also keep the integral territorial identity of the new state-nation by overcoming Protestant objections. The Home Rule party also had a conservative instinct. From Butt's conviction that Ireland should be protected from the dangers of democracy, through the party's embracing of 'liberal' majoritarian, representative and egalitarian principles (Macmillan, 1993) the Home Rule Party was only interested in as much social change as was compatible with its limited social base. This was manifested in attitudes to taxation, education, insurance and pension reform in the first decade of the twentieth century. For instance the budget of 1908/09, when the Liberal Party introduced plans to raise income taxes to create a welfare system, was intensely debated in Ireland and proved especially unpopular in those parts where it struck at the distilleries and publicans, who were the backbone of the party (Lyons, 1973, p. 266).[11]

The social base of the party, in its formative years, was built upon the same petit-bourgeois habitus and interests as that of the Catholic church. From the beginning, clerics were made honorary members of the party. The same church-sponsored virtues of respectability, sexlessness, obedience, communal solidarity, familism, were prominent within the party though the party was to some extent in competition with the Church to decide who would have the dominant hand in constructing the new Ireland. While nationalism in Ireland was not the secular phenomenon that it was elsewhere, it did have a secular component revealed in part in the capacity of nationalist politicians of different kinds to defy the Church in certain situations, notably in supporting the separatist doctrine of Fenianism, in the protracted split of the party caused by the demise of Parnell in the 1890s, and in support for the Republican side in the civil war (Whyte, 1980). In part, too, Home Rule politicians could not easily succumb to a narrow confessional identity while, sincerely or otherwise, they sought solutions to the Irish question which involved the British state and political parties as well as northern and southern Protestants seeking the continuation of the Union. Participation in the broader context of British constitutional innovation had an expanding effect on horizons. As Strauss (1941) has argued, the question of Home Rule for Ireland was a central aspect in the shaping of British democracy. As British politicians became progressively more involved in the Irish question, they became increasingly more democratic (Heyck, 1974).

Considerations of wider horizons were undoubtedly important for the Parliamentary Party at all times during its hegemony because, apart from very occasional rhetorical aberrations by its leaders, it held true to a constitutionalist line. In so doing, it made an indispensable contribution to the establishment of a democratic political culture within southern Ireland that has only once been threatened, during the civil war (Prager, 1986). Notwithstanding this, the environment of the Irish Parliamentary Party became all the more chauvinistic as the new nationalism gained ground in the early twentieth century. This was fuelled both by the church, animated by the desire to establish a collective political identity to match its cultural project, and by the revolutionary nationalists who, especially after 1900, were busy establishing the cultural foundations of a Gaelic-Catholic primordialism. These influences pushed the Irish Parliamentary Party ever more to adopt an 'Irish-Ireland' cultural perspective and to slowly diminish its commitment to a policy of conciliation towards northern and southern Unionists after 1900 (Bew, 1994). The cross-class nationalist appeal and political dominance of the party inevitably led to a populist orientation.

Populism was further promoted by the sharpness of social conflict in late nineteenth and early twentieth century Ireland. Dissatisfaction with existing arrangements was prominent in both town and countryside. In the one case, dissatisfaction was manifested in lower middle-class disenchantment at career prospects, in labour radicalism whose great symbolic expression was the Dublin lock-out of 1913 and, in the other, by continuing rural agitation throughout the first decade of the century. Rural tensions were absorbed directly into the party from the late 1890s through the influence of William O'Brien's United Irish League, which started off as an explicitly anti-grazier movement but reunited with the Parliamentary Party in 1900. After the last of the great Land Acts in 1903 that enabled the tenant farmers to become owners of the land, the rural discontent that had emerged could no longer be contained by a united agrarian movement due to spiralling tensions within the rural classes between labourers and tenant farmers and the owners of the land as against the still landless (Bull, 1988a). Agariarism, therefore, continued to be an unavoidable factor in Irish nationalist politics and a major hindrance to ambitions of nationalist consensus (Bew, 1987). Given these pressures the party had to choose and, though it sought to postpone it, it sided with the conservative wing of the social base of nationalism. The party became increasingly representative of the better off tenant farmers. Hence, though the party was able to hold its own constituency, its position of electoral dominance was always likely to be threatened by the expansion of the suffrage to include disaffected lower class elements in the population. This, as much as the particular circumstances of the First World War and the Easter Rising, explains the replacement of the Irish Parliamentary Party by Sinn Fein as the dominant party of rural Ireland in 1918. Ultimately, the party remained true to the agrarian and professional elite and pursued a politics destined to preserve that elite's coherence. Towards the rest, it practised a symbolic politics which was fuzzy about the sharing of either power or resources.

What enabled the party to retain its coherence was its professional organisational basis which was very advanced for the time. The organisational structure of the party not alone ensured party discipline but also gave it control over the emerging national movement. Parnell achieved this with the foundation of the Irish National League in 1882 which, unlike the Land League which had been founded to progress tenant interests, he was able to control directly. The National League was effectively an adjunct of the Parliamentary Party with local branches which rallied support, constituency committees who selected candidates and ran campaigns and a national executive, who organised, co-ordinated and directed the other two levels (Travers, 1988). This organisational basis, first made possible by the charismatic leadership of Parnell, allowed for effective control of the grass-roots while also remaining sensitive to changing currents of opinion. It was the basis of the party's continuing hegemony over Irish politics after the era of Parnell's charismatic leadership came to an end.

(2) The Identity Project of the Irish Parliamentary Party

The primary contribution of the Parliamentary Party to the forma-tion of Irish national identity was to counter-act the exclusivist, anti-modern and even tendentially anti-democratic aspects of other wings of the national movement by anchoring in national identity a rational democratic component. The Home Rule Ireland sought by the party might bear witness to the ideals of a Gaelic past but its form of life would also be informed by a respect for parliamen-tary democracy. This commitment to democracy might be described as the universalistic accomplishment of the party. It survived the vicissitudes and violence of nationalist revolution to ensure the post-independent state would have a democratic political culture. How-ever, its particularistic accomplishment was to anchor institutionally the particular value syndrome of its petit-bourgeois constituency, especially the affinity between propertied respectability and con-fessional identity. This petit-bourgeois constituency veered between relatively stronger and weaker religious influences but became rec-onciled to an increasingly pro-clerical line after the re-unification of the party in the 1890s. The ambivalence of the party from its origins on the relationship between democratic-pluralist and con-fessional identity continued to shape Irish political culture throughout the twentieth century.

The party's ambivalence as to the appropriate demarcation of the spheres of politics and everyday culture led to it becoming an institutional conduit for two characteristic phenomena of Irish twen-tieth-century political culture. On the material level, it facilitated localised political clientelism, the pragmatic politics of small favours conferred by politicians on their citizen 'clients', especially after gaining control of local government by the turn of the century. On the cultural level, it facilitated the advance of confessional morali-sation into political culture and the constitutional order. The diag-nosis of the existing situation carried by the party emphasised the relationship between Irishness and confessional injustice. While its initial programme did not wish to open vistas of difference between the newly empowered Catholic lower middle-class and the existing Irish elite, nor did it wish to eschew some of the advantages of empire such as the relatively high participation of Irish people in imperial service, it did use its gathering institutional power to facilitate the newly emerging powers within Ireland, the recently propertied, the Church, and the symbolic power of cultural nationalism.

In its organisational form and political activity the party contributed hugely to the style of politics of twentieth century Ireland. Its local political dominance and direct political influence contrasted with its highly indirect influence over the macro-institutional order of the state. This divide helped to establish in the twentieth century the political role of a public opinion that could not appropriately direct an irresponsible and distant state. To be effective, public opinion had to be filtered through the institutionalised political channels of the party. The early modern disjuncture of state and society, as argued in Chapter 3, continued in the period of high nationalism. This left the recurring legacy in the post-independence state of a disempowered public opinion imbued with what was substantially only an historical kind of symbolic power. It had allegedly had its say in its support for nationalism and now the organisations that interpreted the nationalist legacy could speak for public opinion as a whole. Further, in post-independence politics up to the 1950s, the state was construed in the dominant political culture as a suspicious outsider whose influence should be minimised.

A further contribution to the southern Irish national identity code emanating from the party was the idea of a society which emphasised duties rather than rights. This may seem rather curious given the explosion in the politics of rights in the 1880s associated with the party. But the party had fought predominantly Protestant landholding, electoral, social, and occupational power in the interests of the rights of an emerging Catholic elite. Once these had been substantially achieved, insofar as it was possible within the United Kingdom framework with the extension of such formal rights as electoral power and the substantive re-balancing of informal rights such as occupational and educational opportunity between the confessions, the party was satisfied on the social question. The importance of the generalisation of rights to subaltern elements in the population, who with greater or lesser intensity pursued these rights through the period of the Irish national movement, did not concern it to an extent comparable with its initial social radicalism. It was expedient, in the context of the national question, and the future Ireland that would satisfy the new elite, to turn from rights to the symbolic construction of duty with the exception, of course, of the 'inalienable' right to national self-government. The manner in which the social question was redefined and ultimately suppressed by the party instituted the elements of selective perception and authoritarianism in Irish political culture and shaped its conceptions of citizenship.

THE REVOLUTIONARY WING OF THE NATIONALIST MOVEMENT

(1) The Social Location of the Revolutionary Separatists

Many chapters in mainstream historical texts addressing the rise of Irish nationalism around the turn of the century are now entitled in whole or in part 'the new nationalism'.[12] After the extraordinary excitement of the Home Rule period, followed by the Parnellite split and the failure of the second Home Rule Bill, Irish constitutional politics was heading into a period if not of quiescence then of 'normal' politics. The emergence of the new cultural nationalism enlivened the political scene in the 1890s though the main issues of the period were still dominated by this 'normal' politics: Home Rule, the divisions of the Parliamentary Party, alleged over-taxation, and local government reform. The term 'new nationalism' signifies above all the politics of cultural radicalism which began as an eclectic search for a new identity basis for a mass politics and finished more than thirty years later as a self-confident politics of Irish separatism.[13]

Two dimensions of the theory of differentiation may be used to locate the origin of the organised separatist nationalism that matured in the 1890s with the founding of the Gaelic League and the growing importance of the Gaelic Athletic Association. The first is that in the process of functional differentiation and specialisation in the second half of the nineteenth century, associated inter alia with the expansion of state activities and the rapid expansion of the service economy, a new lower middle-class had been formed in both urban and rural locations. The first indications of its potentially radical politics had come in the 1860s with the Fenian movement which had staged an ill-fated revolt in 1867. But Fenianism was overwhelmingly a rural movement, supported by some sections of the rural lower middle-class, whereas the further expansion of the state, law, education, commerce and health had greatly expanded the urban lower middle-class by the 1890s. Functional differentiation and specialisation generated significant social pressures in the form of blocked occupational mobility for a new actual or potential lower middle-class who had acquired educational capital but whose gateway to prosperity and social status was blocked by declining middle-class career options (Garvin, 1987, 1988). The second is that the new nationalism gave the structural outcomes of the transfer of political and socio-economic power to the Catholic middle-class a culturalist twist. Intellectuals were crucial actors in constructing the nation (Giesen, 1993; Goldring, 1993). In Greenfeld's (1992) Durkheimean terms, 'anomie' created by structural contradictions took on a cultural form and education became a means of cultural subversion. But the new nationalism represented more than the cultural legitimation of the social interests of the 1880s or of forming a new oppositional momentum associated with the dissatisfactions of the nineties. It also represented the development of new weapons for the *cultural* interests of the nineties. It was becoming the vehicle of an alternative vision of a social order.

In the 1890s, the scale of blocked mobility for the Catholic lower middle-class in the cities and towns became evident. Imbued with a significant degree of educational and cultural capital, their employment prospects neither satisfied their motivational requirements, their sense of self-worth, or their desired levels of prosperity. In part, this can be attributed to the adjustment problems of a society undergoing rapid modernisation, experiencing the first major wave of expansion of knowledge work, and generally finding itself too small to generate the complex division of labour that opened career prospects commensurate with available talents (Garvin, 1987, pp. 43–9). From the standpoint of those affected a more immediate grievance was the relatively advantaged position of Protestants who commanded a disproportionate number of higher positions in the rapidly expanding civil service, in the professions, and in commercial activity. These Protestants served as proxy for a wider assumption, that the modernisation process in Ireland had followed an English model which was unsuited to Irish conditions and had led not alone to poor material prospects but also to low self-esteem, a situation which needed to be corrected by a new moral valuation of the national culture (MacDonagh, 1983, p. 116). The Gaelic

Athletic Association was an Irish response to contemporary developments in British culture which espoused militant Christianity and a culture of heroic virtue. More generally, the Gaelic movement and Victorian racialism could be seen as two examples of Social Darwinist inspired patriotism (Bew, 1991; Boyce, 1987; Mandle, 1987).

The idea of a revaluation of the native culture was spun out of the feeling of marginalisation of the lower middle class. Sufficiently educated and modern to require a legitimation model of equality of worth, convinced as only the lower middle-class can be convinced that it is the unfairness of the situation they find themselves in, and not structural causes or any deficiencies of their own that explains their perceived low achievement, they were concerned to demonstrate their equality of status in relation to the metropolitan culture that did them the double disservice of loading the dice against them and then morally disdained them for their backwardness. With this animus, the lower middle-class made a virtue of their own local habitus much as the characters in the rural Norway of Ibsen at the same time. Internalised feelings of inferiority turned to joyful release as they apparently found in the very point of their weakness, rurality and peripherality, the basis of their new cultural strength. As Garvin (1987, p. 47) points out it was difficult for these lower-middle class intellectuals to acquire middle class respectability, but they could, as Catholics, acquire and promulgate a certain spirituality and the revival movement gave them a kind of psychological comfort. For the discovery and sustaining of this new strength they needed a cosmology that, moreover, would unite them in feelings of solidarity with those around them, making up for the rootlessness of the new urban form of life.

The cosmology required intellectual creators and interpreters and these were ready to hand. The expansion of knowledge work created in a rough and ready fashion a new intelligentsia that were not so much oriented to high-cultural forms as to nostalgic, sentimentalising local cultural production (Leerssen, 1996).[14] That some of the figures of the Gaelic revival, for instance Douglas Hyde and Eoghan MacNeil, were fine scholars was not the point. The intellectual productions of the Gaelic Revival were not so much troubled with truth or artistic form as with the creation of communal meaning in the form of socially effective myths. These myths were revolutionary myths as the separatist component of the cultural nationalist imaginary became stronger in the early twentieth century and contemplated the complete de-Anglicisation of Ireland.

As Hutchinson (1987, p. 153) points out, the Gaelic Revival was primarily an educational movement attempting to build a new pedagogy of the nation-to-be. This pedagogy first addressed the manifest basis of what they understood as an exhalted, Gaelic civilisation that, far from being the subject-matter of derision, had in their eyes actually guaranteed the continuity of European civilisation in early medieval Europe. Hence, at least a sympathy for language and history became necessary perquisites of the newly Gaelicised person.

The ideology of Gaelic Ireland took on a more defined shape in the early twentieth century. It moved away from an urban to a rural idyll, though organisationally still remaining predominantly urban, and with its vision of society as an aesthetically transformed totality it progressively moved into a more intimate relationship with Catholicism. In the former sense, the distinctiveness of the Irish situation appeared to reside in its rural civilisation while, in the latter sense, Moran's[15] view that Irish and Catholic were synonymous began to have increasing resonance, a position rapidly taken on board by sectarian organisations such as the Ancient Order of Hibernians, who helped to politicise Catholicism in Ulster and eventually acted as a recruiting base for the Parliamentary Party (Fitzpatrick, 1989, p. 185). Notwithstanding, its commitment to a new, simple and virtuous rural civilisation, the Revival's main contribution was to mobilise urban Ireland, including the intelligentsia and Catholic lower middle-class, for nationalist politics. It therefore filled a gap that the Parliamentary Party had been unable to fill given its rural origins and focus as well as its engagement in secular liberal imperialism. While the Gaelic League was shaping a new identity code for Irish nationalism, the ground for violent mobilisation was being prepared by the Irish Republican Brotherhood (IRB) which had revitalised the old Fenian tradition and was to become the key influence on the 1916 Rising. When Sinn Fein eventually emerged as a populist movement in 1918 it was able to profit from both the identity politics of the League and the militarisation of the society by the separatist Republican movement. As a secret militia, the IRB did not engage in an open identity politics of its own.

As a social philosophy, the Gaelic Revival was nebulous (Murray, 1993). Its ideology of Gaelic civilisation created a platform for rural values that was ambivalent and evasive about urban problems. On the whole it embraced two sets of contradictory utopian values.

On the one hand, in its rural variant it stressed an anti-industrialism which envisaged an Irish development path quite different to that of England. On the other hand, it argued that protectionism would allow Irish industries to flourish freed from the debilitating competition of English imports. In general, however, its position on Irish development was vague and its main orientation was to stress the virtues of a separatism that would allow the construction of a distinctive identity that would mobilise society towards nationally appropriate goals. It did adopt political positions on certain cultural matters but it steered clear of major ethical and political issues such as the political expression of rural grievances by small tenants and landless labourers or conflict over the rights and conditions of labour in the cities. Its main cultural achievement was, negatively, to define 'Irishness' as non-Englishness and, positively, to create a new 'race project' that answered the psychological needs of the times for solidarity based on primordial and quasi-egalitarian feelings of collective identification before the nation.

The emotions unleashed by the new nationalism were sectarian and even racist. An organic unity of Catholicism, nationality, culture and race was forged in promoting extreme Anglophobia. The movement towards a sectarian frame of reference in Irish and Anglo-Irish politics was reflected in the right-wing Catholic counterparts to the Protestant sectarianism of the Orange Order, the Ancient Order of Hibernians, the Catholic Defence Society, and the Catholic Association of Ireland formed in 1902, whose declared objective was the destruction of Protestant influences (Foster, 1989, p. 453). The strong emphasis on exclusivity in the construction of Irish national identity was also directed at Freemasons and Jews. Anti-Semitism was deeply rooted in Sinn Fein, *The Leader*, and in the Irish church. In 1904 there was a pogrom against the Jews in Limerick and the Irish clergy generally took an anti-Dreyfus stance in the case that deeply divided France (Garvin, 1987, pp. 69–72).

The task of creating a nationalist cosmology involves the building of appropriate norms while drawing heavily on the re-interpretation of history. The cosmology is meant to have universal appeal to all those defined to fall within it. In the cosmology of the Gaelic Revival, these were the Catholic Irish. The cosmology has to be teachable, answer the social psychological requirements of identification, direct grievance into a cultural project of national destiny, and command universal adherence. This cosmology had already achieved considerable success by the end of the first decade of the twentieth century in spite of the continuing electoral success of the Parliamentary Party. As long as cultural nationalism was unable or unwilling to engage in constitutional or non-constitutional politics there was no necessary conflict with the party's control of southern Irish electoral politics.

This situation was to change radically after 1912. The new cosmology of the Gaelic Revival had succeeded in broadly diffusing its identity project. In the years from 1898 to 1916 the League was gradually taken over by the revitalised IRB under the leadership of Tom Clark, who had returned from America, and Douglas Hyde resigned from its board (Foster, 1989, pp. 475–6). The Parliamentary Party was pursuing Home Rule for what appeared to many an interminable time and it was to be further delayed for the duration of the First World War. The symbolic violence against the established order, aimed at delegitimating the existing state and creating within Ireland a new cultural basis for political legitimation, had established the moral and sacrificial basis for physical violence. While commitment to physical violence remained a minority phenomenon, the cultural idea of violence as a legitimate response to the national situation had been established. This idea, and the capacity to give it affect through military training and the militarisation and masculinisation of culture (Mosse, 1985), was further sustained by the violence all over Europe in the First World War. The *ennui* of the long nineteenth century was now giving rise to excitement on a terrible scale.

Nationalists like Pearse wanted to be part of this. They combined the idea of the general, historically given will of the Irish people, which overrode any merely empirical will, with a cult of violence (Dudley Edwards, 1977). The 1916 rising was the culmination of this *fin-de-siècle* cult of violence (O'Brien, 1994; Gerson, 1995; Thompson, 1982). They therefore built on the identity code developed in the Gaelic revival which attempted to create a project and a destiny for a homogeneous 'race' consistent with the social and psychological needs of the population. Republican nationalism in this tradition appealed in urban Ireland to those who had less to lose, the radicalised lower middle-class constituency of the Gaelic revival. In rural Ireland, Rumph and Hepburn (1977), Garvin (1987) and Fitzpatrick (1977) agree that it was the lower middle-class in the countryside, though not in the small towns, that supported Sinn Fein, the new party of Irish Republicanism. In general, the new Sinn Fein elite was non-agrarian and middle class, but of recent rural origins and highly educated with nearly half having third level education (Garvin, 1987, p. 53).[16] Much has been written about the dramatic reversal of fortunes of the Irish Parliamentary Party and the corresponding rise of Sinn Fein in the 1918 elections. Various arguments have been advanced to explain the electoral turn to Republican separatism. They include the symbolic legacy of 1916, the conscription issue fuelled by the strong anti-conscription movement that was prominent in the latter stages of the war, disaffection with the experience of war, the change in suffrage rights that extended the vote in class terms much lower down the male electorate and to women,[17] and the growing international attraction towards 'self-determination. Of the possible explanations, and they are intertwined with one another, it is probably suffrage change, and its political anticipation in the re-alignment of nationalist politics in 1917 and 1918, that was most decisive. Changes in suffrage rights provided greater incentive for all social classes to participate in nationalist politics. The earlier efforts of the cultural nationalists ensured that the new voting constituencies were familiar with the Republican messages of the separatists which appeared to give them a stake in the benefits of nationalist revolution. In any case, Sinn Fein won a landslide victory in the 1918 election.[18]

Historians such as Fitzpatrick (1977) and Foster (1989) stress the continuity between the Parliamentary Party and Sinn Fein. Sinn Fein after 1918 took over the populism, the organisation, much of the sources of finance and much of the constituency of the Parliamentary Party. But Sinn Fein reached further than the party in two dimensions. It extended to a new socio-economic constituency which posed, at least partly, new social questions. And it marked a transition in the politics of Irish nationalism from an empirically-based, compromise-oriented movement to one which put the nation as transcendental value on a spiritual plane developing a quasi-theocratic notion of sovereignty. This transcendental idea is captured by Garvin (1993, p. 15) in the notion of the 'public band', a male brotherhood of revolutionary activists who defended their own right to a revolutionary-communitarian will that transcended all empirical wills. In the independent Irish state, the weakly-formulated social question associated with Sinn Fein did not entirely disappear but it was subordinated to transcendental notions of the nation and feelings of identification with the nation that actually promoted inegalitarian outcomes.

(2) The Identity Project of the Revolutionary Separatists

The revolutionary ideology drew directly off an older tradition of cultural nationalism, which had first emerged in the eighteenth century and was further elaborated in the early nineteenth century. This nationalism was largely associated with Protestant romanticism but also included Catholic historians and antiquarians. Two major names associated with this movement were George Petrie and Samuel Ferguson who emphasised the foundations of Irish national identity in the Gaelic past. With the emergence of Young Ireland in the 1830s cultural nationalism took on a more political shape (Davis, 1987). Young Ireland's most important leader, Thomas Davis, introduced German romanticist ideas into Irish cultural nationalism, in particular the organic historicism of Herder (MacDonagh, 1983, p. 110; O'Neil, 1976, 1977). These romanticist ideas were combined with ideas of the autonomy of civil society drawn from the French revolutionary tradition. French revolutionary ideas also had an impact on O'Connell's movement for the repeal of the Act of Union with which the Young Irelanders were associated (Petler, 1985). Romanticism and ideas of the legitimacy of the revolutionary will of the people created what was to become in later decades a potent nationalism in Ireland (Mansergh, 1968, pp. 245–67). However, this nationalism was to have two streams which were based on a similar cultural inspiration but with very different strategies, constitutional parliamentary nationalism and violent revolutionary nationalism. These two currents were ambivalently connected by long-run historical myths and as time wore on by a common Catholicism.[19]

The common origins and cultural affinities of both kinds of nationalism drew from a 'base' literary nationalism which drew from a long tradition of scholarship on Gaelic themes in both Irish and English. They also drew political inspiration from the United Irishmen of the 1790s (Gibbons, 1991; Thuenete, 1994). The literary movement was a predominantly urban middle class movement of intellectuals (Hill, 1980) and while it increasingly became more political it remained non-sectarian. The movement was in fact predominantly Protestant. Its importance lay not in its status as a social movement or as an organisation of any significance – by mid-century it had ceased to exist – but in its cultural resonance which kept alive interpretations of a distinctive nationality.[20] It bequeathed cultural codes which were used in new ways by later generations of nationalists. The Gaelic Revival movement which emerged in the 1890s was at the outset predominantly a cultural movement. In it early stages, it did not have any obvious connection with revolutionary nationalism or political mobilisation (Hutchinson, 1987, 1994, pp. 54–63; MacDonagh, 1983, pp. 104–25).

By the turn of the twentieth century cultural nationalism can be divided into two groups united in their opposition to Anglicisation and modernity: Anglo-Irish revivalism which was elitist, Gaelic-romanticist and non-political and the 'Irish-Ireland' movement which was Catholic, sectarian, also Gaelic-romanticist and increasingly political, though displaying more of a romantic cultural politics than one attached to a clear programme for secession (Lyons, 1982). The Anglo-Irish tradition going back to Davis retained the view that English should remain the dominant language of culture (Boyce, 1991b, p. 252). Unlike Davis, the later Anglo-Irish revival remained in the tradition of non-political nationalism, though under the influence of writers such as Yeats and Hyde it adopted a revolutionary aesthetic form which indirectly legitimated political radicalism. By contrast, the separatist animus of the Irish-Ireland movement was rapidly gaining ground, striving to make a connection between language and religion.

Irish cultural nationalism went through many manifestations from its eighteenth century origins, to its philosophical maturation in the Herdian counter-Enlightenment, to the revolutionary ideas of the Young Irelanders and Fenians, to the antiquarian scholars and artists of the Revival of late Victorian Ireland, to the revolutionary IRB and the moralising tone of the Irish Irelanders of the Edwardian era. The identity project that consolidated from the 1890s was a mixture of cultural despair directed at the existing social order and utopianism based on future oriented and often invented memories. As with German cultural nationalism, a transcendental idea of its own superiority crystallised around Irish culture. Radical cultural ideas could offer apparent remedies for political problems by promoting the aesthetically inspired integration of a society that could somehow transcend real differences if all were prepared to take the leap. Eisenstadt and Giesen (1995, p. 89) show how the nation-form became central to this way of constructing the world:

> The centre of this aesthetic integration is the transcendental idea of *Volk* and Nation. The romantic idea of nation did not refer to the 'superficial' reality of state and economy, but located the collective identity in the transcendental realm of sublime essences

and forces of history. Because *Volk* and Nation are conceived as the eternal and sacred centre beyond the fluidity of modern communication, these processes of communication cannot touch them: an entirely new and detached form of communication is required in order to penetrate the opaque surface of modernity and to reveal the hidden core of history: the nation.

The language of the nation is like a secret language which outsiders have great difficulty in following. Its logic does not pretend at rational coherence but is based on an overwhelming sense of sympathetic self-identification by a group of people who feel their collective experience cannot be understood by outsiders, only felt by themselves.

The combination of ideas of cultural superiority and a self-sympathy beyond rational reflection created a structure of values on which arose a potent aesthetic politics. Unlike the cultural codes which the Parliamentary Party relied on, these codes were particularly amenable to diffusion in the age of mass communication, thus facilitating the 'nationalisation of the masses' (Mosse, 1975). As a cultural nationalism imbued with primordialism, the aesthetic politics of radical separatism was explicitly anti-statist. It was therefore suspiciously disposed to any state, be it Irish or British. This cultural suspicion survived the foundation of the Free State to be a continuing source of political instability.

The identity project of the separatist nationalists involved the generalisation of the national idea to all social strata. It contained above all the idea that injustice produced new community-based rights that were self-evidently true and therefore did not depend on rational legitimation against contending ideas and traditions. In this sense, firstly on a formal plane, the ideology of separatism in Ireland was distinct from the social interests of its lower-class base constituency and could more easily be aligned with conservative Catholicism. The nationalist cultural basis of social mobilisation hindered the emergence of a social democratic consciousness. In the early twentieth century, this formal potential became increasingly substantively aligned through the promotion of the common identification of Gaelic and Catholic. The reciprocal legitimation of Catholicism and nationalism prevented social criticism that went beyond the conservative straitjacket of Irish Catholicism from emerging. Cultural nationalism was a critical architect of this anti-critical spirit towards interest conflicts within the nation. Neither the Parliamentary Party, which was anyhow generally agnostic on myths of the nation, nor the Church which was socially cautious, morally defensive and organisationally hierarchical would alone have been able to institute such powerful, inclusive myths of we-feeling. This we-feeling was, like the Catholic ideology, both primordial and conventional. It extended beyond the Catholic moralisation of the world by introducing subjective-aesthetic meaning complexes directed at extra-religious dimensions of social life and the frustration and disappointment that comes with not achieving life ambitions. It therefore represented not just a diffusion of communal norms in the modern, national setting but a powerful re-elaboration of cultural codes, an exercise in what has been described as the 'invention of tradition' (Hobsbawm and Ranger, 1983).

The subjective-aesthetic figurations of the culture of separatism involved the articulation of a collective identity code that included a curious hybrid of religious and secular-spiritual motifs as criteria of political legitimation. A pre-given spiritual bonding with the solidary community of the nation supersedes the articulation of individual or collective rights. This in turn led to a particular normative account of rights. Rights are what were denied historically by others not what should be in the present. To postulate rights before the establishment of the nation-state, that in any sense qualified the ideal of national freedom as the transcendental basis of all rights, was inherently wrong. This laid the foundations of a transcendental and illiberal ethical code in Irish political culture according to which rights were given by the national community not taken by the individual or group. One consequence was a powerful coincidence of individual and collective identities: Irish identities were thus less based on the peculiarities of economic and political interests as on a communitarian identification with the nation. It also created the related idea that the negativity of Irish experience of historical persecution was so overpowering that the act of assertion of freedom itself did not require justification. Nobody needed to take responsibility for the foundation of the state, therefore no baseline needed to be set for the evaluation of its consequences.

This abdication of positive, ethical responsibility is paralleled by the *episteme* of the Gaelic revival. Much has been made of the Irish love of history. This may be traced to the mythical constructions of the separatists who, first of all, excavated tradition to satisfy the present, and then, in the post-revolutionary period, used the often spurious historical results as legitimation of the nation-state. This answered the partly mythical and spiritual basis of the model of sovereignty of the Free State. History became the 'necessary' realisation of a mythical national consciousness, imbued with a teleology that left aside everything other than the destiny of the national project as an irrelevant bye-way. The myth of communalism was a nostalgic one that hearkened back, like other nationalist cosmologies, to a golden age which, in this case, was alleged Celtic communalism. This myth of a pre-modern pristine Gaelic nation that defined the primordial origins of the culture-nation and legitimated the foundations of the state-nation was an important component in fomenting a selective amnesia. This amnesia was not alone applied to everything that had happened in-between, written-off as 'seven hundred years of colonialism', but also to the legacies of what had happened, chiefly the existence of a Protestant community in Ireland who could not share this myth of origins.

The separatist wing, especially after the militarisation of culture after 1913 which led to armed militias emerging in both Protestant and Catholic communities had an answer for dealing with the problem of an Irish 'other', Protestantism.[21] The answer, which was not confined to the Catholic separatists but extended also to Protestant cultural representations of their 'other', was denial and violence. This violence did not have to be physical. It could also be symbolic or cultural in the form of the denial of difference in the assertion of an imposed homogeneity (Galtung, 1990). This was more possible in southern Ireland where the Protestant population was relatively small – in the pre-Free State period about ten per cent and declining. Not rational reflection and recognition of difference prevented the separatists from laying claim to the whole island, only power did. Hence, to the symbolic shaping of a communitarianism that, at its separatist extreme, could be violently homogenising could be added the device of actual or threatened violence. In terms of the construction of a new society, this code in fusing the cultural with the primordial, had determined that there could be no middle ground on issues concerning cultural mediation: the nation-state was to be shaped in the image of Catholic traditionalism. The Irish Ireland movement had opposed the idea of cultural fusion in the belief that Irishness had to be opposed to Englishness and modernity (Lyons, 1979, p. 61). Fused with the moral technology of the Catholic church, this became a powerful ideology when it joined forces with national separatism.

THE RADICAL WING OF THE NATIONAL MOVEMENT

(1) The Social Location of the Radicals

Radical demands from within or without the nationalist front was the dog whose bark was stifled in late nineteenth and early twentieth century Ireland. The broad sweep of social change, together with potent social and political mobilisation, had created the conditions for the emergence of an elite as the first instalment in remedying one kind of exclusion, that of the Catholic lower middle-class. Other kinds of exclusion remained: landless labourers, the landed class without significant capital, the urban working-class and women. For the Catholic lower middle-class the extension and legitimation of their gains in both the Land War and through the gradual displacement of Protestants in many professional occupations was an important goal. For this, they required a cross-class romantic ideology that could embrace the masses of the periphery. Irish nationalism from 1880 is full of examples of radicalism twarthed or postponed: the Parliamentary Party's control of Land War agitation kept it within acceptable bounds; the absorption of the more radical aims of the United Irish League, which aimed at greater equity in rural Ireland, into a cross-class populism; the separatists lack of interest or even, in Griffith's case, hostility to the demands of labour; the general lack of support by all nationalist fractions of the aims of the workers in the 1913 lockout; the Parliamentary Party's and in particular Redmond's opposition to the extension of the vote to women (Ryan, 1994); the lack of enthusiasm to support radical, agrarian action initiated by local elements of Sinn Fein in 1918.

Agrarian radicalism had a long history in Ireland, going back to the peasant revolt of the late eighteenth century when secret societies, such as the Defenders and the Whiteboys, created rural unrest (Smith, 1992). These organised societies of rural labours and small farmers shaped radicalism in prefamine Ireland. As with many protest movements in this period, they were seeking to defend traditional forms of life rather than to achieve new goals and were able to draw on long standing rural traditions (Calhoun, 1982, 1983). Organised radicalism did not develop on a mass scale until the foundation of the Land League in the period known as the Land War between 1879 and 1882 (Bew, 1978). This movement built upon the tradition of nationally organised collective action such as the United Irishmen, the movement for Catholic Emancipation, the movement against tithes and the movement for Repeal of the Union. But its tactical repertoire was enhanced by the tradition of secret societies and the tactics of violence and ostracisation that were permanent features of the Irish nineteenth century.

In the conditions of intense politicisation that characterised late nineteenth-century Ireland, rural protest was transformed from local to national organisation. In this process, agrarian radical collective action became increasingly proactive, less communal and more associational in its organisation structure (Clark, 1979). In the 1880s, the goal of peasant proprietorship became the overriding goal of the Land League. The late establishment of the goal of peasant proprietorship shows how movement goals were related to mobilisation capacity. Peasant proprietorship could not be contemplated until a powerful movement could impose significant political pressures in pursuit of it. This capacity was enhanced by the formation of new links between rural and urban areas from the 1870s: there was an advancement in literacy, railways were extended, and there was increasing commercialisation of agriculture. As peasants became drawn into the cash economy links with urban areas increased and the urban lower middle-class became more and more dependent upon the farming sector with whom it had kinship bonds (Clark, 1975, pp. 490/1; 1971; Kennedy, 1983). The Parliamentary Party provided agrarian radicalism with political direction and at the same time made Home Rule central to the agrarian issue. This had the predictable effect that rural Protestant agrarianism in Ulster distanced itself from the Land League.

Those who benefited from the Land Acts were mostly the bigger farmers who, once their own objectives were secured, showed little sympathy with smaller farmers excluded from the land settlement or with landless labourers (Bew, 1987; Clark, 1975, 1978; Jones, 1983; Townshend, 1989; Vaughan, 1994). In addition to tensions within rural Ireland, Graham and Wood (1994) further emphasise tensions between town and countryside. In their (1994, p. 57) view, late nineteenth and early twentieth-century Ireland was characterised 'by a markedly more disparate array of interests and social protest than the notion of a homogeneous, autochthonous society might allow'.

A further implication of the gradual transfer of ownership of the land brought about by various British government financed Land Acts was a crisis of identity for radical politics which began to be absorbed into nationalist politics. The polarisation of the Irish peasantry into those who benefited from the Land Acts and those who did not was later politicised in the relationship between the Parliamentary Party and Sinn Fein, which at least initially in the period after 1916 took on the cause of the poorer elements in the countryside. Thus agrarianism was absorbed by two varieties of nationalism, the petit-bourgeois constitutional nationalism of the Parliamentary Party and republican populist nationalism. The former ultimately failed to respond adequately to the resolution of the land issue (Bull, 1993) with the result that the way was open for revolutionary nationalism to profit from the eclipse of the parliamentary party and the widening of the electorate. Up to this point, which did not really develop until the war years and the emergence of an alternative political force, the Parliamentary Party sought to contain the constant class tensions that beset the countryside.

Irish radicalism was weak for more reasons than the symbolic integration of agrarianism by nationalism. Irish labour was, from the outset, structurally weak in the south (Berresford Ellis, 1985; O'Connor, 1992). The Irish Trade Union movement was dominated by the British-based amalgamated Unions up to the foundation of the Irish Transport and General Workers Union in 1909 and was reluctant to throw in its lot with nationalism in the early twentieth century for this meant cutting itself off from both the industrial base of North East Ulster and from the wider British labour movement (Pimley, 1988). The labourist ideology of the early twentieth century emphasised the international solidarity of labour[22] and to turn to a nationalist framework, when nationalist organisations and intelligentsia afforded them little sympathy, seemed a particularly unpromising option. Given the structural weakness of urban labour, an alliance with landless rural labour could have been highly beneficial to both parties. However, landless labourers had great difficulty in effectively organising or in sustaining organisation. They were unable to break easily the shackles of local communalism, or patriarchal employment relations on the farm. They worked in isolated pockets which made organisation difficult. And, in any case, their numbers were rapidly declining as with the break-up of the large estates some of them became converted into small-holders and the new owners of the land had less need for labour outside the immediate family.

Beyond structural reasons, Irish social radicalism was also weak in a cultural sense. Many potential radicals had nationalist feelings and their political identities were often nationalist first and trade

unionist second. This became more true as time went on. This had
the effect of making it very difficult to stand outside the nationalist consensus or even to establish dissident interests within it. After the bitter strike and defeat of 1913, Irish Trade Unionism
increasingly came to accept the nationalist consensus and to seek
a place within it. This was a response both to the sense of isolation as a result of the failure of the English Unions to adequately
support Irish workers in 1913 and to the growing realisation that
Irish Trade Unionism would have to earn its corn within an Irish
state rather than as part of United Kingdom. It is in this context
that Connolly has his place (Morgan, 1988). The Irish national
movement was therefore able to absorb the labour movement at
relatively low cost to its overall aims. The issue of underprivilege
and disadvantage would have to await the internal politics of the
new state and here labour would start from a position of relative
weakness as much in ideological as structural terms.[23]

The Irish suffragist movement was one radical movement in pre-
independence Ireland that did achieve its most prominent goal,
the vote for adult women.[24] The movement was composed of a
cross-sectarian alliance between Protestants and Catholics and its
main political struggle was to prevent Ireland being excluded from
the provisions of the Representation of the People Bill in 1918
(Ryan, 1994). Though suffragists cannot be counted as operating
within the nationalist movement, they did try to influence the institutional development of nationalism in a direction that exhibited
greater sympathy for women's weak legal and everyday positions.
However, the hostility of Irish constitutional nationalism to the main
objective of the movement indicates how difficult it was for women
to mobilise within the nationalist framework. The replacement of
the institutional order of the British state with that of the Free
State and its concomitant, the immense rise in the political significance of the Catholic Church, made successful mobilisation on
women's issues impossible for many decades.

(2) The Identity Project of the Radical Wing of the National Movement

Much of the national identity project of Irish labour owed its inspiration to Connolly, who provided the perfect range of symbolic
devices for the inclusion of labour into the national consensus. He
was a radical Catholic, held a spiritual view of the sanctity of the

Irish people, was a Germanophile and was convinced of his view that imperialism was operative in the Irish case. These were the perfect ingredients for left-wing populism. He envisaged the possibility of a structurally inspired redress of Irish labour's grievances within a nationalist institutional order and did not consider that gaining cultural resource and institutional standing for radical politics would be problematic within such an order. In Connolly's view, an Irish institutional structure offered a more ready basis for socialist influence or domination than did participating in the larger UK context. Irish nationalism promoted the fragmentation of international capitalism and made proletarian organisation more likely to be effective. The essential contribution that this made to Irish national identity was that oppositional positions in society could still belong to the overall cultural consensus and did not require to engage in constructing their own counter-culture. For this and other reasons the culture of the Irish working-class has on the whole stayed resolutely local and conservative; orientations to the collectivity are as often as not expressed in terms not of 'first-order' discourses of exclusion and difference but through the 'second-order' channels provided by the more powerful, institutionalised discourses of nationalism and Catholicism.

In return, Irish nationalism was grateful enough for Connolly's view that the cause of Ireland is the cause of labour and the cause of labour the cause of Ireland. It had symbolic value in heading off labour radicalism in the twentieth century. It also contributed powerfully to the negative, anglophobic definition of Irish identity. Connolly's anti-capitalism and anti-imperialism could easily be converted into anglophobia and anti-modernism. Irish nationalism, overwhelmingly right-wing and conservative in its foundation phase, never really had to worry about its left flank.

The agrarian radicalism which continued after the Wyndham Land Act of 1903 could not symbolically contribute to the nationalist identity project in a potent way. Agrarian radicalism was socially powerful enough to become one of the dominant issues in Irish politics in the first decade of the twentieth century, but though it regularly convulsed the Parliamentary Party the class basis of that organisation was sufficiently middle-class as to preclude taking up support for the anti-grazier aims of radicalism in a central way.[25] Similarly, Sinn Fein from 1916 onwards also sought to tap rural disaffection without it ever become pivotal to its political identity. The agrarian radicalism of the early twentieth century was presented with no institutional outlet until, mellowed by the Free State experience, it re-emerged with Fianna Fáil in the thirties.

Women's radicalism sought to raise issues of repression in Irish public culture in the early part of the century. According to Murphy (1989, 1993), women were effectively excluded from symbolically shaping nationalist politics which was built around male groups. This politics in common with nationalist discourses all over Europe at the time was characterised by founding myths of male heroism and a cult of male brotherliness (Mosse, 1985, Benton; 1995). It wasn't women's radicalism and problems that was sought by nationalist discourse, it was images of purity, domesticity and obedience that were promoted. It was fateful for the passive representation of women in codes of national identity, and for their position in twentieth century Ireland, that a nation-state was founded at the high tide of images of maleness and militarism.

THE IDENTITY CODES OF THE NATIONALIST MOVEMENT

The second half of the nineteenth century was a time of profound social change as the consequences of industrialisation and the communications revolution changed cultural perceptions at alarming speed. A new kind of mass, society-integrating national identity began to develop to provide a basis for the symbolic integration of society and the stabilisation of its institutions. This process was a cultural universal of the age though it took different forms. In those smaller countries where secessionist nationalism took hold in the period such as Norway, Hungary, and Ireland, nationalism had the double function of re-integrating society which threatened to become differentiated and absorbed into larger aggregates and of articulating a code of belonging based on a distinct people. This process was driven by newly empowered peripheral elites whose opportunities expanded with social change.

In Ireland in this period cultural creativity, responding to the pressure of international cultural change and to the society's own modernisation, ran at a very high level. This creativity was ultimately rooted in the institutional breakdown of the old cultural interpretation models which had underpinned the previously dominant social order. Ideas of 'natural' Protestant domination of social and political institutions, deference to the virtues of Anglo-Irish gentility, and liberalism as the foundation of political culture were rapidly replaced. The Irish national movement organised the replacement and defined new codes. As outlined in this chapter, the most important of these new codes were those carried by the powerful clerical elite who progressively dominated the intelligentsia, the new political elite of the Parliamentary Party, the cultural and revolutionary ferment of separatism, and the emergence of organised radicalism. In synthetic form following from our analysis above, these wings were associated with the following cultural value complexes:

Catholic Church: rurality, respectability, sexlessness, the extramundane moral code of sin and unreflective obedience, theocratic sovereignty, domestication of women, conservative anti-modernism, anti-radicalism, commitment to hierarchy as principle of social organisation, the conventional personality, the necessity of the Catholic way of life, naturalisation of culture, controlled production of culture, anti-intellectualism, the evil of the external world.

Parliamentary Party: democratic, adherence to legality, clientelistic and dutiful ideas of citizenship, the importance of locality, weak commitment to pluralism, political populism, respectability.

Revolutionaries: masculinity, militarisation of culture, intellectual popularism, irrationalist nation code (asocial, ascriptive), self-esteem, anglophobic, national communitarianism (hostility to liberalism, republican political philosophy), aestheticisation of politics (spiritualisation of sovereignty), denial, danger of moral pollution from outside.

Radicals: anchoring justice in national community, compatibility of social radicalism and Catholicism.

It would be wrong to assume that there was no convergence between these codes as the boundaries between them were fluid. But each of them added distinctive elements to the shaping of an overall code of national identity. Each of them was related to the social location and organisational resources of their principal carriers. They were formed in a period of distinctive cultural openness and yet one that was converging towards new institutionalised selectivity. The major question raised by the national movement would be what ultimate code would guide the Irish institutional order in the twentieth century. We turn to this issue in the next two chapters.

5 The Alignment of Nationalist Politics: Self-Determination as Goal and Achievement

THE CONSTRUCTION OF A MASTER FRAME

The dominant view in Catholic Ireland by the 1890s was that Home Rule was necessary as quickly as possible if good governance was to be realised. The political field was dominated by political actors carrying nationalist messages. As time wore on, an equivalent nationalist political culture was created, though nationalism remained ambivalent about its ultimate goals. The success of nationalism meant that other political actors, the state and Protestant-Unionist counter-actors, adopted positions that were increasingly a response to it, varying between accommodation and repression in the one case to outright opposition in the other. Given its electoral power and growing institutional power – Catholics were increasingly prominent in the professions and they dominated local government by the end of the century – the state had to adjust. The Liberal Party's conversion to the Home Rule agenda was one response, the Conservative strategy of 'killing Home Rule with kindness', the dominant strategy during the Conservative hegemony of the 1890s and the early twentieth century, was another. The cultural impact of nationalism was a creative product of the actor wings described in the last chapter, though the creativity was shared with other cultural producers such as intellectuals and journalists and conditioned by other forces such as shifts in international public opinion or electoral reform. The nationalist political culture that was gaining in strength and self-confidence existed within an institutional structure that denied its power by placing it in a larger context in which it was neutralised. An institutional order that prevented a dominant political culture for a long time from realising the structures it desired led to a continuous and deepening crisis of legitimation in the period from the 1880s to 1918–21.

The first and longest manifestation of this legitimation crisis was expressed in the persistence of a constitutional nationalist politics in which the structure of the British polity continued to be important. In this phase, the dominant goal was the constitutional one of Home Rule. This phase which had two sub-phases, the Parnellite and post-Parnellite campaigns for Home Rule, lasted between the late 1870s and up to the First World War. The second legitimation crisis variously involved a new degree of alignment amongst the components of nationalist political culture leading to the emergence of a populist movement with mass appeal, a massive decline in the significance of the British institutional structure, and a new dominant political goal, self-determination.

The nationalist mobilisation that gathered momentum in this period increasingly absorbed the imagination of Catholic Ireland. In the first era of legitimation crisis, political actors adopted positions that were oriented by, and directed towards, the wider institutional framework of the United Kingdom. This could be seen in the importance for many Irish of the imperial connection which was a major outlet for employment, in the strength of British Trade Unions in Ireland, in the continuing social importance of the Anglo-Irish elite, in the ambivalence of the values guiding institutional orders such as health, marital relations, education. By the early twentieth century, the orientation to British institutions and to the general British path towards modernity was on the retreat on all fronts. Nationalism was the expression of a society taking stock about the values of modernity in its late nineteenth century forms of urbanisation, secularisation, industrialisation, liberalisation, and principles of social justice inspired by the labour movement, social reformers and the counter-cultural movements striving for artistic autonomy and equality for women. It succeeded in representing its opposition to modernity as above all an opposition to the British path to modernity but this could not disguise the fact that the values of modernity in the period, British or otherwise, did not find favour with the cultural constructions of Irish nationalism.

The negative attitude to the values of modernity shows the extent that Irish nationalism was not simply a straitjacketed response to prevailing conditions but a force in shaping a set of values that reflected *freedom of choice*. This freedom was counted in the ability of different social groups to develop and project images of the future society they would wish to emerge. As shown in the last chapter, they did not all adopt a similar stance. Their identity projects represented considerable divergences in *ideological perceptions*. The particular perceptions of the actor wings or the general perceptions of the movement as a whole, which became more convergent over time, did not simply rationally respond to a given situation. The situation was more fluid, more contingently driven, more socio-emotionally constructed than that. But amidst the contingency two social facts were inescapable and enduring; Irish nationalism, with a Catholic worldview as its heartbeat, was sceptical of the values of twentieth century modernity and the Catholic lower middle-class was the most cohesive group in the society, had most experience of networks of power and most actual power in Catholic Ireland, and knew best what it socially desired.

The successful construction of revolutionary will, of which separatist nationalist movements are an example, ultimately requires that the revolutionary movement develops a clearly expressed programme of action that unites its own divergent wings and provides a clear common goal. In the recent language of social movement theory (Snow and Benford, 1988, 1992; Snow et al., 1986; Swart, 1995; Tarrow, 1992, 1994, 1995), a revolutionary movement needs a 'master-frame'. In this context, a master-frame can be understood as a unifying position amongst the diversity of frames associated with the identity projects of the various wings of the nationalist movement. These wings 'framed' or codified social reality through their identity projects. Since the cultural logic, or 'framing', of the different identity constructions of the various wings is determined by their respective identity projects, the issues of the immediate success and long-term effects[1] of a social movement as a whole, which is always more than its constituent parts, is determined by the alignment of identity projects. Alignment depends not only on sharing a common goal or goals and contributing common resources to achieve these goals, it also depends on possessing an identity that makes agreement on goals possible, stabilises the interpretation of goals, and decides whom the attainment of the goals shall benefit and whom they shall not. A master frame emerges when the alignment of the various identity projects results in a common movement identity which is combined with a new frame of meaning capable of resonating in its discursive context (Swart, 1995). A master frame is thus a 'synthetic' identity project that is capable of connecting the various wings of a movement together in the diffusion of a symbolically potent situation-interpreting and strategy-guiding frame.

The identity projects of the nationalist actors, presented in the last chapter, did not occur in a vacuum. They occurred in a live, dynamic context influenced by their reciprocal relations and by the broader political and social context. The word 'dynamic' is central in that it indicates the creative power of political action. The aims of Irish nationalism as a political movement were not given in an uncomplicated way in some historically ancient telos of the movement but constructed in reciprocally determined action by a variety of actors in which historical-mythical constructs were only one of the elements. Over time, all the important actors in nationalist Ireland came to agree on the key goal of self-determination which acted as a master frame within the movement. However, the means to be attained to achieve self-determination and the purpose of self-determination were highly contested. Different value complexes and institutional arrangements were associated with self-determination. These included Home Rule within the imperial context with some allowance, never clearly worked out, for confessionally-structured political cultural differences, a monarchy, and, ultimately, late in the day, a completely independent republic. Within these institutional forms there were also different ideas of which social interests should be given precedence. Should it be the newly propertied lower middle-class or should it be those disadvantaged within the nation such as workers, landless labourers or women. These divergences, and their ultimate convergence, characterised the relational field of Irish nationalism.

The relational field of Irish nationalism was constructed from the articulation of identity projects by the wings of the movement and their complex interplay. Each of the identity projects worked from interpretations of existing cultural forms, the value complexes that were embedded in Irish culture. The interpretations both matched their needs as cultural producers and appealed to and re-shaped the needs of their constituency. The cultural projection of these interpretations as identity projects were filtered through what were described in chapter two as opportunity structures. The opportunity structures of access to and influence over state authorities and the public sphere, the readiness of the public sphere to accept their messages, and the receptivity of other movement wings to these messages determined how successful was the identity code of a particular wing. Success in this case is measured in how influential it became in shaping the consensual master-frame governing the movement as a whole in its consensus phase, an influence that translates into opportunities to specify the values guiding the institutional order of the nation-state later on. But to understand the process whereby a master frame is produced attention must be given to the opportunities that decide the fate of the different identity projects. By plotting these projects against the opportunity structures that condition the ability of actors to realise them, the structure of the relational field of nationalist politics comes into view. Actors' identity projects were refracted through the prism of their contexts of opportunity before contributing, to a greater or lesser extent, to the outcome of an Irish national identity code. This national identity code, stabilised through cultural meaning and social power, was then applied to reshaping the institutional structure of post-Independence Ireland.

In this chapter, the identity projects described in the previous chapter are considered in relation to these opportunity structures so that not just the manifest outcomes but the latent suppressions of nationalist identity politics becomes apparent. The three periods chosen are the first wave of Home Rule politics from 1870 to 1893, concentrating on the aftermath of the death of Parnell. The second is the long period when the British state sought to defuse Irish grievances in the form of accelerated reform which, in the end, included a commitment to Home Rule. The third phase is a crisis phase when the war-induced fateful delay in the introduction of Home Rule, together with the rise of cultural separatist nationalism, led to the addition of military to constitutional methods and the new goal of a complete break with the UK.

PHASE ONE: THE CONSTRUCTION OF MODERN
NATIONALIST POLITICS (1870–1893)[2]

The first wave of modern Catholic nationalism was over by 1893. In this first wave, its distinguishing characteristics was the claim to independent political institutions and the motive power of agrarian social interests. The ideology of the movement in this period was based on clearly discernible social grievances that were simultaneously given the status of being national and religiously based grievances. In this first phase, which distinguished it from the two later phases of nationalist mobilisation discussed below, status-resentment could be addressed in terms of a coherent social programme. In the historical work on this period, much emphasis has been placed on the inclusion of agrarian grievances within a national fold but less on the absorption of wider radical activity within the straitjacket of a conservatively-oriented leadership. The nature of the Land-War to this point created a division of interest between those who clearly stood to profit from the direction of the land settlement and those who remained excluded, temporarily or permanently. Also excluded, in whole or in part, were structural options for a land settlement other than peasant proprietorship such as the more radical co-operative pattern of agricultural organisation in Denmark, which provided not alone an alternative model of rural organisation but also broke the linkage between a predominantly rural social structure and social and political conservatism (Ostergard, 1992).

In this first period of 'classic' Home Rule politics early alignment processes between the principal wings of the national movement can be discerned. Three alignment processes are particularly noteworthy. The first alignment process was the alliance between the Parliamentary Party and the separatist Irish Republican Brotherhood in 1878 in the initiative that was known as the New Departure by which the IRB slowly adapted themselves to constitutional politics and the Parliamentary Party accommodated radicalism. With the New Departure, Home Rule evolved from being a demand for the reform of the Union and switched to more radical ideas of self-government. Through the New Departure electoral power and access to the state – at the disposal of the Parliamentary Party – were combined with the revolutionary movement, which had strong support in the United States.

A second alignment process can be discerned in the Plan of Campaign of 1886 in which the Parliamentary Party supported the aims of the Land League, thus bringing about increased unity of purpose with the agrarian radicals. This alignment process allowed the Party to gain access to a powerful social force and to compensate for a limited electoral base. On the other side, it allowed the Land League to gain access to the political representation system. The overall effect was that local issues became transformed into national issues.

A third alignment process can be seen in the Parliamentary Party's tacit concordat with the Church from 1884 and the Church's gradual endorsement of the Land League from 1888, when the Irish bishops refused to enforce the Roman decree condemning it (Larkin, 1987).[3] By 1886 the bishops under Archbishop Walsh had defined their aims for the Party, which included control over education and the right to be consulted on the suitability of parliamentary candidates.[4] Parnell knew the Church had to be accommodated by being given a constitutional role and that the Party could ultimately benefit from this, though ironically it would later cause his own downfall (Larkin, 1975). Other factors also played a role in the Church's gradual distancing of itself from the Gladstonian Liberals and embracing of Home Rule, such as Gladstone's anti-Catholic turn in 1874, a reaction to the papal doctrine of infallibility, and the failure of the Liberals to deliver university reform in 1877 through which the Church would have got a state financed Catholic university.

These alignment processes had created a solid base for nationalist politics by the early 1890s in Catholic Ireland. But the nationalist politics of the 1890s were by no means cohesive. On the contrary, there was a continuous tendency towards fragmentation on social and moral fronts. Looking at the situation in relation to the interplay of identity projections and political and cultural opportunities for each of the key nationalist actors demonstrates how the enhanced power of nationalist politics had created its own problems of integration.

The Church: The early 1890s represented the arrival of Catholicism as a more independent and self-conscious political force, one that moreover had gained considerable political power as a consequence of its role in the 'moral' deposition of Parnell. This had been presaged by the involvement of Catholic clergy in direct political activity in the 1880s. In the 1890s, however, they co-existed uneasily with secular politicians, leading to an uncertain combination of secular and denominational politics. After the Parnell split, the Catholic Church became a leading player in the new cultural politics. This new cultural politics added to the politics of material interests a more defined and less negotiable politics based on the continuously asserted difference in values of Catholic Ireland. The politics of interest and cultural identity fed off one another enhancing, on the one hand, what Callanan (1992, p. 175) calls the 'Catholic proprietorial nationalism' that had matured as a political movement in the 1880s and, on the other, generating a new politics of symbolic inclusion that spread to more and more constituencies in and after the 1890s. There was also in this period a progressive strengthening and independent articulation of the cultural interests of Catholicism as an organised political movement.

The Irish Catholic Church was a Victorian organisation, obsessively concerned with Victorian moral values and centrally engaged in what Inglis (1987), following Elias, describes as the Irish civilising process. As it had developed organisationally and ideologically by the late nineteenth century, it was perfectly in position to avail of the opportunity offered by the circumstances that had occasioned the Parnell split in the Irish Parliamentary Party. Parnell had been named as a correspondent by a Captain O'Shea in a divorce suit and moral condemnation in Ireland precipitated the split of the Party. The political opportunity provided by a split in nationalist politics, together with the moralisation of its cause, gave the Church the perfect opportunity to step in as moral arbiter not just of life conduct but also of political behaviour. The Parnell split, therefore, marked the advent of the Church as a moral authority in Irish politics. Since the departure of Parnell, Protestants ceased to be central to the nationalist movement and for this reason the Church could more rapidly adapt itself to that movement.

The immediate outcome of the Parnell split also marked the beginning of the realisation by the Church that the politics of the nation could be more profitable than continued involvement with the British state. Three key elements were added to the Church's social imaginary as a result of the Parnell split and succeeding political activities. These were, firstly, the explication of a principle of quasi-theocratic sovereignty where the Catholic movement would not seek to become politically institutionalised, as in some European countries of the period, but would determine the permissible space of political variation from behind the scenes. The second element was a stronger conviction of both the virtue and desirability of an exclusively Catholic society. The third was the intervention of the Church into secular politics as a culture-producing organisation that wished to shape basic political cultural values. The second and third elements required the Church to have a stronger influence in the public sphere. The Church's advantageous position in its role of moral leader of the anti-Parnellite movement helped to achieve political prominence for its cultural messages. Together with the cultural power over private life it already held, it now began to attain expanded cultural power over public life also, because its cultural messages were so well-suited to the broader ethos of respectable, Victorian provincialism that characterised Irish society in the period. The mass resonance of the Church's message was strong, although political and cultural Parnellism, with its mild anti-clericalism, sometimes made life uncomfortable.

The Parliamentary Party: In contrast to the Church, the situation for the Parliamentary Party worsened in the early 1890s. Together with its own sundering into two distinct wings, the 1890s were generally a difficult period for the Party as the Church and, to a lesser extent, the various strands of cultural nationalism re-shaped the civic culture and changed the cultural environment of subsequent nationalist politics. The failure of the second Home Rule Bill, and the demise of Liberal government, marked the end of a propitious opportunity for the Party in relation to the immediate capacity to achieve its dedicated objective of Home Rule. Divisions in the Party also made its relative domination of nationalist media coverage in the 1880s less secure. Further, the Party did not have the same attraction for intellectuals as the new cultural nationalism. This is not to suggest that it completely lost educated support, but it was unable to dominate political-cultural interpretations in the way that it dominated parliamentary representation. Both wings of the Party faced ideological competition: the anti-Parnellites found themselves forced to operate within an agenda defined by the Church and the Parnellites increasingly had to reckon with the new cultural nationalists. The Party was losing its capacity to shape the deep agenda of nationalist politics that it had with Parnell's charismatic leadership and the more favourable circumstances of the 1880s.

In these circumstances of regrouping in the early 1890s, the role of the Parliamentary Party as political co-ordinator rather than leader of Irish nationalist politics was first established. The creative currents that flowed into institutionalised political decision-making were from more varied sources and these sources held power resources that qualified the power of the constitutional politicians. The capacity of the Church to subvert the secular basis of politics and to shape the Party's internal agenda was the harbinger of this new situation.

The Agrarian Radicals: The opportunity conditions for the agrarian radicals remained relatively promising. The Land Reform of 1893 marked the end of landlord domination of rural society. But for social reasons, connected with status, lifestyle and even continued presence in the society, and for economic reasons connected with the propitious market situation, proprietorship of land remained a goal of many who were still excluded from it. Agrarian radicals disposed over considerable social power. They did not merely depend on access to the media-based public sphere and formal politics but had at their disposal the full repertoire of political tactics including lawful demonstrations, boycotts where they were the initiators of the tactic, unlawful demonstrations, damage, violence and, finally, even sabotage and assassinations. For reasons connected with their often unconventional tactics, their power was frequently more impressive on a local scale than on a national one.

Notwithstanding the radical nature of the tactics used, and the social change that was initiated, the term agrarian radicalism induces a degree of confusion. The struggle for social rights on land faced in both a radical and conservative direction. Typically, those who did not have land, or did not have it on the right terms, were radicals, but when they got it, or when the terms improved, they became conservatives.

The organised power and tactical acumen of agrarian radicalism was such that it could constantly re-position itself within nationalist politics. In the period in question, agrarian radicalism tended to be split between the two wings of the Irish Party as anti-Parnellism tended to be more in tandem with the conservative foundations of Irish rural society whereas Parnellism had considerable attraction for those still excluded from social and economic power. The period after the death of Parnell and the failed Home Rule Bill of 1893 marked to a considerable extent a new fragmentation of nationalist politics in which the divided Parliamentary Party and the Church engaged in often conflictual exchange over the political power of religious authority and continuing uncertainly prevailed on the social front about who would be the winners and losers on the land. There was some potential that in certain circumstances these moral-political and social differences would lead to rival socio-moral political bases. However, the structural situation which imposed an imperative of unity on nationalist Ireland, if it were to remain nationalist, along with the continuing structural power of the Church over the expanding social services, together with cultural change represented by the arrival of a new and socially agnostic nationalism, moved the pendulum in the direction of an alternative cleavage structure that favoured dissensus within overall 'consensus' as a mode of conducting oppositional politics.

PHASE TWO: NATIONALIST POLITICS IN THE ERA OF REFORM (1893–1914)

The departure of Parnell and the failure of the second Home Rule Period ushered in a new political era in Ireland that was to last up to the First World War. Of course the pure politics of Home Rule never disappeared from the political agenda but it became absorbed into a wider framework of political positions and actions. What was at stake was not the issue of some form of devolutionary government for some or all of Ireland, up to and including Home Rule, for everyone except the British Conservatives and Ulster Unionists accepted this would happen, but on what terms it would happen. The issue of Home Rule had been repugnant to many in British politics, leading to major structural change through the formation of the modern Conservative Party, not so much because of its implications for Ireland but because of its implications for the legitimacy and integrity of British domestic constitutional arrangements and its governance of a vast empire. After 1895, the opportunity arose to devise policies that would put into practice their view that the Irish Home Rule movement was not the outpouring of some primordial nationalism but a product of failed social and economic modernisation and that enlightened policies in the latter dimension would obviate the need for at least the more radical claims of the movement. In this way the state responded to the rise of contentious action in the preceding phase by major reform.

The conservative regime in Ireland therefore turned to the policies of constructive Unionism (Gailey, 1987). These policies were expressed in five areas: land, tax, local government, work and education. They were designed to create an enlightened Catholic elite who would respect the imperial context while conducting, to the limits of their constitution-unthreatening powers, good local governance in Ireland. The international context of constructive unionism must also be borne in mind for at this time the idea that every nation should have its own state had not yet won the popularity that it was to gain in the post-1918 period (Hobsbawm, 1991). To some extent, and perhaps to an extent greater than is historically recognised, an opportunity arose to organise a context that would lead to a new definition of Home Rule from the 1890s. The primary positive reason was the first indications of the sundering of the social-democratic code and the nation-code in this period. In the earlier period, an encompassing populist coalition had made the identification of national and social politics appear complete. But the nature of the land settlement led to the problem of those who were excluded fighting anew to acquire proprietoral rights and fair treatment. Hence, on the agrarian side a social politics of the land question was emerging (Bew, 1987) that asked new questions about the direction of nationalist Ireland. The rise of the new Trade Unionism from the 1890s, and the first serious indications of a labour politics in Ireland, led to further questioning of the inclusivity of the nation-code. Both these developments raised the question, for the first time, of whether the nation-code exhausted the democratic code, especially in the manner in which the latter addressed issues of resource creation and allocation.

A second, related dimension of the re-definition of the Home Rule question was the reaction of nationalist politicians in the Parliamentary Party to constructive unionism. Home Rule politicians had always been clear about the critical relationship between social politics and nationalist politics. Without the former, nationalist politics would lose its drive but, if it became dominant, nationalism might lose its *raison d'être*. But the Parliamentary Party had to recognise the importance of a variety of social questions to various groups in Ireland. This was so for a number of reasons. Firstly, the Party was conscious that the drift towards widening the electorate, together with the rapid development of a mass and contested public sphere, meant that it had to work harder to stay in touch with nationalist public opinion. Secondly, the Party saw itself as not simply responding to social pressures but as actively shaping the future institutional structure and principles of justice it would inherit under Home Rule. Thirdly, the Party had to work to maintain enthusiasm for Home Rule, and for nationalist politics generally, in a period of quiescence. Fourthly, the Party found itself in an ambivalent position in relation to British state-induced economic and social modernisation. Much of the Party did not want it, or at least only selectively in relation to rights to ownership of land, as it raised expectations and fiscal burdens that a Home Rule Ireland would inherit, but others, especially in urban Ireland and in deprived regions who faced no future in the society without major social change, clearly did. Finally, the Parliamentary Party actively followed a policy of conciliation towards Unionist opinion in the belief that the support, especially of southern Unionism, would be vital to securing a Home Rule settlement in the given constitutional conditions.

The tableau facing the various actors in the nationalist movement after 1893 consisted therefore of the emergence of an extended and internally divisive social politics, the growing influence of cultural factors and public opinion in politics, and the challenges created by a modernising but ideologically hostile government. The new situation complicated the field of nationalist politics. The nationalist movement itself, both in response to these developments and due to the historical legacy of previous experience, became more differentiated with the major nationalist political organisation, the Parliamentary Party, itself internally divided even after the formal unification of the Party in 1900, and joined in the nationalist fold by a more radical cultural wing, by a politically mobilised Church, by the rise of a politics of labour, and, finally, by the continuation of a recalcitrant and fluctuating politics of land. In these circumstances, while Home Rule was the undisputed goal a series of sub-goals were emerging with the cultural deepening of the various wings of the movement in the context of a more mobilised populace. This is can be seen in relation to the adaptation of identity projects undertaken by each of the wings of the overall movement.

The Church: The position of the Church at the end of the nineteenth century was overwhelmingly favourable. The ratio of clerics to population had continued to rise, the major building programme was well-advanced, it had profited from the Irish version of the ambiguous but powerful Victorian return to religiosity, it had a well-established organisation with a coherent, integrating ideological programme, it had developed a strong foothold in health, education and voluntary associations, and it was positioned in a powerful, mediating position between state and nation. In these circumstances, the Church had the capacity to promote central elements of its identity project and to construct the social conditions for their realisation. The period therefore saw the symbolic politics of Catholic community building as the Church generalised the localised, rural absorption of Victorian petit-bourgeois culture into a Catholic version of the nation-code. This 'civilising project' was based on moving its identity project in a primordial direction, equating Catholic and Irish, and thereby developing its own nation code. This period therefore saw the establishment of close and enduring links between the Church and the lay intelligentsia in the public sphere, of which Moran is the exemplary figure. This was created and maintained both by the dispositions of the intelligentsia, including the journalists, but also because of the immense behind-the-scenes power the Church was beginning to establish with a well-oiled machinery specialising, on the one hand, in criticism of 'un-Catholic' behaviour or opinion and, on the other, equipped with an immense capacity to influence behaviour through its prominence in social networks, cultural, sporting, and educational, as well as religious in the narrow sense.

The issue of networks brings into focus a vital factor in the social power of the Church, the role of the clergy as a trained, ideologically coherent occupational group who were professionally available for cultural politics. The active shaping of the nation as a Catholic nation was, in substantial part, the occupation of these clerics. They therefore had the time as well as the disposition to penetrate the wide range of networks that underpinned nationalist politics. The flowering of associations in the period under questions created a formal organisational basis for networks of solidarity. Some of these had an explicitly Catholic orientation such as the Catholic Association of Ireland, founded to advance Catholic interests, whose goals revealed a sectarian frame of reference.

The reform politics of the early twentieth century interested the Church in one key sphere, education, revealed most clearly in the long controversy over the University Question. The University Question revealed both the political capacity of the Church and the political limits of working within a secular, political order which the British connection, at bottom, secured. In a formal sense, the Church was not successful in its goal of achieving a Catholic University based on the organisation framework of the so-called 'Godless' Queen's Colleges which it had opposed for more than fifty years and into which it had forbidden Catholics to enter. The establishment of the National University of Ireland on formally secular lines represented a setback for the Church's aim to dominate education in Ireland. The key issues for the Church, here revealing a key element in its identity project, were, firstly, to prevent the emergence of a literate, secular, humanistic intellectual culture that would impede the Church's aim to dominate cultural production in Ireland. Secondly, to create a cradle-to-grave experience of organised, Catholic shaping of occupational as well as personal life and, thirdly, to securely dominate the formation of the Catholic elite. The University Question concretised the Church's ambition but final victory would have to await Home Rule Ireland.

The shift from the first to the second period in our framework reveals the growing centrality of the Church to political networks. The first period of land and Home Rule politics were secular projects into which the Church was absorbed because of its social and cultural importance. But the manner of the fall of Parnell, allied to the broad thrust of the social and cultural change we have been documenting, propelled the Church directly into a political role. The Church now occupied a progressively more important role as moral arbiter of the politics of the Parliamentary Party, a position that was admittedly not easy to maintain in the eddying flow of Irish politics in the period. But the fall of Parnell, the decisive entry of the Church into political communication, and the growing Catholic primordialism of southern Ireland as more social, cultural and political power passed into its hands made the Church a central pivot of nationalist politics. The emergence of cultural nationalism in the 1890s in the end strengthened this phenomenon but in no simple manner. It took considerable time before the identity project of the cultural movement shifted from the economic and social goals associated with urban life to a preoccupation with a virtuous rural civilisation, more consistent with the Church's own cultural model. But the Church was always important to the rural basis of cultural nationalism through its key role in the Gaelic Athletic Association and other rural associations. Notwithstanding this overlap, it retained a suspicion of cultural nationalism whose lay basis appeared as a threat to the Church's hegemony of Irish cultural life. Its position on the labour movement and radical agrarianism went further and was often expressed as a thinly-disguised hostility to radical manifestations of these movements.

Finally, the resonance of the Church's messages was more and more extensive. While the density of cultural production in urban regions, chiefly Dublin, was relatively high and relatively differentiated, this was not so in rural Ireland where the Church was the only nationally-based cultural organisation. Moreover, from the time of the Parnell split, it had extended its hegemony from its own networks into the political networks of the Parliamentary Party in rural areas. The Church was unique in having direct access, beyond the public sphere, to its political audience through the technical activity of organised religion and through religious and non-religious social networks. It worked with the powerful moral technology of sin and with the social authority of the clergy. Together with its prominence in the public sphere, the Church, therefore, was in a position to progressively extend its symbolic power over rural Ireland which the conservative outcome of the land settlement greatly facilitated. In urban Ireland the situation was more complex as the Church was rivalled by the cultural nationalists for cultural influence amongst a population that manifested a wider range of political and cultural beliefs. But even here the Church's message was not so much opposed as placed in a wider, more differentiated context.

The Parliamentary Party: We have already seen in the introduction to this section how the Parliamentary Party was affected by the opportunities and constraints offered by the period of unionist government and its reform programme. The identity project of the Parliamentary Party, with its rationalist and conciliationist approach located within the broader imperial context, continued fitfully in the post-Parnell era. But the more complex environment in which it was located began to powerfully affect the Party. Though it felt it had little choice but to go with the reform politics of the period, whose main lines were of major concern to its constituency, it did so with the uneasy feeling that its cross-confessional, conciliationist politics of post-1900 was being outflanked by a cultural-political movement that had no such responsibilities and that increasingly held to the values of a separatism that felt little or no obligation to mediate with other concerned parties on or off the island. From a social-structural perspective, the Party was squeezed from below by the new vitality of social and cultural politics and from above by a reform-oriented government, and even more generally by the political-cultural reform climate in the UK towards general welfare provision that threatened to throw into relief the conservative socio-economic programme of the relatively prosperous leadership of the Party. The Parliamentary Party therefore found itself embroiled in a politics, founded upon social and cultural differentiations, which its dominant conservative strand did not want.

The opportunity conditions within the public sphere were less favourable for the Party in this period than in the first Home Rule period for a number of reasons. Firstly, the Party did not speak with an united voice even after 1900 when it formally re-united. In the small-holding West, the United Irish League, which had for long periods a strong anti-grazier animus, was dominant. Elsewhere in rural Ireland, the Parliamentary Party was mostly the Party of the graziers and the emerging middle-classes. In the cities, the Party was generally a middle-class Party which contained both liberal and conservative currents. In these circumstances, the political identity of the Party had no recourse but to a weakly-defined political populism that, far from commanding the public sphere, did not even have a consistent message to offer it. In relation to the support of the intelligentsia, much has been written about their loss of interest in constitutional politics. There is some truth in this as the Parliamentary Party's structural position and political goals made it more difficult for it to win a foothold in circumstances that gave a new centrality to a cultural politics of identity. This may well be explicable on class grounds as the Party tended to win the support of the 'higher' intelligentsia while the cultural nationalists appealed to the disaffected lower middle-class intelligentsia.

In the fractured political alignments of early twentieth century Ireland, the Parliamentary Party still remained the pivotal player. The farming element in its membership increased after 1906, enhancing the affinity of interests between agrarianism and the political elite. In relation to the state, its command of electoral and, after 1898, local government politics in nationalist Ireland ensured it of wide-ranging institutional influence. Its monopoly of political power meant, too, that other manifestations of nationalist Ireland had at some level to compromise with its agenda, extending from cultural nationalists, to the Church, to radical, social politics. The environmental pressures operating on the selection decisions of the Party, as well as the internal dispositions of the leadership, was to prevent a secondary front becoming dominant that would threaten the elite interests that had been staked out in the first period.[5] The resulting strategy of building a populist coalition focusing on the national question to the neglect of the social one was the overwhelming alliance-building goal of the Party. This is what made it a Party of de-differentiation and conservative rationalisation.

The public resonance of the various messages of the Parliamentary Party in the period presaged the difficulties it would later have with the rise of Sinn Fein. The identity project of the Party, and the dominant habitus from which it sprang, produced a limited sociopolitical imaginary that was unable to satisfy the solidaristic needs that were mushrooming in the social networks of the period. It was unable to symbolically appeal to a lower middle-class urban milieu in a real and satisfying way and its social politics were too conservative for large areas of the country. But the commitment to a democratic politics while pursuing an ambivalent politics of state de-legitimation had wide appeal. More specifically, the desire to continue to engage in British and, above all, imperial, social opportunities continued to be attractive to the Irish middle-class public. It has to be remembered that Redmond, the leader of the re-united Party after the turn of the century, and the dominant strand in his Party did stand for Home Rule in the British context and this remained relatively popular politics in the first decade of the twentieth century even if the storm clouds were gathering.

Cultural Nationalism: The major factor that changed the align-ment of Irish nationalist politics after 1893 was the emergence of cultural nationalism. This nationalism penetrated emotionally into the deepest recesses of the collective unconscious of large sections of the Irish lower middle-class creating a satisfying symbolic basis for possible and desirable political mobilisation. The cultural orien-tation of the new Gaelic revival was dedicated to the de-Anglicisa-tion of Ireland and this made the de-legitimation of the state in Ireland its overwhelming priority. The major formal opportunity structures that facilitated radical, nationalist politics, the existence of liberal freedoms of association and expression, were already given. Beyond this, the cultural nationalists had little interest in develop-ing relations with the British state.

By contrast, they had a strong desire to penetrate the public sphere. The basis of cultural nationalism was the advancement of the cul-tural rights of the Catholic Irish. This co-existed uneasily with the social politics of rights. In some instances, such as Protestant influ-ence in the occupational sphere, the two coincided nicely, but, in other areas, the articulation of cultural identity based on Catholic-national primordialism retreated to an increasingly asocial and aestheticised politics as the politics of the social forced choices that the cultural nationalists were unwilling to make. Cultural national-ism was a politics of identity that was not securely aligned with social interest cleavages. This made the modality of communica-tion extremely important.

The successful diffusion of the identity project of cultural nationalism required that a virtuous relationship be established be-tween the resentment anchored in social networks of family and peers and its political dissemination in the public sphere. The possi-bilities of such a project ultimately depended on the vast expan-sion of capacities of literary production and reception. The conditions of reception were based on the expansion of literacy, higher levels of education, greater leisure time and enough disposable income to enjoy it and of production by the growing intelligentsia and the corresponding flourishing of newspaper, magazine and fictional outputs in response to demand. Cultural nationalism therefore re-sulted in a large profusion of new publications such as the *Free-man's Journal* founded in 1900 and the *Irish Peasant* in 1905 and a large number of pamphlets and periodicals. The cumulative conse-quence was the infusion of new nationalist themes into the public sphere sponsored by an emerging intelligentsia. This intelligentsia could be described as political-cultural entrepreneurs who were specialists in the new modality of mass political communication.

The lay entrepreneurs of cultural nationalism were ably supported by the extensive cadres of the Church. While from a formal, organisational point of view the Church exhibited considerable suspicion towards the secular intelligentsia,[6] there was considerable thematic continuity in the identity projects of the two wings. The formal and informal pedagogical activities of the Church[7] supported those of the cultural nationalists directed at an adult lay public. On the whole, both were anglophobic and anti-modern and convinced of the spiritual supremacy of the Irish nation to all others. The clerics were an important diffusion agent of the nationalist's identity project and, progressively, the nationalists began to define themselves exclusively as Catholics. The myth of common Gaelic origins remained important but insufficiently differentiated for social application. The assertion of discrimination against Catholics had much greater resonance, simultaneously invoking collective feelings of outrage and justifying a classically reactionary, primordial politics.

The relationship with the Parliamentary Party was more antagonistic on both the organisational and symbolic level. Both competed for attention on the crowded stage of nationalist Ireland contending for nothing less than the right to define the goals and tactics of nationalist politics. From the standpoint of the Parliamentary Party, the existing commitment to Home Rule would probably have endured without the efforts of the cultural nationalists who had the negative effect of forcing the Parliamentary Party into mass politics on terms often not of their own choosing. On the other hand, the cultural nationalists took some of the sting out of the politics of the social, turning perceptions of injustice outwards, and naturalising the politics of national resentment. In creating a new cultural politics they did what the Party was ill-equipped to do itself, though in the end they exacted a high price.

In terms of public resonance, the cultural nationalists grew rapidly from a low base. They effectively colonised a substantial part of the public sphere and rapidly came to play a vital role in cultural life, providing an alternative popular culture to the English one that, up to then, had been rapidly gaining. This occurred in the realm of sports where Gaelic games relatively rapidly acquired a dominant position and in theatre and literature. Cultural nationalism appealed to the relatively educated young (Hutchinson, 1987,

p. 179) in both urban and rural Ireland. Its success in appealing to both urban and rural educated elements was of great importance as on this basis a national rather than a localised cultural politics was made possible. The extent of the appeal of cultural national-ism is hard to gauge precisely but it would not be unreasonable to claim that by the end of the first decade of the century it had changed the reception conditions of nationalist politics in Ireland and shaped images of Irishness amongst the population into a more spiritualist and primordial mould.

The Radicals: The identity project of the radicals stressed an egalitarian code within the nation. Its most obvious manifestations were the protracted battle over the period 1890 to 1918 between graziers and radical agrarians over land ownership and the labour unrest that was unleashed most characteristically in the Dublin Lockout of 1913 but which had begun with the new mass unionism in the 1890s. In spite of this evident conflict over the social implications of egalitarian principles, the most characteristic fea-ture of radical, social politics in the period was the incorporation into nationalist politics of the justice code of the radicals. Right up to 1918, the battle was enjoined to rein in the radical politics of rural disaffection and after 1907 the labour movement increasingly adopted a nationalist frame of reference. The Boer War, which saw strong support in Ireland for the Boers, escalated the popu-larity of revolutionary nationalism and the polarisation of the nation from the state.

The two radical wings, however, experienced quite different op-portunity structures. The radical agrarians had access to the core of nationalist politics and operated as a strong pressure group, first within the Parliamentary Party and later within Sinn Fein. Their kind of radicalism could on the whole be satisfied within the popu-list coalition, even if with considerable difficulty, resistance and exclusions. In the capacity of belonging to the organised national-ist movement, the radical agrarians were able to influence govern-ment land policy. They also had an important presence in the public sphere where they did not depend on conventional media of com-munication but practised a wide repertoire of protest tactics inside and outside the law. The ability to form alignments was strong as nationalist politicians constantly sought to incorporate them within the nationalist fold rather than allowing the emergence of an inde-pendent social politics which might have been accompanied by a move leftwards. Such developments might even have led in certain circumstances to an alliance of radical agrarians and the labour movement though the likelihood of this happening was much reduced by the conservative nature of the Irish co-operative movement as well as the benefits for individuals of peasant proprietorship. Their identity project was certainly localised in both a social, and mostly in a geographical, sense, but within the given milieu and locale they experienced convinced support on the basis of being founded on material interest.

The situation was different with the labour movement. It had little influence on the state and for most of the period it was unwilling to enter the nationalist consensus, in part due to its own attempt to keep religious and national questions out of labour politics (Rumph and Hepburn, 1977, p. 12). It had some limited presence in the public sphere but, until 1913, the issues raised were not able to command public prominence except in a negative sense connected with the fear of socialism. Further, unlike the rest of Western Europe, the Irish socialist movement won very little support from intellectuals. It was therefore almost entirely Trade Union based in the early part of the century. The labour movement was generally in a poor position to form alliances as it was regarded with suspicion by the Church,[8] was of little interest to the conservative Parliamentary Party leadership, and was largely opposed by the cultural nationalists. Its resonance was therefore limited and confined to urban areas. But this resonance was not negligible and, especially in Dublin, as the labour radicalism of 1913 demonstrated, the social politics of labour could not be lightly disregarded.

By outbreak of war in 1914 the dominant frame of reference for Irish nationalism was still the existing state which it sought to both reform and transcend through Home Rule. The addition of the new dimensions of cultural nationalism and a more strongly marked political Catholicism, however, marked a new departure and created the conditions whereby radical separatism came onto the agenda in a central way. While this would in time lead to a consensus on the virtues of such separatism across all actors, this was by no means fore-ordained in circumstances where the more moderate politics of Home Rule still held sway. Finding a Home Rule solution to the Irish question within the limitations of the British constitutional order and the divisions occurring in Ireland was never going to be easy. The impact of the First World War ensured that it would never happen.

PHASE THREE: NATIONALIST POLITICS IN THE ERA OF CRISIS (1914–1921)

The period from the beginning of the First World War to the War of Independence, and beyond it to the Civil War which immediately followed, has left a legacy of division and confusion in the twentieth century. By the outbreak of war, the long sought-after Home Rule legislation had been passed by the imperial parliament and on the whole no major problems remained over the proposed institutional framework within nationalist Ireland. But the problems with Ulster Unionist rejection of the Home Rule settlement were profound and the British state had no clear answer for this problem, compelled on the one side by its agreement, after long struggle, to the principle of Home Rule, but on the other unable and unwilling to consider wider constitutional reform within the UK polity. The devolution of powers to a Dublin parliament might presage a stable epoch of Ireland continuing within the Union along the lines of what happened subsequently in the case of the Northern Ireland state. Or it might presage a gradual constitutional distancing along the lines of what actually happened quite rapidly within the quite different terms of the Anglo-Irish treaty in 1921.

In the circumstances, and standing outside the spectrum of interests and events, it is hard to imagine why precisely the turn to violence occurred within nationalist Ireland. The violence succeeded in eradicating problems from the political agenda that as a result remained unresolved throughout the twentieth century. This applied both in relation to the problem of accommodation with the very different religiously-based political views of Irish Protestants and also in relation to the possibility of an authentic social politics that stood on its own ground rather than on the elusive ground of the nation. The question that then remains is whether addressing such problems was in everybody's interests.

The Church: There was a clear, structural logic in the Church's position that suggests that it would have been quite comfortable with the idea of a Catholic Ireland distinct from and untroubled by accommodation with alien Ulster Protestantism. Irish Catholicism, in association with cultural nationalism, had been progressively moving towards a primordial code of identification after 1900. The Church was clear about what it opposed: cultural and social modernisation and what it perceived to be non-Catholic morality, which in Ireland was most explicitly anchored in the Protestant population. The Church was gradually forming an alliance with cultural nationalism. However, in the period of revolutionary nationalism proper after 1916 the Church was less able to exercise cultural power than it had been in the preceding period and in the subsequent period of institution-building in the Free State. In the revolutionary period, the Church was forced to withdraw to adjudicating between the contending nationalist forces.

In this period the process of de-legitimation of the British state progressed rapidly after 1916 and as it advanced the alignment of forces within the nation was becoming ever more important. The UK was embroiled in a huge war effort and 'normal' politics as such scarcely existed. For both these reasons relations with the state were less important for all nationalist actors including the Church. The clerical agenda while remaining influential also lost some of its centrality within the public sphere as the secular politics of the nation took over. The issues of the day were not those to which the Church was central as it had been to educational issues in the preceding period. The Church remained an indirect moral arbiter, but it did not have compelling power over political behaviour. This is most notably revealed in the Civil War where the Republicans defied the threat of excommunication in continuing their struggle. The Church did not regain its pivotal position until after the Civil War, when circumstances were to propel it into a very powerful position. In the public communication of the period in question, the Church did not so much lose adherence as other forces gained in centrality. The capacity of the Church to form alliances amongst the other wings of the nationalist movement on its own terms temporarily declined. In many respects, however, the Church had already achieved what it felt it could achieve in terms of positioning in the future Irish state. What it now awaited was the shape that state would take and this it was unable directly to control.

The Parliamentary Party: In this period the Parliamentary Party was replaced by Sinn Fein as the major political force of nationalist Ireland. The opportunity conditions that opened up before the Parliamentary Party contained within them a devastating paradox. The promise of Home Rule had resulted in the most propitious conditions for the Party in nationalist Ireland in its history. The conservative institutional structure of the British state had at last been breached. A further, important consideration which improved the 'feel-good' factor, and might have been assumed to have propitiated a long-term bias towards 'constructive' constitutional politics, was that economic conditions had been noticeably improving for those in possession of significant property or educational capital, which in the main were supporters of the Parliamentary Party. But the class and opportunity-based disposition and requirement to support the state in its war-effort required that the Party identified with the existing institutional order to a very significant extent. Consequently, if this order became unpopular it was probable that the Party would be damned by association. What Redmond needed was a quick war and a rapid return to the implementation of the Home Rule legislation. The precise opposite in fact happened.

An important consideration in increasing the volatility of the Parliamentary Party's situation was the relationship between recruitment and social class. Support for the war, and its encouragement of recruitment, reflected a class interest that probably correlated well with the upper echelons of Parliamentary Party support who had an interest in persuading large numbers of the working-class to sign up in order to head off the imposition of conscription and thereby protect their own sons. Southern Irish recruitment levels ran well below those of Protestant northern Ireland, Wales and Scotland and when the war situation became critical in 1917–18 the extension of conscription to Ireland seemed a logical response on behalf of the state. Redmond therefore became a double loser. The impact and consequences of the war on Irish society resulted in the demise of the Party (Fitzpatrick, 1988). Like Parnell before him, Redmond himself died in 1918 when his Party had collapsed. The war had brought great trauma to those who had fought in it and their relatives, and in the more nationalistic climate after 1916 had seemed at best a less important moral commitment than it might once have appeared to be. The Parliamentary Party's support for the war, especially its encouragement of recruitment, was remembered. With the threat of the extension of conscription to the Party's core supporters there was a haemorrhaging of support from the Party to Sinn Fein, which was, above all, the anti-conscription Party. If in the 1918 elections the Parliamentary Party didn't lose the absolute level of support it enjoyed in the pre-war period, rather in the main losing to Sinn Fein as a consequence of the extension of the suffrage, it certainly lost whatever opportunity it may have had to increase support significantly and to compete seriously with Sinn Fein.

After 1916, the degree of support enjoyed by the Parliamentary Party in the Irish press rapidly eroded. Not alone had the Party lost credibility on account of its war stance, but its moderate and constructive legitimation politics, balancing state and nation, was rapidly overtaken by events and the rise of a more extreme nationalist climate. In a relatively short time the situation changed adversely both in relation to the sympathy of the press and to the resonance of its messages in nationalist Ireland. The Irish public rapidly became disaffected with the state regime in Ireland and the Party's continuing association with this regime brought it into disrepute. The rapid decline of the electoral hegemony of the Parliamentary Party needs, of course, to be understood in relation to what was happening in revolutionary politics. From the standpoint of the Party, the rise of Sinn Fein represented a force that could previously have been accommodated within the Party but now represented an independent electoral force. The populist coalition had split.

Revolutionary Separatism: In this period, for the first time, cultural nationalism and radical separatism begin to unite behind a common programme. The separatists were able to profit from the power of organisations such as the Ancient Order of Hibernians and the United Irish League to shape political consciousness (Foster, 1989, p. 279). However, according to Hutchinson (1987, pp. 184–8; 1987), the Gaelic Revival was already on the wane by 1906, represented most volubly by the decline of the language movement and ancillary organisation from 964 to 388 branches between 1906 and 1913. Hutchinson identifies three factors as central to this decline: firstly, the resurgence of political nationalism with the return of the politics of Home Rule after the Liberal Party's victory in the General Election of 1906, secondly, the alienation of the Church after the League's campaign against the Catholic hierarchy on the subject of compulsory Irish, and, thirdly, growing class conflict in Dublin from 1908 which focused attention on the social question neglected by cultural nationalism and which internally polarised the Gaelic revival movement. While the Gaelic League as a cultural force may have been on the decline in organisational terms, circumstances were to favour the continuation of separatist nationalism by other, violent means after 1913.

Six key factors propitiated the rise of violent revolutionary nationalism. These were, firstly, the success of cultural nationalism in instilling a near-fanatical devotion to the establishment of a culturally distinct national community amongst an avant-garde. It also succeeded in widely diffusing a nationalist cultural sensibility of significant motivating power. Secondly, the general militarisation and masculinisation of culture (Mosse, 1985) all over Europe in the first decades of the century which, together with the revolutionary idea of national self-determination, provided ideological orientation. Thirdly, the unanticipated consequences of the founding of the Irish Volunteers in 1913 as a recruitment vehicle for the British Army which placed weapons and military expertise in the hands of revolutionary separatists who were protected by the voluntary nature of recruitment from serving in the British Army. Fourthly, both the Parliamentary Party and the previous generation of cultural nationalists had shown themselves unwilling to intervene in social politics, either ignoring it or adopting conservative positions. Therefore, a Party that indicated a propensity, if not real commitment, to social radicalism such as Sinn Fein after 1916 would profit hugely from the ossifying conservatism that the habitus of the Parliamentary Party exhibited. In the period after 1913, this was a problem in both urban and in rural Ireland. Fifthly, the Irish Volunteers were given major impetus by the emergence of the Ulster Volunteers the year previously. In southern Ireland the Volunteers were perceived as a response to the militarisation of Ulster. Finally, the cultural messages and style of the Party were designed for middle-class opinion and they were unable to compete with a party like Sinn Fein that was built around mass cultural politics.

The relationship between the separatists and the state was one of piecemeal repression. The state's failure to act on the Home Rule issue, shelving the implementation of the legislation during the war years, played into the separatists' hands. By the outbreak of war Home Rule had been at the top of the political agenda in nationalist Ireland for more than thirty years without resolution and still had to pass further major obstacles in the unshakeable objections of Ulster Unionists. In these circumstances of protracted political negotiation, which was itself suspended after the outbreak of war, a powerful ennui had developed following the decline in the excitement offered by cultural nationalism and the delay in the emergence of a new, institutional order in a Home Rule Ireland. In these circumstances, the democratic basis of the public sphere itself appeared to some as politically incomplete. Structurally, the war led to the situation that a state, without legitimation, continued to govern, a situation that disconnected the politics of the nation from a democratic politics of de-legitimation that had continued throughout the preceding reform period. Subjectively, the

idea of revolutionary will had become instilled in the minds of revolutionary activists like Pearse and they were prepared to go beyond democratic recourse to violent methods. To them, the situation
of continued 'British rule' had become intolerable and they were
prepared to 'strike for freedom'. They were unconcerned as to the
nature of that freedom. They certainly did not define it in terms of
the extension of liberal, political rights or, in the main, of enhanced
social justice but rather in terms of a national community that could
be trusted to work out its own destiny. They transformed a discursive modality of political communication into a violent, conflictual
modality of political exchange. In so doing, Sinn Fein made a large
component of the Irish nationalist tradition obstinately self-refer-
ential, recurringly convinced of its own right to violence in pursuit
of its aims. This would later be decisive in plunging the country
into civil war and in constituting the ambivalence about the legitimacy of armed struggle characteristic of twentieth century Irish
political culture.

Much has been written about support for separatist nationalism
after 1916 and, as already observed, in the absence of intense quali-
tative and quantitative study no confident conclusions may be drawn.
What is known suggests that 1916 occurred in a period of immense
political uncertainty, even emptiness, and that the event succeeded
in grabbing the national imagination. The execution of the revolutionaries gave their actions a sacrificial character that rendered
them potent symbols of British state insensitivity in the period afterwards. Together with the conscription issue, which was also a class
issue, and the broader social politics of distribution in the countryside in which Sinn Fein for a time succeeded in appearing socially
radical, the symbolic potency of the myth of martyrdom put Sinn
Fein politics on an entirely new footing quickly displacing the old
politics of consensual and constitutional nationalism.[9] The consequences were that the identity project of cultural nationalism, with
the legitimacy of revolutionary violence added, now became a critical
part of the political identity of the nation. Given the constitutional
barriers that remained in the way of Home Rule, the identity code
of the separatists, which conveniently placed Ulster Protestants
outside the nation, provided a short-cut towards the founding of
the nation, though on terms that had fateful consequences.

Fitzpatrick (1977, p. 233) points out that Sinn Fein as a loosely
organised mass movement seeking support from a national consensus inherited much of the style and character of the Parliamen-

tary Party. Sinn Fein after 1918 absorbed the Party into a new national coalition that combined the more radical lower middle-class and working class elements that had become electorally politicised through its own efforts with the more conservative constituency represented by the old Parliamentary Party. Sinn Fein's electoral success had occurred in extremely propitious circumstances for a revolutionary nationalist party at a time when a new social imaginary based on the inclusion of all social classes and milieux had fused with a national imaginary that would square all circles. Sinn Fein, brought down to its simplest, could be understood as the old populist coalition surrounding the Parliamentary Party, with the addition of the newly enfranchised and socially excluded, all equipped with a more radical nation-code that appeared to profit the under-privileged and excluded altogether the problem of Protestant opposition. Further, Sinn Fein had the advantage that it was not a secret society and could therefore engage in mass political communication.

Sinn Fein also benefited from what Swart (1995) believes was crucial to the eventual emergence of a separatist master frame, the international master frame of 'self-determination' associated with the Versailles Order and the League of Nations. In the aftermath of the War it was widely believed that the best solution to the dissolution of the Central European empires was the formation of ethnic nation-states. Thus a major theme used by Sinn Fein leaders was to align their cause with the Fourteen Point Plan and the general rhetoric of the League of Nations by characterising Britain as an imperialist 'Prussian' power forever thwarting Ireland's right to 'self-determination'.

Radicalism: The opportunity structures facing radical politics after 1913 definitely advanced. Organisationally, the labour movement had shown itself capable of mounting a long and complicated campaign against the Dublin employers in 1913. While it had lost the long confrontation it marked the real beginning of significant labour politics in Ireland on a national scale.[10] The issue of agrarian radicalism, as ever bound up with exclusion from the ownership of land, also remained on the agenda and recurred in a new cycle of intensity in association with the rise of Sinn Fein after 1917. However, the twin structural weaknesses of radical politics in Ireland remained: firstly, the numerical weakness of the Irish working-class and, secondly and more decisively, the absence of rural radicalism aimed at social transformation. Those excluded from land simply pursued the politics of seeking to be excluded no longer, a situation that pointed ultimately to the prospect of a conservative settlement which was largely achieved in subsequent land reform. Radical politics was further undone by the convenient fact of high emigration and the presence of the British market which provided sufficient demand to underwrite inefficiency in production until well into the twentieth century. Emigration and steady demand for agricultural products reduced structural pressures to innovate.

Hence, radical politics after 1913, though, especially in urban areas, structurally more advantaged and organisationally stronger than formerly, nevertheless exhibited the presence of structural strains rather than a revolutionary imaginary committed to societal transformation such as an ideologically developed socialism. The absence of such a revolutionary imaginary, in the sense of perceiving an alternative vision of societal institutions, both in this period and subsequently, left labour politics appearing as a mere adjunct to nationalist politics. Rumph and Hepburn (1977, p. 20) perceive this process as decisively occurring between 1913 and 1916. Taken as a whole, Connolly excepted, the labour movement made this choice reluctantly. In Britain the origins of the welfare state were being established and the state was accepting responsibility for the welfare of labour in areas other than the classic liberal concern with health and safety conditions. The desire to remain associated with the powerful British Trade Unions, the tradition of internationalism in the labour movement, the fear of being separated from the industrial base of Ulster, all caused labour to hesitate. But, nationally, the politics of the nation were becoming irresistible as British governance had entered a terminal crisis of legitimation and, internationally, the behaviour of labour in the First World War where it had without exception followed the nationalist line in all European countries, forced a major re-evaluation of the position of the Irish labour movement. Like the Church after 1913, the labour movement moved substantially to the sidelines, as the two major nationalist strands fought it out.

Fitzpatrick (1977, pp. 283–5) describes a process whereby the agrarian radicalism that had been manifested in 1917 and 1918 had been dampened down and a locally organised Sinn Fein had returned to a position that was 'extremely socially and politically conservative'. He claims that Sinn Fein showed a poor capacity for institutional innovation, merely replicating the British system when it established alternative courts and other administrative machinery between 1918 and 1921. Its dependence on the same financial support base as the Parliamentary Party was a major factor ensuring a conservative return. Both Fitzpatrick (1977) and Rumph and Hepburn (1977) conclude that while at various times and in various places there were indications of radicalism in the Sinn Fein coalition nonetheless the 'equilibrium condition' was basically conservative.

The identity project of the radicals therefore ended up back inside the conservative nation-code. Yet enough social unrest existed from the 1880s to the 1920s in both urban and rural Ireland to indicate how a more radical, and, at least, relatively independent democratic code of social democratic politics might have become institutionalised. What was absent was the crystallisation of an alternative imaginary in which a new institutional order could have been foreseen. The co-operative movement might have given a decisive lead, but the Irish co-operative movement was conservative and content to operate within rather than beyond the organisational basis of peasant proprietorship. And the breathless pace of a largely conservative nationalism, racing to control the direction of societal modernisation, strangled any other rationalisation than the de-differentiating drive towards a conservative Catholic nation-state.

THE RELATIONAL FIELDS OF NATIONALIST POLITICS

Each of the wings of the nationalist movement has been analysed within the relational field of nationalist politics. A synthetic account of this relational field is presented in Figure 5.1, below. Three parts of the figure, a, b and c, have an horizontal axis ranging from commitment to political pluralism to commitment to primordial/communitarian[11] nationalism. The same horizontal axis is present in the other three parts, x, y and z. In a, b and c, the vertical axis ranges between strength of identification with the state and strength of identification with the nation and, in the second set, between commitment to social conservatism and commitment to social radicalism. The various actors are plotted on these polar diagrams for each of the three time periods analysed above: a and x relating to the first time period, b and y to the second, and c and z to the third. The representation of radical politics is given two designations in these figures, respectively S1 for the labour movement and S2 for the agrarian radicals.

124

Figure 5.1 The relational field of nationalist politics, 1870–1921

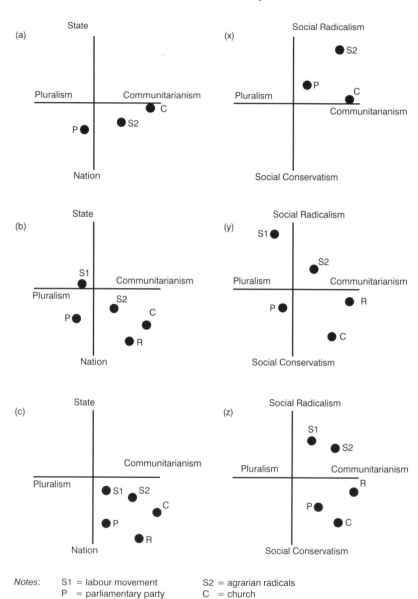

Notes: S1 = labour movement   S2 = agrarian radicals
        P = parliamentary party C = church
        R = separatist revolutionaries

Notes: S1 = labour movement; S2 = agrarian radicals; P = parliamentary party; C = Church; R = separatist revolutionaries.

Analysing each of the first set of figures, a, b and c, in turn presents the following picture. In the first period, the relational field of nationalist politics revealed a more pluralist and state-centric alignment than was to emerge over the entire cycle of the movement. This may be partly attributable to the stage of evolution of nationalist politics, partly to the limits of the relevant electoral constituency, partly to the incomplete movement of the Church in the direction of the nation, and partly to the overall political culture and opportunity conditions of the period. In the second period, a powerful movement towards the nation may be discerned. This may be attributed to the arrival on the political scene of a radical, separatist politics of the nation, the corresponding rise of the nation as a theme in an expanding, mass public sphere, and the new alignment of various political actors as the nation-code becomes the effective, thematic basis of Irish politics. Lastly, in the third period, the emergence of Republicanism as a dominant theme after 1916 pushes all actors into the communitarian/nation axis. In this period a transcendental nation-code becomes dominant for a time, achieves relatively rapid political success, and is absorbed into the general code of Irish national identity which it powerfully influences.

Analysing the second set of figures produces the following picture. In the first phase there appears to be a concentration of all actors in a socially radical and communitarian axis. The radicalism is, in one respect, real and, in another, illusory. There is no doubt that vast and transforming forces were unleashed in the Land War extending across this period, but there is equally no doubt that the long-run tendency of this phase of agrarian radicalism was the establishment of a socially conservative outcome, peasant proprietorship. The second period saw the best opportunity for the establishment of a social cleavage that would qualify the nation-code with a social-democratic code. There were two movements, urban and rural, that were engaged in significant campaigns for social change but, for a variety of reasons they did not complement one another. In these circumstances the strengthening nation code revealed in the alignment represented in Figure 5.1(b) was in a good position to absorb the existing social cleavage and to prevent it from being institutionalised. The full implications are manifest in the third table where the radicals in the social radicalism/communitarian quadrant are isolated from the major nationalist political actors in the communitarian/social conservatism quadrant. The social question has been stifled both because the politics of the social were secondary in momentum to the politics of the nation and because social radicals could not come up with a sufficiently integrated, radical vision and organisational base. The temporary victory of transcendental nationalism, and the less temporary suppression of the social question, were firmly in place.

Central conclusions, which link the mobilisation phase to the institutionalisation phase, may be drawn from the establishment of a socio-political identity based upon conservative Catholic communitarianism. The first is that the Irish national movement was far from monolithic, either in terms of social support bases or tactical preferences, but it became a monolith for a brief period. In this brief period a cultural consensus was forcibly established that locked the society within a cultural model that often offered evasive solutions to urgent problems for a long time afterwards. Second, the emphasis on the nation-code led to the sidelining of the social-democratic code and left a legacy to social-democratic and other oppositional politics suggesting that enhancing the nation-code is somehow consistent with social justice. Since the revolutionary separatists came more from the lower classes, nationalism and social-democracy would be perceived as at least potentially compatible in the future nation-state. Third, nationalist cultural categories, though having mass appeal, were consistent with the interests of a propertied social elite if the spectre of social radicalism could be purged. This was made to happen after 1918, in the civil war and in the early years of the Free State.[12] An ethical code based on nationalism, could therefore provide a blueprint for the social and functional reconstruction of the society on conservative lines. Fourth, the political actors active in the mobilisation phase were re-translated into the dominant political actors in the new state; the Irish Parliamentary Party bore an elective affinity with Cumann na nGaedheal, pre-1918 Sinn Fein with Fianna Fáil, and, of course, the Church and the social radicals remained themselves. Fifth, the nationalist consensus established in the course of the First World War collapsed within a very short time plunging the country into civil war.

The mobilisation phase of Irish nationalism issued in the production of two consensus movements that were capable of mobilising on a wide range of fronts. The first consensus movement and master frame was that of Home Rule, the second that of republican separatism. Both were variants on the theme of self-determination. The shift from the first to the second master frame contained within it an apparent contradiction. In spite of Irish nationalism appealing to a wider constituency in the second consensus phase it had become ideologically more conservative and less pluralist. The answer is to be found in the increase in compulsiveness of strong identification with the nation which, as more groups adhered to it and adhered more strongly, became less defined as to its future programme.[13] The obfuscation of the politics of the real revealed an ideology of deferment. Those who had resources adhered to the collective sentiment but did so without prejudice to these resources. Those who lacked resources felt they could acquire them with the institutionalisation of the nation-state. However, the power of conservatism and primordialism had increased as forces that necessitated accommodation were swept aside and made irrelevant whether in the form of the British state framework or Irish Protestants. Within the true core of a national identity for all a conservative social vision had been forged that would dominate the twentieth century.

In assessing the genesis and nature of this conservative turn, social forces in Ireland were not the only conditioning factor. A little-observed factor is the extent to which Irish conservative nationalism was in tune with what Freeden calls 'Tory Democracy'. This concept of democracy which became the guiding principle of the Conservative Party from the 1890s was oriented to 'the taming of change through the guiding hand of the past, the appeal to the masses to put their faith in established institutions, and the bestowing of extra-human sanction on the existing state machinery by means of the Church.' (Freeden, 1996, p. 352). Freeden also quotes Balfour to the effect that a psychological climate should be produced that could maintain the beliefs and morality of a society: 'that interior assent should be produced in countless cases by custom, public opinion, the contagious convictions of countryman, family, Party or Church, seems natural, and even obvious'; and that a confined notion of reason should operate to direct 'the public policy of communities within the narrow limits of deviation permitted by accepted custom and tradition' (Balfour quoted in Freeden, 1996, p. 353). Each of these conservative beliefs was part of the gathering synthesis of Irish nationalism though it was forced to use an equivocal symbologism due to the unresolved social question in Ireland and the continuing support of the Liberal Party for Irish Home Rule. This homology between conservative thinking in Ireland and in Britain is not altogether surprising. Prior to the advent of agrarian radicalism in the late 1870s the southern Irish parliamentary tradition had been conservative. In addition, Conservative policies designed to slow the progress of social reform advanced by their liberal and socialist opponents found favour in Ireland on issues such as taxation, local government, land tenure reform, and the establishment of the Congested Districts Board.

The conservative turn in Irish nationalist ideology sought to head off the 'problems' likely to follow the anchorage in Ireland of the progressive movements of the period such as suffragism, welfarist policies, and educational progressivism. This is not to say that progressive politics would have been opposed by all social forces in Ireland. In fact, many in Ireland including women, workers, landless labourers, smaller farmers, emigrants from all social classes would have stood to benefit materially from liberal and social reformist policies and institutions. The reason they did not turn to these ideologies was that they did not have cohesive ideological awareness, lacked the social power to introduce them on their own and were convinced that in the end the nation would somehow address their concerns. This latter conviction cannot be understressed. The communitarian conservative strand within Irish nationalism was immensely successful in promulgating its ideology. The conservative forces in the Church and the Parliamentary Party were already organised prior to the advent of mass electoral politics. The extension of the suffrage occurred at a time when mass Irish political culture was in its infancy and could easily be swayed by well-packaged, emotionally resonating arguments that appeared to promise the generalisation of rights and opportunities. Nationalism was used to hide social and political conservatism, a process which continued throughout the twentieth century, taking on a variety of forms.

Freeden (1996, p. 344) identifies two devices that are used to maintain basic conservative beliefs. He identifies these beliefs as resistance to change that is not perceived to be organic and natural and subordinating change to the belief that the laws and forces guiding human behaviour have extra-human origins and should not be subordinated to human whims and will. The two devices are, firstly, the fashioning of relatively stable beliefs out of reaction to progressive values and, secondly, flexibility in the application of decontested concepts so as to maximise under varying conditions the preservation of the conservative conception of acceptable change. These two devices were well entrenched in the Irish nationalist movement in its consensus phase. Its conservative core ideology reacted against progressive ideologies and developed a stable ideological configuration of its own and it exhibited extreme flexibility in using the communitarian-conservative interpretation of the nation to arrange other conceptual world-understandings in a fashion consistent with its own core conservatism. It therefore reacted against a whole host of modern ills but still succeeded in institutionally constructing a populism that presented itself as simultaneously conservative and egalitarian.[14]

The naturalisation of conservatism was therefore the final mobilisatory ideology of the national movement. While the society seethed with latent conflict the interpretation systems of nationalism de-emphasised and de-legitimated the expression of social and cultural differences. The national movement ended up on the Victorian and Edwardian right, an ironic outcome given that its main opponent was British conservatism and its main ally was British liberalism.

6 The Institutionalisation of National Identity in the Irish Free State

INDEPENDENCE, CIVIL WAR AND IDENTITY

The consensus movement that won the right to establish a separate nation-state in the early 1920s was characterised by a primordial communitarian political philosophy and social conservatism. This political and social identity, which represented a move towards a new confidence in national 'we-feeling', occurred in a context of insecurity and contradiction. It can be understood in part as a product of the internal rationalisation of the movement impelled by perceptions of needs, the distribution of social power, revulsion at war, the martyrology of revolution, unprecedented prosperity, and the international context. It was in part also the movement's response to problems in its external environment. The dominant problems in this environment were, on the one hand, the power of both the British State and Irish Unionism to block a political settlement that would be satisfactory to all strands of Irish nationalism and, on the other, the unresolved social question in Ireland. The euphoria of inclusive we-feeling, both of its own and its unionist other, led Irish nationalism away from a dialogical politics with other political and confessional traditions on the island. The social question was suppressed: propertied conservatism and social injustice were never to receive a fundamental challenge.

The construction of ideological consensus within Irish nationalism around the master frame of separatist self-determination (Tambini, 1996) was built upon a tenuous surface agreement hiding real differences. Within the overall hegemony of Sinn Fein still lay the different wings of Irish nationalism which, while cohering on how the nation should be constituted on certain points, differed on others. The ideology that emerged from nationalist politics at the end of the First World War was still without institutional foundations. To some it showed the way to a conservative, Catholic social order. To others, it promised a society that would be fairer and more just. To yet others, it revealed the power of force as a means of settling disputes over political authority. These differences, expressed in opposing value systems, were sufficient to fuel a civil war which broke out in 1922 and lasted until 1923. Prager (1986), whose interest is in the cultural bases of democratic order, describes the value differences than animated civil war participants as Irish-Enlightenment and Gaelic-Romantic respectively. He ascribes to Irish enlightenment values a cosmopolitan and democratic character, while Gaelic-romantic values are characterised as local and based on a violent, revolutionary community of the will. To this value cleavage, Rumph and Hepburn (1977) would add a social cleavage. The Civil War in their view to some extent reflected respectively the class and regional bases of republican and constitutional nationalism. Support for the Republican cause emanated mainly from the poorer farmers of the West who retained an interest in land distribution. The proximate cause of the civil war was the outcome of the Anglo-Irish Treaty negotiations that followed three years of guerrilla war. What Prager calls the Gaelic-Romantics rejected the treaty – which committed all who wished to enter the Irish parliament to give an oath of allegiance to the British crown – and turned to arms after a parliamentary and electoral defeat.

The Church committed its support to the pro-treaty camp, though it did not share enlightenment values, when the Republicans turned to violence. The Church and the Republicans carried sometimes complementary, sometimes competing visions of primordial identity, one Catholic and the other Gaelic. In the mobilisation phase, the Church feared the secular undertones to the separatists politics since it potentially competed with their own spiritual monopoly though they accepted much of their cultural programme if it did not deny them institutional and moral domination. Their relationship with the constitutionalists had matured in the early twentieth century and, while not possessing the cultural complementary they shared with the separatists, it represented a safe haven for the preservation of Catholic influence.

The break-up of Sinn Fein created the new fault-lines of post-Independence politics which were genetically related to the fault-lines of the nationalist movement. The Church remained an actor in its own right as did the labour movement. The constitutional nationalism of the Irish Parliamentary Party went substantially over to Cumann Na nGaedheal while, similarly, the separatist wing became associated with extreme Republicanism before being constitutionalised into Fianna Fáil founded in 1926. In the Civil War, the constitutionalists and Church were opposed by the separatist republicans with the labour movement not taking sides explicitly but standing more on the government side. The republicans, drawing inspiration from the romantic irrationalism of cultural nationalism, held out for a complete break with Britain. The constitutionalist Free State side were prepared to settle for the outcome of the Treaty negotiation. Under the Treaty, the Irish Free State of the partitioned Ireland was to have more or less full autonomy in domestic though not in foreign policy. The military divisions of the Civil War align fairly closely with the main fault-lines of the preceding guerrilla war for a separatist state. The Republicans were substantially drawn from those who had fought the British and were strongest in those parts of the country that were most active in this preceding struggle (Rumph and Hepburn, 1977). On the Republican side, the idea of revolutionary will gave its military proponents a strong conviction of their superiority to merely democratic will, a feeling all the more strengthened by the perception that they represented the authentic and singular national imaginary. The republican side were thus ostensibly prepared to settle for nothing less than a nation-state that would embrace the geographical territory of the island: democracy was subordinated to the will of the nationalist 'Self', embodied in Sinn Fein ideology, and they were not prepared to allow Ulster, or a part of the province, to secede from their secession.

The Republicans were relatively easily defeated in the Civil War, which was fought exclusively in the south (Hopkinson, 1988; Fitzpatrick, 1977). The majority of the Irish population could not see the importance of the distinctions they drew between partial and full sovereignty with respect to the oath, which was a more important issue in the Civil War conflict than the Ulster question.[2] The civil war division shows that the legacy of the Parliamentary Party had not disappeared with the victory of Sinn Fein in 1918 but transferred into Cumann na nGaedheal which, in the new circumstances of Free State politics, found itself in a more restricted and more local context. In the Civil War, Cumann na nGaedheal was supported by the Church, which was in any case happier with an homogeneous Catholic 26 county Ireland than one embracing a Protestant Ulster, which would have to be accommodated in political culture and institutional arrangements and which would not have accepted the power of the Church.[3] The victory of the government or Free State forces meant the marginalisation of Republicanism for a period and gave free rein to Cumann na nGaedheal and the Church to institutionalise their imaginaries of the nation. During the Civil War the Free State government, Cumann na nGaedheal, relied for support on the Church, which branded the IRA irregulars as murderers (Foster, 1989, p. 534).

Three interrelated factors explain why, after the Civil War, the new government increasingly looked to the Church as its indispensable ally in the building of new institutions. Firstly, they had been allies in the Civil War and the government perceived that it needed church support in the complex task of regime stabilisation in which many difficult decisions had to be taken. This regime stabilisation was undertaken in a situation of great uncertainty created by the continuing presence of a potential armed conspiracy against the state, by the challenge of state-building in transformed institutional conditions, and by adverse economic conditions created by the economic depression of the 1920s. The Catholic church with its long history of institution-building was clearly useful in these circumstances. The Church's influence was felt across the full range of institutions, but it took full control over an expanded voluntary sector which extended in the Irish system to such key institutional complexes as welfare, heath and education.

Secondly, the old nationalist aspiration for an Irish nation-state had arrived in unpropitious circumstances. Nationalist revolution had ended in a bitter civil war, with 4,000 casualties including 77 executions (Lee, 1989b, p. 69). With partition as the effective outcome of the struggle for independence, and given the bitter divisions of the civil war, the new state could not so easily appeal to the unqualified we-feeling of nationalism for its legitimation. The Church provided a new pole of legitimation. The struggle for Irish independence became represented as the struggle for the right to live a Catholic form of life free from the alien impositions of modernity.

Thirdly, the Cumann na nGaedheal party inherited the difficulties of the Parliamentary Party in its poor capacity to play cultural politics. It could only rely on legal authority, lacking what Weber has called traditional authority (Macmillan, 1993) and, certainly, unable to draw upon charismatic authority. In the case of the Parliamentary Party this arose both from the particular social interests and cultural dispositions of its dominant elite and because its cultural ground was taken both by the Church and by cultural separatists. In the

1920s these same conditions were once again apparent as Cumann na nGaedheal on its own lacked symbolic creativity. It turned increasingly to the Church to supply cultural legitimation. Alternative codes of identity construction had not succeeded: linguistic nationalism was a failure both ideologically and in real terms. The relatively narrow base of Cumann na nGaedheal's core constituency, chiefly the urban middle-class, big farmers, shopkeepers and former Unionists, accentuated its problems of legitimation and political appeal. Soon after the party was launched in 1923 it failed to win a significant majority of seats – 63 out of 153 – in the election later that year (Lee, 1989b, p. 94). The Church, ideologically not comfortable with democracy in the first place, favoured authoritarian governance which also suited the temperament of the secular leaders. The Church contrasted with them, however, in its capacity culturally to reach a wide constituency while continuing to imbue in them a respect for its unchangeable authority.

RECONSTRUCTING THE INSTITUTIONAL ORDER IN POST-INDEPENDENT IRELAND

In Chapters 4 and 5, the main components of the identity project of the Catholic church and the Irish Parliamentary Party were represented respectively as:

Catholic Church: rurality, respectability, sexlessness, the extramundane moral code of sin and unreflective obedience, theocratic sovereignty, domestication of women, conservative anti-modernism, anti-radicalism, commitment to hierarchy as principle of social organisation, the conventional personality, the necessity of the Catholic way of life, naturalisation of culture, controlled production of culture, anti-intellectualism, the evil of the external world.

Parliamentary Party: democratic, adherence to legality, clientelistic and dutiful ideas of citizenship, the importance of locality, weak commitment to pluralism, political populism, respectability.

In the aftermath of the Civil War these two traditions came together to mould the institutional project of the new state according to their particular identity projects. This required, in the first instance, a consolidation of the twin identity projects and their institutionalisation as the national identity of the new state. The institutionalisation of a dominant project of national identity in a nation-state is very different to establishing a collective identity for part or whole of a national movement. The former aims to pressurise an external, dominant, governing power according to the fusion of idealised images of the nation-to-be and social interests while the latter involves the mobilisation of an identity project which can be directly applied to the organisation of society. National identity codes, especially those of the late nineteenth century, are morally prescriptive to a high degree and aim at a morally-based transformation of society.

The precise form that a national identity code takes in a given case depends upon a number of factors. These are, firstly, the nature of the identity project itself. This depends on whether it is accommodating or radical, i.e., whether its major proponents aim at the accommodation of competing interests or at a 'fundamentalist' project. The second factor determining the national identity code is the balance of powers that emerges from the dynamics of the nationalist mobilisation phase itself. The composite identity project which emerges is based on both the historical concretisation of interests and capacities for action in the society and on the opportunities offered by the current situation including the institutional powers of the sponsors and the existence or absence of competing projects. The degree of instituting power that a particular identity project can muster will depend on the power and cohesion of the groups sponsoring the project and their capacity to publicly legitimate their project.

The national identity project of the 'clerical-constitutionalists' in the 1920s can be classified in relation to the above dimensions as follows. Firstly, the project was fundamentalist. It promoted a conservative moral order for society that involved the restriction of the free play of cultural and personal innovation. The normative foundations of conservative social order were designed to dominate new patterns of thinking or new expressions of individuation. Secondly, the general outcome of the dynamics of nationalist mobilisation in Ireland pointed, as we saw at the end of chapter five, to a conservative political consensus. The temporary neutralisation of the republican nationalists, the losers in the Civil War, and the absence of a significant non-nationalist project, aided the dominance of clerical conservatism over the exact definition of conservative communitarianism that would be institutionalised. Thirdly, both Cumann na nGaedheal and the Church were organisationally coherent and, by and large, culturally and politically compatible.[4] They also had a relatively easy time in the context of a social structure that was predominantly conservative, with a majority commitment to democratic order and ideologically of nationalist persuasion.[5]

With access to the institutional power of the state, the national identity project of cultural conservatism could no longer subsist on negativity towards the established order. It had to deal with a reality in which the positive content of its programme had to be socially realised. It was a matter of transferring a revolutionary nationalist ideology into a programme of state-based patriotism. National identity projects in these circumstances gain power over society but are also tested and reconstructed by society. Both organisations were unwilling to countenance an open, democratic politics. The identity project they mutually developed was immunised from testing by means of a strong, agreed authoritarianism. In the absence of a social programme of its own, Cumann na nGaedheal adopted that of the Church and transferred the Church's social authoritarianism into the state's basic attitude (Nolan, 1975; Schmitt, 1973, p. 47; Prager, 1986, p. 217).

THE INSTITUTIONALISATION OF CLERICAL CONSERVATISM

The dominant socio-political actors in the 1920s were the Church and the repackaged constitutional nationalists. The conservatism of the constitutionalists had increased since the nationalist mobilisation given the demise of Irish Protestantism as a political and cultural force and the disappearance of the more complex and pluralist UK institutional order. Together Cumann na nGaedheal and the Church put in place a social project that combined a defensive lower middle-class project with an anti-modern religious one. The latter project was the primary cultural inspiration about what should constitute an Irish way of life and how the institutional order inherited from the British should be modified. It was composed of three strands: (1) a process of re-enchantment in the extension of the authoritarian, religious values to the whole of society with a consequent de-differentiation of institutional spheres; (2) the development of a cultural ideology that maintained tight role ascriptions in the social structure; (3) repressive opposition to the emergence of reflexive individuation. Each of these is considered in turn below:

(1) *Re-enchantment and de-differentiation*: The position of the Irish Catholic church in the twentieth century marked a classic reversal of the trend towards the differentiation of religion into a single, specialised sub-system and the accompanying differentiation of its concentrated power across different social spheres (Luhmann, 1982). With the progress of secularisation and the differentiation of other social systems, religion had to recognise that its theocratic principles of integration could no longer dominate other social systems without endangering their ability to function. Modern citizens acquire the power to make decisions in different spheres according to their own discretion. Religion either has to recognise this power or to re-impose a society of lower complexity based on a religiously-regulated normative order. Otherwise, individuals will only act nominally as members of a religious community and will in various contexts act according to non-religious codes. Religion has to acquire enormous institutional power and social prestige before it can attempt the task of de-differentiation.[6] The chief requirement for such a 're-enchantment' of the social order is the presence of a fundamentalist anti-modernist identity project and a suitable environment for its realisation. Both these requirements were present in Ireland in the 1920s.

Directly and indirectly, the Church was able to impose wide-ranging de-differentiation on Irish institutional spheres, viz., health, education, art, education, economy and welfare by building a dominant religious code into their own operational codes. Prior to independence, the Church already had direct control over religion, health and education and strove to consolidate and extend those powers. The Church also acquired immense power over family life and intimacy through its control of sexuality, especially the subjugation of the female body. Religious norms also prevailed in the spheres of art and culture rendering them affirmative and uncritical. Finally, in the economy, religiously inculcated cultural values were antithetical to economic development. These developments need to be considered in more detail.

The Church was firmly focused on controlling socialisation in Ireland to ensure that it fulfilled the central function of reproducing a traditional, Catholic inner nature. According to Schmitt (1973, p. 49) education, family and democracy in Ireland are authoritarian and not democratic. In school and family unresisting obedience was demanded whether to the figure of the teacher or the patriarchal head of household. The Church was dedicated to the exclusion of

all secularising influences and any form of post-traditional pedagogy or socialisation practice. In the school, the model was a strictly
transmissive one of inculcating received, traditional and patriotic
norms and corpora of knowledge. Control over family life and intimacy was achieved, according to Inglis (1987, p. 5) by the dependence of mothers on the Church for moral power within the home.
It was also maintained by strict control over sexuality in all its aspects.
In the domain of family life, the Church was able to use the power
of the confessional and the pulpit to regulate behaviour. In the
area of health, a rigid Catholic ethos was imposed on Irish medicine which conditioned the behaviour of medical personnel. Nuns
ran the Catholic hospitals and priests and sympathetic lay people
sat on hospital boards. The Catholic clergy were given institutional
power over children.[7] In these areas of life, education, health, family,
the Church benefited from concentrated and inter-connected circuits of power. Peoples' relationship to religious authority and values
was the primary determinant of their experience of social organisation
and personal freedom in most areas of everyday experience. After
independence, when the power of the state was harnessed to support
and expand the existing institutional power of the Church, Irish
society was organised to a very substantial extent on theocratic
principles of social integration.

This can be seen further in the Church's successful campaign for
the suppression of the autonomy of art and culture (O'Callaghan,
1984). Laws censoring films were imposed in 1923, in 1924 the
dominating position of the Church in relation to education was
affirmed and, in 1925, debates began on matrimonial law leading
to a prohibition on divorce (Nolan, 1975). W. B. Yeats, then a senator
in the Upper House, protested against the new measures arguing
that they would only alienate Northern Ireland from joining the
Free State.[8] In 1926 a Committee on Evil Literature was set up
and in 1929 the Censorship of Publications Act was passed which
made it possible for any Catholic action group, such as the Vigilance Association, to apply to have a book banned if it did not
meet the requirements of the Catholic dominated board. Under
Fianna Fáil in the 1930s repressive legislation was continued, with
the Public Dance Halls Bill and the Criminal Law Amendment
Bill of 1934 tightly regulating sexual behaviour. Catholic pressure
groups skilfully manipulated politicians (Fitzpatrick, 1989, p. 223).
The result of these measures was the achievement of a kind of de-
differentiation between law and morality that pre-figured the Con-

stitution of 1937: Catholic social teaching re-moralised law and through law controlled everyday life.

The Church extended its power indirectly to control much of university life leading to the strangulation of any critical impulses that might have emerged in philosophy, psychology, and sociology.[9] Whyte (1980) speaks of the rise of a 'Catholic social movement' in the early decades of the Free State with such as bodies Muintir na Tire.[10] The Catholic Workers' College and others contributed to the creation of a Catholic social order. An Irish Catholic sociology developed along with societies such as Christus Rex Society which was founded in 1946.

In short, the Church partly through the agency of the state managed to prevent the cognitive and moral basis of criticism of the institutional order from emerging. Territorial insularity and powerful cultural nationalism were major allies in this denial of a central aspect of the culture of modernity. Beyond active repression through censorship, clerical and nationalist dogma was also applied through intimidation. Careers could be endangered by speaking out. Lay Catholic organisations such as Catholic Truth Society of Ireland, the Irish Vigilance Association, the Legion of Mary, the Irish Christian Brothers, the Knights of Columbanus and others extended the already potent clerical surveillance of dissidence.

Finally, in the area of the economy, the Catholic church had little interest in promoting an economically vital culture (Keating, 1992; Daly, 1985). In line with Cumann na nGaedheal policy in the twenties, the economy was left to find its own level while the Church acted to maintain the ideological cohesiveness of society. According to Keating and Desmond (1993, p. 5), 'the canon of identity into which the Irish are encultured came to be located in an ideal of civilisation that subordinated economic activity to non-economic interests.' Keating and Desmond view the Church as having been the main upholder of this identity and its main transmission agent through the socialisation system.

(2) *Ascribing Roles*: The virtues of a propertied, predominantly rural civilisation were at the heart of the Church's anti-modern project from the late nineteenth century. In the 1920s, the institutionalisation both of its organisational powers and its identity code conduced to legitimate and reproduce the existing social structure. The dominant social base of partisan Cumann na nGaedheal support in the 1920s were rural or small-town property owners, precisely those who were most active in Catholic organisations. The

dominance of this social class who stood for resistance to change and the construction of an institutional order that would ensure this resistance led to a process of institutional design and an ideological ethos that would reproduce for most of the century a disproportionately rural domination of the setting of societal goals. This social structure was predominantly non-entrepreneurial and the cultural ethos and status order, reproduced in substantial part through clerical influence, was indifferent to socio-economic innovation. The task of legitimating and institutionally reproducing this order was made easier by the new numerical importance of the rural and small town petit-bourgeoisie in post-independence Ireland. In Lee's view (1989b, p. 159) the obsession with censorship 'suitably symbolised the impoverishment of spirit and the bareness of mind of the risen bourgeoisie, touting for respectability'. The problem of unemployment was easily solved through emigration: Britain was always there as a reliable safety-valve for social problems. In this way Ireland solved the problem of the opposition that might have followed social mobilisation (Schmitt, 1973, p. 41). The industrial entrepreneurial class and proletariat of the North-East were no longer an issue. Nor were the Protestant landholding elite. Protestants generally were in relatively rapid decline and emigration siphoned off the population that was not needed and that might have proved troublesome (Lyons, 1979). This social-structural simplification, together with the advocacy of a rural civilisation by nationalist ideology since the early part of the century, made the project of deliberately engineered social stasis – or paralysis, to use Joyce's term – possible.

The project of mostly coercively and partly persuasively maintaining social roles was at the core of the Church's anti-modernism since the nineteenth century. As Inglis points out (1987, p. 6) the popular legitimation of the Church's coercive power was connected to how the propertied and advantaged sought to maintain various kinds of power, but especially 'economic possessions, occupational positions and social prestige.' The Church advocated a societal model based on simplicity and peasant virtues and was unenthusiastic about social, cultural or economic innovation. In league with the lay middle-class the Church created an hierarchical societal model through the educational and socialisation system in which women and those lower down the social class scale were ascribed a position within the family which was extremely difficult to alter and which in time led to very low participation rates of females in work.[11]

(3) *Repression of autonomy*: The Church was dedicated to op-posing political liberalism with its dangerous doctrines of individual choice and pluralistic politics and to any manifestations of moral individualism or the privatisation of decision-making. Irish Catholi-cism was a folk Church that depended on social conformity and the secure handing-on of a narrative of national holiness with the Church at its core. This tied the Church to a narrative that put it at one with the nation. Irish tradition, and the Church within it, was timeless and transcendent. The Church therefore spoke for the collectivity and could define what adherence to this collectivity meant. In a whole variety of institutionally interconnected ways, the individual experienced this narrative from the moment she or he entered the world. The objective structuring of the habitus maintained, above all, by the silence of power, appeared as a seamless web of social obligations. It appeared as a world without rights, except for the right to command held by an almost exclusively male band of property owners, by government functionaries and by reli-gious hierarchies. Yeats spoke of the dangers of unchecked auth-oritarianism when he described the implications of the 1929 Censorship of Publications Act 'our zealots idea of establishing the Kingdom of God upon Earth is to make Ireland an island of moral cowards' (Brown, 1985, p. 131).

Religious authority in Ireland demanded more than mere sym-bolic compliance, it demanded committed moral compliance. The good life did not consist of the exploration of autonomy but, in true conservative style, of the acceptance of tradition. Inglis (1987) describes in detail how the Church set about establishing a distinc-tive civilising process in the nineteenth century that laid down ex-haustive rules for individual conduct. This was backed by increased institutional power after 1922. To the unconscious power of guilt for sin and the dogmatic moral power of Church teaching, was now added additional statutory and even, after 1937, constitutional power. This extension of the Church's power created terrifying intra-psychic tensions for many. Socially, the dissident had little chance and many emigrated for cultural reasons.

In the division of authority over society in the 1920s, the Church was confirmed and enhanced in its domination of community and societal institutions. This established a structure of power that was to endure substantially for the following fifty years. It revealed the clerical inclination in the implementation of civil authority in Ire-land, a factor which grew with the national movement and was institutionalised as one major consequence of its success. The other, major and related complex of power was that derived from the state. The two were related in the sense that political legitimation in the broadest, trans-regime sense depended to a high degree on clerical approval via a process that might be described as a clericalisation of political culture.

The Cumann na nGaedheal government found itself in a very difficult position after the Civil War. Power was assumed in precarious circumstances with a divided population and an uncertain institutional context. Economic options appeared relatively few given the government's class base and ideological commitment to maintaining the British connection.[12] The defeated Republican side in the civil war presented for election but refused to take their seats in the Irish parliament (Dáil) though they continued to win a substantial share of the vote, twenty seven per cent of the total poll in 1923 and forty four seats. The composition of parliament was made up of a majority Cumann na nGaedheal representation, a Labour party that won around 10 per cent, a farmers party who won a little less, and a scattering of independent parties that also won about 10 per cent in the general elections of 1923 and 1927. Cumann na nGaedheal, now Fine Gael, therefore won a comfortable majority in 1923 and remained in government even after the entry of Fianna Fáil to mainstream constitutional politics in 1926.

Prager (1986, p. 140) describes convincingly how the new Fine Gael party became increasingly reduced to a politics of power as the decade wore on in contrast to the cultural politics of Sinn Fein and, later, Fianna Fáil. Fine Gael, partly through the pressure of events, partly through its own ideology and inclination and partly through its alliance with the Church, increasingly adopted an authoritarian pose as it constructed a bureaucratised and centralised state. Prager documents the growing adoption of authoritarian measures and attitudes as the government responded to challenges to its sovereignty such as the Army Mutiny of 1924, the Boundary Commission crisis of 1925 and the assassination of its Minister of Justice in 1927.[13] He claims that the model of authoritarianism was derived from the Church and the Church's shaping of social relations. In his account it was carried by political elites as an 'unquestioned vision . . . expressed through an irrational commitment to absolutist leaders unaccompanied by an ethic of individualised, critical judgement concerning the purposes of politics . . . political accountability extended no further than the elite's articulation of that vision'

(Prager, 1986, p. 213). The government's confidence in its vision increased as the twenties wore on and as its hold on power grew more secure. This vision became increasingly conservative and became obsessed with anti-communism which was used as an ideational adversary to emphasise the virtues of conservatism. Dunphy (1995, p. 21) describes its interest in the revival of the Irish language, the prosperity of large farmers, the social teachings of the Catholic church, together with clericalist and anti-foreign tendencies as indicators of conservatism as the decade wore on.

After Cumann na nGaedheal/Fine Gael survived the initial legitimation crisis it became apparent by the later 1920s that the party lacked creative vision. It was effectively a party living out of the nineteenth century and in this sense in tune with the stasis and regressive inclinations of Irish society in the period. It was a party uncomfortable with the era of mass politics (Mair, 1987, p. 122), committed to conservatism and with little to offer those not at the higher echelons of the social structure who were comfortable with more of the same.[14] It was therefore a party that effectively ran out of policies after it had achieved the stabilisation of the institutional order.

The legacy of the first decade of Irish party politics was the production of an authoritarian and remote state whose distance from civil society was bridged by clientelistic and personalistic political procedures.[15] Prager (1986, pp. 220–2) describes personalism as the mediation of political decisions through personal reciprocities. He associates personalism with authoritarianism. One balances the other in given personalities and situations. Personalism indicates a tendency to prefer chains of personal influence to meritocratic means of making decisions. While personalism was not fully institutionalised as a key element in the Irish political system until Fianna Fáil came to power in 1932, the development of a centralised and distant state under Fine Gael was an important condition of its emergence.

Apart from its authoritarianism, its dependence on the Church for purposes of legitimation (Whyte, 1980, pp. 34–5) the state under Fine Gael was a minimialist state except in the areas of security and moral policy.[16] In the former case, it acted to secure the legal foundations of the state in an increasingly authoritarian fashion staying with the themes of order and responsibility throughout the decade (Prager, 1986, p. 203). In the latter area, it supported Church power over formal institutions and the societal community. In

Schmitt's (1973) path-breaking analysis of Irish political culture, the authoritarianism and personalism that characterises Irish social relations is a product of church dominance and comprises the political culture that is the source of stability in the political system. The normative implications of this claim do not concern us here, but it does indicate how Cumann na nGaedheal in the 1920s accepted the religious domination of civil life and the production of a political culture that would grant the government political stability.

A major factor explaining the conservatism of the Irish institutional order after independence is the degree to which a stable institutional system preceded the foundation of the state. The transfer of power after Independence from the British to the Irish authorities was peaceful and Ireland never experienced a significant Fascist threat. Given the emphasis of the national movement on cultural change rather than revolutionary social change or widespread institutional reform, it was completely unsurprising that the British institutional model should have been taken over. The fact that the Free State political leadership was composed of mostly young men, who were not likely to tamper with the existing model, also played a role as did the fact that the Free State was founded after a Civil War. It was imperative, from the standpoint of the government, to establish the institutional order of the state as rapidly as possible. This applied also to the constitutional order. A constitution was written in considerable haste in 1922 and approved by the British authorities. According to Prager's detailed analysis, the constitution represented a compromise between the Gaelic-Romantic and Irish Enlightenment value traditions. The constitution, like the subsequent, more enduring, one of 1937, derived all rights from God and emphasised the power of the nation over the government though on the whole it was a constitution that balanced liberal democratic elements with communitarian ones (Ward, 1994).

A critical element in the construction of democratic values is the role and functioning of the public sphere. The Irish public sphere stood between civil society with its authoritarian and personalistic political culture and a centralised, bureaucratic, and authoritarian state. In these circumstances the public sphere reproduced marginalisation and de-autonomisation. In the pre-Independence period, the public sphere in Ireland had at least been vital. Now a host of new forces conspired to render it less than central as a means of thematising political issues or the overall national identity of the society. This was so for a number of reasons. Firstly, much of social life in civil society was de-politicised under Church control and not directly subject to public controversy. This also applied to the workings of the state bureaucracy where a culture of secrecy prevailed. In this situation, political legitimacy was rendered both formal and indirect. Secondly, as we have already outlined, cultural control was exercised through censorship, suppression of critical thinking, and through the construction of an intimidating ethos of compulsory cultural intimacy. Nobody was allowed to be different or to carry deviant opinions. Thirdly, the public sphere was to a substantial extent by-passed by the development of clientelistic and personalistic political arrangements. Political clientelism in developing societies where important issues are often discussed and decided upon without meaningful public debate results in the location of the 'public' sphere within the state sector itself where a 'real' public sphere substitutes for the liberal model. Whyte (1994) speaks of a situation where political clientelism represents the real public sphere, a state of affairs which also applies in some part to the Irish case. This tendency was enhanced by the high ratio to population of public representatives of all kinds. It is also very closely related to a further aspect of Irish political communication which is the greater importance given to local over national issues. Fourth, the public sphere as it was constituted in the Independent Ireland of the 1920s bore the imprint of the Civil War. Decisions were made by other means. This was reflected in the public culture that matured in the twenties in which public accountability was not regarded as a major priority. Beyond immediate situational factors, this attitude was anchored in a national identity construct which stressed the formation of the Catholic and conservative Irish nation as a 'natural' development whose logic was being revealed in the historical process and required no exhaustive process of critical scrutiny.

Looking at the situation in general, the institutional construction of the Free State under Catholic and conservative authority involved a wide-ranging institutional project of de-differentiation. The symbolic order was reduced to a national identity that emphasised the values of Catholic conservative communitarianism in which culture was forced to function like an eternally given nature. Other, more liberal traditions of political pluralism were dispensed with as not consistent with the nation's Catholicism. This all involved a kind of collective amnesia because, as Foster (1989, p. 535) has written, 'the real nature of pre-1916 society had to be glossed over, including, among much else, the hundreds of thousands of Irish who had volunteered in the Great War.' The institutional order was de-differentiated by a restoration of the functional primacy of religion and its secure institutionalisation in the structures of the state including the reconstruction of educational curricula and the legislative suppression of cultural autonomy. Everyday life was brought firmly under Church control and secured with various kinds of sanctions. The relation between politics, the state and society, substantially by-passed the public sphere which lost the degree of autonomy it had possessed to that time and lost whatever capacity it might have had to clarify possible alternatives. The not-insubstantial Protestant population left the state in large numbers, fearful of discrimination, mindful of loss of privilege, and opposed to living in an atmosphere dominated by political Catholicism. The number of political actors was also reduced. The labour movement lost its militancy as it identified closely both with Catholicism and nationalism and sought a perspective of integration rather than opposition. Agrarian radicalism disappeared and any form of political feminism petered out.

However, by the 1930s this project had over-reached itself even as it succeeded in establishing the dominant collective identity and institutional foundations of twentieth century Ireland. It had over-reached itself because the emphasis on moral and evaluative dimensions of identity, and the corresponding need for social stasis, were so extreme as to allow virtually no breathing space for addressing social inequality, the suppression of individual rights, or the poor performance of administration or the economy. It was time for Fianna Fáil to step onto the stage to redress the balance, albeit in a manner that was to add to the collective illusion that modernity could be indefinitely denied in a society that was already substantially modern.

NATIONAL IDENTITY AND POLITICS UNDER FIANNA FÁIL HEGEMONY

Peter Mair (1987) argues against the view that Civil War divisions explain the stable alignment of the Irish party system. He argues instead for the autonomy and dynamism of politics in Ireland in which the party system is neither determined by history nor by social structure. He points, therefore, to the organisation, strategies, ideological appeal and policies of Irish political parties as determinants of their relative success. The fact that Irish politics appears to operate without the social bases that characterises other European societies does not permit the conclusion that Irish politics is aberrational. It is normal by virtue of the way its political parties contend for electoral support and by their active engagement with the electorate. And this engagement extended beyond the symbolic play of positions on the national question to dispute over social and political issues. Hence, Fianna Fáil hegemony cannot be explained only by cultural and historical factors related to divisions over nationalism but by the way that party mobilised a dominant electoral coalition. Richard Dunphy (1995) accepts Mair's view on the creativity of political action but argues more strongly for the social embeddedness of party politics. He claims that the party programme of Fianna Fáil aimed 'at realising the economic project of the class of relatively small producers and native industrial manufacturers, numerically strong and fairly homogenous in terms of ideology, *but without restricting itself to that project*' (Dunphy, 1995, p 25). In other words, Fianna Fáil created a populist coalition on a relatively secure core support by initiating policies that were of relevance for a sufficient number of the electorate.

As an attempt to demonstrate the co-existence of nationalist and non-nationalist themes in Irish politics, the two authors mark an important advance over any kind of civil war fatalism. However, one can accept these perspectives while emphasising the decisive importance of the limits imposed by the identity project of Irish nationalism as a whole on institutional projects. These institutional projects must be understood in terms of the Catholic-communitarian cultural model of national identity that circumscribed what was possible or desirable. They must also be understood in terms of the structural configurations that the new state inherited and the types and scales of action that were available. When these conditions are taken into account, a degree of autonomy can be granted to political initiative or allowance made for changing circumstances while still holding to the view that the permitted range of variation was set within boundaries established by the institutional consequences of the nationalist movement.

The only way in which this can be demonstrated is by relating actors and their programmes to those of the pre-institutional phase of the movement, for only in this way can it be ensured that the collective identity formed in that movement actually remains and is not transformed into something else. In this respect, there is a striking continuity between the evolution of the movement and the evolution of the nation-state that followed it. Just as the limitations of the Parliamentary Party were transcended first by the Church and then by the more radical cultural nationalists so too was the Cumann na nGaedheal/church axis by the more radical nationalism of Fianna Fáil. Fianna Fáil in the late twenties and thirties appealed once more to the national 'opposition', those who were excluded or less well looked after following the social cleavage of Irish society into the more prosperous propertied strata and the rest, a division which became apparent for the first time at the end of the first phase of Home Rule and land reform.

The social cleavage in Irish politics, which was real but weak, was culturally over-determined by the cultural forces of nationalism and Catholicism. These ideologies under Fianna Fáil became means of ensuring social integration beyond its core constituencies of small farmers, small propertied and small industrialists. Nationalism, which Mair (1987, p. 204) admits may have been important in establishing core loyalties to political parties though it does not by itself explain their electoral appeal, was different from Catholicism in that it facilitated a clear distinction to be drawn between the parties. Fianna Fáil, like the cultural nationalists before them, represented the appeal of quasi-secular nationalism. It appealed to those who had less to lose from change and whose nationalism was bound up with a vaguely defined perception of the importance of social change that would favour them. The republicans could not carry enough of this constituency if they proposed actions that could lead to the abandonment of democracy. When their nationalism was constitutionally relativised, it could be expressed more persuasively as a social programme.

Fianna Fáil certainly marked a new departure in some dimensions of societal change, notably the economy, welfare, and the constitutional framework, but it built securely on what had been established by its political opponents in the first decade of the Free State. In the 1920s, democracy had been stabilised and Church power had been extended in a wide-ranging process of de-differentiation. Fianna Fáil began to assiduously court the Church from the late 1920s for a number of reasons. Firstly, the Church's institutionally-rooted cultural power was critical to the maintenance of political legitimacy. Secondly, the party needed the Church to maintain social solidarity and de-politicise possible conflict in the context of its more radical policies. Thirdly, the national identity and institutional project of clerical nationalism and Fianna Fáil's brand of separatist nationalism was sufficiently close to present the party with no major dilemmas. Finally, on the Church's side, it was aware of the continuing potency of the appeal and programme of cultural nationalism but was confident that its institutional base was now secure and that it could do business with Fianna Fáil in government. The secure power of the Church, together with the party's general inclination, indicated that the party would not tamper with the Church's domination of civil society.

Fianna Fáil's major impact in the period up to the end of the Second World War can be identified along the following dimensions: (1) additions to the national identity code that legitimated its institutional project; (2) socio-economic change that involved further de-differentiation from the external environment but accompanying internal differentiation; (3) significant constitutional change; (4) further erosion of the autonomy of the public sphere with a pronounced increase in the clientelistic and localistic emphasis of politics; (5) a modest commitment to mobilise the power of the state to intervene in society and (6) an enhanced nationalism in inter-state relations. Each of these are dealt with in turn below:

(1) *Additions to national identity*: As already outlined, there was considerable overlap between the separatist's programme and that of the other main cultural identity project of nationalist Ireland, the Catholic one. They shared many aspects; the irrationalist nation code of the separatists matched the communitarian and extra-mundane code of the Church; both believed in the evil of outside influence; both believed that the British were responsible for Irish problems; both espoused puritanical and rural values; both preached a cult of individual sacrifice for the greater good of the community; both were anti-intellectual in disposition; both preferred denial to acknowledgement of cultural and political difference. But there were also significant differences. The separatists' communitarianism was based on raising the self-esteem of members of certain groups and was therefore more socially specific than that of the Church. So, too, in spite of its vagueness was the social programme of the separatists. From the beginning, though never clearly spelled out, it promised social change that would be compatible with the interests of the excluded petit-bourgeois stratum, both rural and urban, and explored themes of protectionism and industrialisation. Also its commitment to egalitarianism was greater even if still did not extend

very far towards policies of radical redistribution. Other manifestations of difference, notably the militarisation of culture and the corresponding aestheticisation of politics, had become much less important by 1932, but lingered in what Garvin (1996) calls the 'public band' and what Dunphy (1995, p. 40) characterises as 'exclusivism', the belief that the republican experience contained a monopoly of truth. Finally, there was a significant difference in the type of commitment to separatism. Cultural nationalism could countenance significant social-structural changes accompanying its programme in a manner that the Church never did.

The arrival of Fianna Fáil therefore involved the most comprehensive mobilisation of the nationalist project, presaged in the rise of separatist nationalism and socially and electorally pre-figured by the success of Sinn Fein. The Fianna Fáil phenomenon responded to the problems of the institutional project of clerical conservatism which had stagnated by the end of the twenties. The Fianna Fáil addition to the code of national identity can therefore be summed up in the idea of 'Ireland for the Irish' and the cult of the 'small man' in the local and rural place. These additions were inserted within the moral code of Catholicism and infused with the populist rhetoric and some of the substance of egalitarianism. An example of the new state patriotism of Catholic nationalism orchestrated by Fianna Fáil was the hosting of the Eucharistic Congress in 1932, when one million people attended an open-air mass in the Phoenix Park (Keogh, 1994, pp. 68–70). This event was important for the initiation of Fianna Fáil into Irish political life in the post-independence period. Through the party's handling of this key symbolic event, they proved themselves as adept as Fine Gael had been at marrying the pageantry of state with that of the Church in a chauvinistic display of Catholic triumphalism.

(2) *Socio-economic de-differentiation*: In its first period in office, Fianna Fáil showed a willingness to offend the interests of parts of the elite in its pursuit of economic autarky and social change. The main policy of Fianna Fáil was economic protectionism achieved through the imposition of substantial tariffs on imported goods. This also served as a kind of economic nationalism of self-sufficiency. Protectionism was inimical to the interests of cattle exporters who lost heavily in the corresponding imposition of tariffs by the UK government on Irish exports which were overwhelmingly agricultural. Trading relationships between the two countries were considerably worsened by the withholding of Land Annuities due to

the British government from Irish farmers as repayment for loans received for the purchase of land in the various pre-Independence land reforms. The combined effects of the withholding of the Annuities and protectionism led to the so-called Economic War between Ireland and the UK which lasted from 1932 to 1938.

The introduction of protectionist policies in Ireland marked a dramatic reversal in economic policy which to that time had been absolutely committed to Free Trade. Though protectionism was not unusual in the 1930s, its implications for an economy that was highly trade-dependent to that point were radical. Many of the goods that were imported now had to be produced in Ireland and the importance of the home market for all forms of economic activity increased. Protectionism significantly strengthened a native small-industrial cadre who became loyal supporters of Fianna Fáil and represented an alternative basis of economic power to landed wealth. Protectionism and the economic war combined led to a significant welfare loss for the mass of the population, a loss that was compensated to some extent by somewhat higher employment possibilities (Daly 1992).

According to Daly (1992, p. 114), Fianna Fáil had the paradoxical goal of pursuing a policy of industrialisation while trying to prevent the emergence of an industrial culture. The party pursued a decentralised industrial policy that dispersed working-class concentration in pursuit of this aim, though this was also intended in part to spread the benefits of economic development to peripheral and Fianna Fáil supporting regions. The antipathy towards forming an industrial culture illustrates how moral and evaluative components of national identity continued to be given precedence over functional considerations even in the context of significant overall changes in policy. Combined social, cultural and political goals, rather than economic ones, lay at the heart of the Fianna Fáil project. Socially, industrial protectionism led to the creation of a small-scale industrial cadre who supplied the home market. The licensing system therefore operated as a major factor in the distribution of profits and the state bureaucracy was equipped with an important new avenue of patronage. Protectionism was also associated with patriarchal goals such as the exclusion of women from the labour force (Daly, 1992, p. 126), a development that would have profound significance for women as female labour-force participation continued on a relatively low plane in post-Second World War Ireland while dramatically rising elsewhere (Coleman, 1992, p. 74). Culturally, protectionist policies and their cultural legitimation contributed significantly to the strengthening of an isolationist identity. Politically, Fianna Fáil gained the reputation of a party who would do something not just for their constituency but also for the country. Protectionism was a badge of patriotism.

Protectionism marked at one and the same time the most radical socio-economic play of nationalism and its comprehensive withdrawal from international economic engagement. In the first case, it marked an internal rationalisation and commitment to a modest degree of social differentiation as a basis for needed change while in the second case it involved a withdrawal from any serious attempt to develop industries oriented to penetrating the huge British market and hence a continuation of de-differentiation. In the latter respect, it is not simply that the nationalists did not register the existence of this market as the most important quantitative economic fact in the economic environment, but they fostered a mentality that made various kinds of production and distribution networks with economic agents in Britain hard to contemplate. Protectionism signalled the end of any attempt along these lines for another thirty years.

(3) *Constitutional change*: Both the 1922 and 1937 constitution involved the articulation of new institutional structures but no new rights. Both constitutions were innovative on an international place, according to Ward (1994), in that key republican values, popular sovereignty, parliamentary control of the war power, and entrenched civil rights are written into constitutional law for the first time. The 1937 constitution, apart from re-designing Ireland's relationship with the British Crown, did not significantly change the framework of responsible government and republican values established in the previous model. But it marked a substantial shift in one key respect: the implicit primacy given to Catholic natural law over positive law (Ward, 1994, p. 252). The constitution could be described as a Catholicisation of the constitutional order. The Constitution in its many explicit principles relating to moral issues displays, as does Irish Catholicism more generally, a suspicion of situated, human reasoning, in favour of a conformity to already established rules derived from the Catholic natural law tradition (Clarke, 1985). In this dimension, the constitution has played an important role in stabilising Irish national identity as a Catholic communitarian one in which neither individual autonomy or reflective reasoning are valued. De Valera,[18] who drafted the constitution with the aid of Jesuits (Faughnan, 1988), believed that the

aim of the constitution should be more than merely to define procedures and formal rights, but should contain substantive values: 'In my judgement,' he said in 1937, 'a constitution ought to do more than define the character of the legislative and judicial regime, and if it is based on the democratic principle, it ought to do more than prescribe how the representative institutions should function. It should inspire as well as control, elicit loyalty as well as compel it' (quoted in Nolan, 1975, p. 156). In other words the 1922 constitution had to be changed to express the fundamental values of a Catholic nation. Thus the preamble to the new constitution, which echoed the declaration of the Catholic Confederation of Kilkenny in 1642 and derived from a decree of the Counter-Reformation's Council of Trent (Nolan, 1975, p. 158), states that all authority derives from God:

> In the Name of the Most Holy Trinity, from whom is all authority and to Whom, as our final end, all actions both of men and States must be referred, We the people of Eire, Humbly acknowledging all our obligations to our Divine Lord, Jesus Christ, Who sustained our fathers through centuries of Trial, Gratefully remembering their heroic and unremitting struggle to regain the rightful independence of our Nation, And seeking to promote the common good, with due observance of Prudence, Justice and Charity, so that the dignity and freedom of the individual may be assured, true social order attained, the unity of our country restored, and concord established with other nations, Do hereby adopt, enact, and give to ourselves this constitution. (*Constitution of Ireland*, 1937)

The Irish Constitution breaks with one of the key ideas of modern constitutional thinking, namely that the foundation of society is individual autonomy and that the aim of a constitution is to give expression to inalienable human rights. In the Irish constitution of 1937, the family and the general Catholic collectivity is generally given priority over the rights of the individual citizen. It is, above all, a 'family constitution' with the state recognising 'the family as the natural primary and fundamental unit group of society, possessing inalienable and imprescriptible rights, antecedent and superior to all positive law' (Article 41, *Constitution of Ireland*, 1937). In the same article, the constitution ties the achievement of the common good to the role of women within the home and commits the state to 'endeavour to ensure that mothers shall not be obliged by economic necessity to engage in labour to the neglect of their duties within the home'. A main aim of the drafters of the constitution, therefore, is that individuals shall be subordinate to the Catholic collectivity and female individuals subordinate to male individuals within the family in which they are to be confined.

Elsewhere in the constitution, the absence of pluralistic intention is revealed both in the recognition of the 'special position' of the Catholic church and the claims made in the still politically contentious Articles 2 and 3 to jurisdiction over the whole island which amounts to official non-recognition of the state of Northern Ireland.

(4) *Erosion of public sphere*: Much of Fianna Fáil's political success has been attributed to its party organisation which builds from local to national levels in a responsive manner. This party organisation has been a major factor in the promotion of clientelist politics. Fianna Fáil in power built a huge web of local patronage which was funnelled through the party organisation. Clientelist politics in Ireland trespasses on what is elsewhere considered the welfare responsibility of the state bureaucracy. In this respect, the Irish model conforms to the experience of developing countries. The effect is to render the political system an arena not so much dedicated to the actualisation of ideals, the competition of ideas, or argument over legislation as to the provision of welfare services to clients in a manner that often has little to do with entitlement on the basis of merit. This has had the effect of a radical privatisation of life and a low propensity amongst citizens to organise politically and participate in the public sphere (Schmitt, 1973, pp. 61–2).

(5) *State mobilisation*: Fianna Fáil can be differentiated also from the previous administration in its willingness to mobilise the state to intervene in society. Though Dunphy (1995, p. 78) claims that the party had no coherent idea of what to do with state power, lacking either a theory of the relationship between state and society or a commitment to the democratisation of the state apparatus, the party was willing to raise taxes to pay for increased welfare spending and, more significantly, as we have seen, to enlist the state in industrial policy. However, when considered as a whole, the first era of Fianna Fáil hegemony is only radical by comparison with the preceding laissez-faire administration with its commitment to the minimal state.

(6) In the area of *inter-state relations*, which in Ireland until comparatively recently has only meant relations with Britain, Fianna Fáil was true to its separatist pedigree. The economic war was fol-

lowed by the constitution which made no reference to the king and, finally, to war-time neutrality.[19] Neutrality was justified by de Valera as an expression of the right to self-determination, as a product of the unresolved issue of partition, and as an assertion of sovereignty (Dunphy, 1995, p. 281). He had much to gain from adopting a policy of neutrality and much to lose by not doing so. Ideologically, to actively support the allied war effort would have been very difficult given the anti-conscription legacy of Sinn Fein in the First World War and given that breaking the British link represented de Valera's main political objective. Neutrality had the effect also of denying Fine Gael one of its main policies, friendly and co-operative relations with Britain. Neutrality therefore made the Fianna Fáil colonisation of Irish national and political identity more pronounced. In other respects, the image of Ireland's wartime isolation, standing outside the major event of a European history, serves as a suitable denouement to more than two decades of progressively greater withdrawal from the world and progressively greater absorption with its own spiritual distinction. Neutrality perfectly served the cultural aspirations of the new state. Secure in the knowledge that Britain would provide the necessary protection for Ireland by virtue of its own survival needs neutrality became associated with extreme isolationism, including the full-scale imposition of censorship and other forms of state repression (O'Drisceoil, 1996).[20] It was also an opportunity to re-assert the code of national identity as rejection of the outsider.

The first twenty years of Independence therefore saw a society endeavouring to roll back the threat of modernity in a whole variety of ways. A national identity code that emphasised the moral and evaluative basis of Catholic identity reflected the norms of a dominant group, a motley assemblage of the middle-class and lower middle-class. This identity code rejected the outside, sanctified the conventionalism of a Catholic way of life for all social strata, and sought to impose a social system in which inequality and functional de-differentiation and stasis were acceptable. The precise parallels between the established identity code and social practices reveals both the power of its proponents, its functional adequacy to prescribe social rule systems that worked well in conditions of elite domination, and its capacity to suppress, absorb or exclude difference. This identity code was projected, with a high degree of success, as superior to legal and public deliberation and private conscience. Given the opportunity of both constitutionalist and separatist wings of the movement to elaborate and apply the code, it was unmistakably the product of the Irish national movement.

Irish nationalism completed its 'classical' cycle by the end of the Second World War. The basic ideas of primordial Catholicism, rejection of foreign influence, conservative social arrangements, patriarchal familialism, restricted justice within the nation, economic protectionism, a minimal state and obedient individuation had been instituted in Irish society. These ideas amounted, in common with much of Catholic European countries, to a rejection of modernity and a determination to preserve the conservative fundamentals of Irish society. The main agents of this order were lower middle-class Catholics of reasonable prosperity supported by their clerical intelligentsia. It was also noticeably rural in origin. In this period, a national identity that was built upon characteristics of a Catholic way of life which included the ethical code of the lower middle-class was the blueprint for the establishment of a society that was comfortable for this class. They had succeeded in unharnessing Catholic Irish development from the British state and political culture, thereby avoiding the 'evils' of socio-political cleavages based on class, the secularisation of institutional life, and a relatively liberal legal code including such undesirable developments as cultural freedom and divorce. Irish national identity had an absorptive quality that assimilated its cultural challengers. What it could not absorb it suppressed. This national identity made the narrative of Irish history a narrative of colonisation and oppression. All the Catholic Irish had equally shared this experience. Now they had to develop together a society that would honour the imputed ideals of their ancestors and not become riven with social envy or excessive individuation. Resentment should be turned outwards, resignation inwards. Inequality and unfairness in the constitution of society were subordinated to the passion of feeling equal before the nation.

7 Social Change and the Transformation of National Identity

THE CULTURAL CONTRADICTIONS OF IRISH SOCIETY

Just under a quarter century after the foundation of the state, at the end of the Second World War, the transformation of the identity project of Irish nationalism into an institutional project for the reconstruction of society had reached its zenith. Society had been reconstructed according to the model of a Catholic and radical nationalist imaginary, an imaginary that had been decisively forged before independence and subsequently institutionalised. The transformation of the identity project of nationalism into an institutional project was not the product of absolute consensus. Profound differences had arisen between the constitutional and radical wings of the movement on political issues though there were no irreconcilable differences between them on social issues. Political differences and the requirement for a theory of the social propelled a conservative Catholicism into a powerful position of compromise. Where both constitutional and radical nationalism was geared to power over the state, Catholicism was geared to power over the extensive non-state institutional order.[1] Catholicism and the evolution of the institutional order in the Free State period brought about substantial consensus which enabled a radical hypothesis to be tested: that the Irish nation was self-contained and scarcely needed the wider world.[2] The success or failure of this experiment was the benchmark of the most radical phase of nationalism. By the late 1940s, society was beginning to take stock of itself. By the late 1950s it had drawn its own conclusion on the radical experiment: it had comprehensively failed.

By the 1940s it became clear to even the most die-hard believers in the potentials of nationalism as a liberating and creative force that the society lacked real capacity for agency. A civil society controlled by the Church was not able to organise itself in a modern way. The society could not go forward because it had difficulty

157

in critically examining its own orientation due to the institutionalisation of a 'timeless' model of national identity that defended a selective and incontrovertible 'truth' about what was right, good, and effective. The power of the state was restricted socially by the institutional power of the Church and the dominant elites (Breen et al., 1990, p. 24) and restricted culturally by the historical British tradition of a non-entrepreneurial state (Daly, 1992, p. 177), though this situation was rapidly changing in the Britain of this period. Hostility to an activist state reached its apotheosis in the conservatism of Catholic social thought, immensely influential in the first quarter century of independence. Catholicism, however, was unable to institute a new principle of social organisation. The idea of full-blown corporatism, based on the functional self-organisation of society without a strong, centralised state, and modelled on undemocratic experiments elsewhere in Europe, was promulgated by the Church for a time. It failed in its purest intent because the secular elite resisted it, because functional organisation was poorly developed in the various sectors with only law and medicine offering the necessary organisation, and because, most basically, it was inconsistent with the power of parliament and the model of responsible cabinet government which had been taken over in Ireland from the Westminster tradition (Ward, 1994). By the 1940s it had become apparent with the inability to institute Catholic principles of social organisation and with the general lack of creativity of civil society that the state was the only agent capable of bringing about radical change.

The state accepted the challenge. The active interventionist state, oriented first to the provision of the social services of a modern welfare state and a little later to creating the conditions of economic expansion, represented in tandem with certain, limited powers of agency in civil society the first challenge to the clerical-conservative model of national identity. The second challenge, building from the new structural and cultural conditions created by the first, came from the growing autonomy of civil society and the enhanced deliberative powers of the public sphere. These processes are conventionally dated to have commenced in the early 1960s. The third, carrying with it once more the accumulated structural and cultural outcomes of preceding waves of change, is associated with the new economic, social and political contexts that produced changed political alignments in the 1970s and 1980s. Finally, the last and most comprehensive challenge is offered by a wide-ranging movement towards a pluralistic society carried by a new politics of identity. These changes and their cumulative affects are discussed in the sections of this chapter below.

In the context of social change in the second half of the century, the reproduction of national identity became more complicated and it lost its consistency and verisimilitude as some of its central tenets were contested. The process of contestation may be described as a 'detranscendentalisation' of national identity, a process characterised by renewed differentiation and disenchantment as various social spheres decouple themselves from religious authority and values.[3] In the process of de-transcendentalisation, the traditional national identity institutionalised at all levels in the society continued to act as a brake on radical innovation. The structural inequality that was so pervasive at the beginning of the period was modified, but national identity codes emphasising conventional values of community and togetherness slowed the emergence of new situation-interpreting models that could have facilitated the exploration of intra-societal differences in dimensions such as class, gender, and political identity. The national identity code proved remarkably capable of institutional elaboration, appearing to preserve continuity in core values while embracing new ones that were, on the surface at least, at variance with them. The level of structural differentiation that was produced by an active state and by socio-economic change was not matched by a similar differentiation or pluralisation of cultural identities. Structural change was accompanied by an unconfident adoption of new cultural values that contradicted older, institutionalised values in areas such as the family and education, but there was little of the manifest conflict out of which learning and institutional adjustment might have come. The cultural legitimation of the institutional order did not need that all or even a majority of the population believes in its central tenets on a particular theme; the power of institutionally legitimated values was carried organisationally by Church and state. Post-war Ireland preferred to live through permanent contradiction rather than openly face its problems.

THE ACTIVE STATE

The pressure for reform-oriented policies grew in the 1940s. The decline in relative living standards, and probably the absolute decline in living standards for sections of the population after the economic war and the war proper, was most graphically illustrated by continuing economic stagnation, high emigration and the rise of tuberculosis as a killer disease. In these circumstances, the Irish state under the governance of first of all Fianna Fáil and then two multi-party coalition governments began to take stock. It was becoming increasingly apparent that innovative capacities for needed social change were not widely diffused in civil society. The normatively regulated sphere of political parties and associations, and within it crucially the state itself, had to act and as is now reasonably well-known a modernising movement began within the political and bureaucratic elite that gradually gained dominance over internal and external opponents (Lee, 1989b; Dunphy, 1995).

Breen et al. (1990, pp. 20–1) provide criteria for assessing the power of the Irish state.[4] They distinguish between the state's autonomy, the ability to formulate and pursue its own goals, and its capacity, the ability to implement them. The main factors affecting autonomy according to these authors were external constraints, partly counterbalanced by nationalist aspirations, the low importance of class interests, the local focus of the political system, and a well-entrenched civil service with a tradition of autonomous action inherited from the British legacy. The factors affecting capacity were the role of the state as financier rather than provider of services, the 'parallel' state of voluntary organisations, charities and vocationalist arrangements, low yield from taxation, the use of semi-state bodies with considerable autonomy to implement many goals, and the heavy reliance placed on expert advisers. The immediate contrast between the relative potential for autonomy and the relative difficulty of realising that potential, revealed in the level of state capacity, is evident. However, to understand why the state was in fact capable of shifting from what Breen et al. (1990) describe as an 'auxiliary' state to an interventionist one requires more than exploring structural features of autonomy and capacity. These remain vital to explaining why state action adopted the forms it did but to understand why it happened at all, and the balance between potential and capacity that emerged, the role of historically conditioned cultural perceptions in facilitating learning and adaptation by social agents also needs to be considered.

The perceived failure of the pre-existing principles and material forms of social organisation was a vital pre-condition for change. This perceived failure was crystallised by pressure on the state to act emanating from Trade Unions, unflattering international comparisons, and the appearance of undeniable social problems. Social forces placed pressure on the governing elite to recognise that the values of efficiency and greater justice to be achieved through collective mobilisation, downplayed in the rural sufficiency, autarchy and general fatalism of the existing societal code, had to be accommodated. In accepting the need for change the state was not simply responding to new structural conditions. It was also impelled by new evaluations of the appropriateness of the cultural order that had established the parameters of what was counted as legitimate social change, parameters that were enforced through the conservative orientation of the institutional order. Irish society began asking questions such as why welfare had to be organised under the aegis of the Church, how acceptable was the level of poverty, were rural values generalisable to an urban society, were the advantages of self-sufficiency greater than participating in the international economy?

Several factors can be adduced to explain why the state, or initially enlightened elements within it, was the main agency of learning and adaptation in the society. Firstly, institutional arrangements maintained from the pre-Independence administration, or acquired in the Free State era, provided a reservoir of accumulated experience that indicated ways of going beyond the passivity of the existing model. Secondly, there was, even in the Ireland of the 1940s, a certain appreciation of the new social politics of the post-war era in Europe, and of the need for ideological re-positioning within the newly emergent welfarist justice model that was reaching the status of an orthodoxy elsewhere. This anticipation, already confirmed by the centrality of social politics in the 1948 election, saw the return of the suppressed heresy of the existence of social cleavage and dictated that political parties would have to occupy new ground. The unstable political environment between 1948 and 1957 which saw the passing of the first era of Fianna Fáil electoral hegemony confirmed this. Thirdly, the Trade Union movement, and, more generally working class political consciousness, was no longer satisfied by the tentative politics of social reform pursued under sixteen years of Fianna Fáil administration and therefore threatened to desert the party in sufficient numbers to bring about government change. The electoral vulnerability of Fianna Fáil without a new departure into social politics was further emphasised by the growing instability of its support base amongst small farmers. The

unresolved issues of distributive justice, suppressed in the later
national movement in the interests of consensus, re-emerged and
disappointed by Fianna Fáil administrations since 1932 was assert-
ing itself against entrenched interests and an anti-innovative climate. Finally, the influence of key 'modernising' individuals such
as Sean Lemass[5] and, in a different way, Noel Browne,[6] should not
be underestimated.

The two areas of greatest attention in this political cultural 'reform'
climate, up until the 1960s, were welfare and economic reforms
respective. Policy change in the former domain ante-dated the latter.
Breen et al. (1990, p. 75) draw attention to Kennedy's (1975) study
of social expenditure between 1947 and 1974. Kennedy divides social expenditure in this period into three main phases; an expansionary phase coinciding with the first coalition government in 1947
in which the proportion of social expenditure relative to GDP rose
from 9.6 per cent to 14.9 per cent, a regressive phase between 1952
and 1962 in which social expenditure as a proportion of GDP con-
tracted and an expansionary phase from the early sixties to 1980 in
which social expenditure grew proportionately faster than any other
area of expenditure and increased from the equivalent of 13 per
cent of GNP in 1961 to 29 per cent in 1980. The early initiatives
were concentrated in the infrastructural areas of housing and health.
In both of these areas, significant headway was made in the period
of the first inter-party coalition between 1948 and 1951.

Over the period to 1980, successive waves of expenditure on social
services led to a transformation in the institutional basis of these
services and to significant amelioration in the life chances of disadvantaged sections of the population. The key shift according to
Breen et al. (1990) was when the state took on institutional responsibility for welfare in the 1960s and broke with the more ad
hoc arrangements of the auxiliary state working closely with voluntary organisations. The impact of the transformation of social services has been mixed. While it has undoubtedly fuelled a greater
welfare and redistributive effort in conditions of higher economic
growth, structural inequality remains high. The life chances of those
who begin in working-class or marginal social positions remain poor
and the expansion of education has improved but not transformed
their mobility prospects.[7] Poverty, highly correlated with employment status and age, remains endemic and at high levels.

The comparative failure of Irish social services to transform the
relative pattern of advantage and disadvantage between sections of

the population owes much to the staying hand of the material and cultural constraints of the preceding institutional order. The constraints on the capacity of the state documented above reflect a highly articulated class programme that represented in the main the interests of the propertied rural and urban middle-class, with those in secure, unionised employment also moderately well looked-after and everybody else marginalised. Hence, from as long before as 1909, propertied interests in Ireland had opposed the expansion of welfare for fear of its impact on a taxation regime that favoured their interests. There was a concerted effort by property-owners and the self-employed in this period and subsequently to reduce expenditure on social programmes or to channel it in the direction of voluntary provision. The Church supported this programme as it accorded well with both its material – the Church dominated the voluntary sector – and symbolic interests.

Social change by the late 1940s led to the consolidation of social forces prepared to promote the freeing of policy programmes from a narrow subservience to the interests of the propertied and professional elite. This challenge was fuelled by the manifest relative failure to raise relative Irish standards of living and by the emergence of a new international welfare model, not least in the Catholic countries with the emergence of Christian democratic movements. However, in Ireland the accommodation of welfare considerations was constrained by the historical situation. Latent structural cleavages were not politically institutionalised in the Free State to any pronounced extent though the Free State was a highly class-divided society. This of course can be explained structurally by the separation of southern Ireland from the UK economy and society in which it had been embedded, a separation that favoured the social power of a propertied middle-class over other classes and class fractions. Potential cleavage was kept latent not only by the device of material power but also by restraints on the deliberative capacity of the society created by a thematically restricted public culture. Such restriction was in part achieved by institutionally limiting the public sphere through imposing legal restraints. Perhaps more importantly, the public sphere was also thematically restricted by the informal but concentrated power of an agenda dedicated to an anti-modern, conservative form of life in which the Catholic Church and the state as the most powerful culture-producing organisations held the dominant hand. These constraints affected the manner in which issues such as welfare were thematised with a pronounced emphasis on Christian verities such as charity and compassion and a corresponding down-grading of liberal concerns for rights and socialist concerns about exploitation and immiseration (Skillington, 1993).

The perceived failures of Catholic corporatism and social and economic isolationism to satisfy new notions of the collective good that emerged in the late 1940s offered a profound challenge to both interests and values held by many in the society. The conjunction of material and ideological moments crystallised in Church opposition to many of the welfare reforms proposed in the late forties and fifties. These included the celebrated Mother and Child Scheme proposed by the Minister for Health, Dr. Noel Browne, which the Church held to interfere with the prerogative of the family in Irish life. The Church was successful in this instance but in the long-run was unable to prevent the emergence of a modern welfare state that, to some extent, broke with the Church's preferences for familial and voluntary solutions. But the power of the Church and conservative forces generally meant that social democratic ideology did not easily penetrate even urban Ireland. The absence of convinced ideological challenge, and the sophisticated capacity to absorb what of it there was through the continuing manifest attachment to the historical code of national identity, protected the dominant actors and ensured that social innovations were confined to a narrow space. Along with the continuing structural consequences of this power, it ensured that the frames of justice in twentieth century Ireland would be based on a Catholic idea of the common good. The welfare ideal became less one of rights than one of 'compassion' and 'caring' and cultural models of social service provision continued to be based on a strongly Catholic ethos. In this sense, the national identity of who 'we' are, conservative and Catholic, has coexisted uneasily with the democratic identity of what moral norms should obtain between institutions and citizens.

This can also be seen in the importance attached to family and to gender role distinctions. The Irish Constitution of 1937 contained a clause emphasising the special position of the Catholic Church and another one pledging to defend the family as an institution. The legal implications of these clauses did not become relevant until the era of judicial activism in the 1960s. However, social and institutional rather than constitutional power was sufficient to maintain a patriarchal social order up to the 1960s. The underlying reality of a social and economic order that emphasised familialism together with the interests and power of the Church and its successful diffusion of a specifically Catholic idea of social life ensured that traditional views of the family persisted. Women were reduced to a subordinate status with their role confined to the home and to domestic life leaving the world of 'affairs' almost exclusively to men. Moral control over women's bodies was exercised by means of social and legal technologies of power that organised domestic life, education, health, the arts, welfare entitlements, religious participation. These technologies had a structural form in terms of barriers to participation and the empowerment of other agents, i.e., men, teachers, religious, and a cultural form in terms of an encompassing discourse of patriarchy that legitimated the imposition of power over females. The late 1940s and 1950s saw the first real challenges to this state of affairs through state policies that sought to develop an institutional relationship between state and family.

In the other major domain of post-war policy reform, economic policy, the fateful decision taken in 1958 to embark on a programme of export-led industrial growth was a response both to pressing structural problems and the wider climate of societal crisis enhanced in the fifties by relatively poor economic performance with a growth rate less than half that of other European economies, high emigration which caused profound self-questioning about the 'vanishing Irish' and the realisation that indigenously-led industrial development had merely led to a concentration on a small-home market with a very low percentage share of manufactured exports to total exports. The half-century old nationalist belief in pursuing industrialisation behind tariff walls had not been a success. The symmetry of cultural and economic isolationism had produced a society paralysed by its own insularity whose self-interpretation had exacerbated its structural disadvantages. In the economic domain, in a version of the thesis of the power of 'revolutionary will', Irish nationalism had gambled that cultural autonomy – the perceived absence of which had resulted in their claims that Ireland was artificially impoverished – would overcome structural disadvantage. It was clear by the late 1950s that it had merely increased it and the ideology of playing off spiritual against material prosperity that legitimated this failure in the 1930s and 1940s was no longer acceptable. In these circumstances, throughout the 1950s, those favouring bolder measures for the economy were gradually gaining the ascendancy as the economy still continued to grow well below the European average and as it experienced an endemic balance of payments crisis.

A series of factors led to a surprisingly positive outcome, measured in the economic growth rate, for the expansionary efforts of the Programme for Economic Expansion, which began in 1958 and lasted through three distinct plans into the 1970s. The most significant factor in this success was external, the willingness and capacity to produce and market on a global scale by Multi-National Corporations (MNCs). In response to this re-alignment in the structure of production, Ireland was able to provide certain important advantages for attracting investment. The first, and probably the most important in relative terms, was political stability which included the relatively low politicisation of the Irish workforce. A second was the relatively good ratio between labour costs and human capital resources. The third, the relative weakness of the position of the Irish government and, correspondingly, the aid-package it was prepared to pay. The fourth, the country's proximity to European markets (Jacobsen, 1994).

The transformation of the economy brought about by multi-national investment had a number of implications for national identity and social change. In the first instance, economic growth was engineered to some extent without the profound upheaval that might have been required in the society's structural arrangements and cultural self-understanding. Institutional arrangements such as clientelistic politics, the property-holding and taxation systems, and educational curricula, were able to continue and to feed off a national identity that continued to be backward-looking. Economic growth without structural transformation protected the socially powerful and yet allowed welfare and distributive pressures that grew in the 1960s to be accommodated. Secondly, in the medium-to-long-term, economic expansion both through its own direct effects, and through its strengthening of the interventionist powers of the state as a consequence of fiscal gains led, together with wider socio-demographic change, to a transformation in the class structure. Breen et al. (1990, p. 60) account for this change as a process of upgrading in which large numbers of the most precarious economic categories such as rural small-holders, landless labourers, and the unskilled working-class were progressively replaced by more affluent strata amongst the skilled working-class and middle-class. Occupational change and the expansion of the education system produced a long-run tendency towards the production of a class structure that was educated and, to a significant extent, reproduced by exchange in educational credentials. This transformation of the class structure in the long-run also laid the structural basis for a very gradual secularisation of the society.

MODERNISATION IN THE SIXTIES: THE OPENING OF A PUBLIC SPHERE

The consequences of the first wave of change were well on their way by the early 1960s. The cultural elaboration that took place in relation to the existing national identity code led to the addition of economic modernisation goals as a key goal of the society and the re-specification of ideas of justice and collective good less in terms of property, frugality and spiritual fulfilment and more in terms of standard of living and fairness of life opportunities. However, the elaboration of the code built in the contradiction that Catholic and conventional identity could occupy pride of place and that a restricted modernity could be introduced through the back door. Structural change should not impinge upon the position of the advantaged and cultural change should, as far as possible, not be recognised. A society began to take shape that could live with the most glaring contradictions. The development path of post-war Ireland began in the late 1940s to create the central contradiction of the last forty or so years of the century. It firstly took the form of hesitant enclaves of modern values within the traditional, anti-modern order and it later began to take its present form with modern values in the ascendant but compromised by the power of tradition.

As in many other countries, the 1960s in Ireland is nostalgically regarded as a period of remarkable social and cultural transformation. Though it has become cliched, the popular memory is in this respect not wrong. A host of things began to happen together and to work in upon one another. The class structure of the society underwent major transformation; the deliberative capacity of the society and its corresponding capacity for cultural innovation increased as the media gained autonomy and new media forms such as television emerged; the expansion of the welfare state led to massive changes in educational and health provision which gradually led to a decline in religious power over these institutions. These changes spurred on, or were part of, a new vitality of differentiation and autonomy of social spheres on the one hand, a new cultural basis for civil society on the other. Both changes created new possibilities for agency across a variety of domains as subjectivity became freed from the tyranny of social convention and as collective organisational forms acquired the requisite institutional autonomy to adequately function. The Irish version of neo-corporatism which began under Lemass in the 1960s was an indicator of the latter.

The sixties saw the beginning of a movement that would sooner or later displace organised Catholicism from its powerful hold over social institutions. Some of the change processes arose from endogenous learning such as the forces unleashed in and through the active state. Others arose from a diffuse process of cultural opening manifesting itself in the form of a gradual release of suppressed needs for expressive autonomy that operated within a large variety of networked forms. The latter process was enormously assisted by the internationalisation of culture in the 1960s. The collective modality of self-perception moved from within to without as the cultural symbols that secured identity no longer warded off the outside world but were re-interpreted through its new cultural legitimacy. The ramparts built by Catholic conservatism to protect against the first wave of mass cultural internationalisation in the early part of the century were unable to prevent the triumph of the second. In the domains of popular culture such as music and magazines, the sexualisation of dress, collective forms of amusement such as first the dancehall and then the discotheque, and the now pervasive television set, cultural innovation proceeded apace.

These processes of change took an almost exclusively cultural form in the sixties. They did not become converted, as elsewhere, into a political radicalism that amounted to a challenge to the social order. Nonetheless, the profusion of new identities that emerged marked a vital change in identification processes. National identity lost its power to dominate other social, cultural and political identities and hence also lost the power to determine society according to a single controllable model. Where previously national identity had a transcending power, now it increasingly occupied one position in a competitive space in which other forms of identity intruded with increasing power and persistence. The emergence of new forms of identification marked a new creativity of culture which began to compete with the norms of a single culture sustained through processes of organised political domination. As cultural creation and political domination began to separate, national identity became increasingly oriented to culture and became somewhat decoupled from politics and extensively decoupled from the economy. As the traditional form of national identity became subject to competition from other sources of identification so it began to be re-elaborated through cultural goods such as traditional music and a reverence for the supposed virtues of the Irish character standing outside the civilisation discontents of modernity. The older national identity retreated somewhat but did not disappear by any means, retaining a powerful hold especially in more rural and peripheral regions but forced to compete to attain institutional efficacy. In this transformation, national identity became only one form of identity and no longer dominated all social spheres. The new national identity code which began simultaneously to interpenetrate with the older code and with the new expressions of cultural identity, was more reflexively articulated as a conscious product of lifestyle. In this sense, its boundary markers were reflexive rather than conventional and primordial (Giesen, 1993; Eisenstadt and Giesen, 1995). The early expressions of this new code began the process of re-orientation that marked the beginning of the drift towards a cultural contemporaneity that signified the growing 'lateral' influence of international cultural forms over the 'vertical', historical legacy of the 'Irish experience'.

SOCIAL CHANGE AND NEW POLITICAL ALIGNMENTS

The accumulated effects of social change in the dimension of, on the one hand, the transformation of social stratification, the rise of the active, interventionist, welfare state, economic development and, on the other, cultural innovation had, by the 1970s amounted to something more than isolated episodes of social change. If it did not amount yet to a new societal model, Irish society had reached a transitional state in which the forces carrying change had gained too much momentum to be resisted in the long-run. This was manifested in a number of critical changes.

Organised religious control over other social spheres had receded significantly. While the economy had never, strictly speaking, between subordinated to clerical power, it had followed the imperatives of an isolationist nationalism. By the 1970s, it was very firmly back in the real world with the interim period largely being seen as a melancholy failure. The welfare state, whose emergence had seen a protracted battle between church and state was now under the control of the state with the constitutionally imposed moral boundaries to its remit gradually being rolled back by legal and statutory change. In these circumstances, rights of social citizenship had expanded significantly in the 1960s and had broken with the laissez-faire model favoured by the Church. Education and health were still formally under the operational control of the Church but the expansion of these social services, bankrolled by the state, saw a dramatic increase in the number of non-religious who worked in them with a corresponding increase in secularisation at the point of delivery. Even the religious sphere itself, had become, to a very limited extent, more open to diverse influences, though this is more explicable through the absence of a clear social project to which it could dedicate its energies (Peillion, 1992) rather than internal change in the allegedly more liberal climate after Vatican Two. The domains of art and culture were still subject to formal and informal restrictions that impeded their autonomy and critical contribution, but there were unmistakable signs of a new vitality of intellectual life which in the humanities and social sciences was most pertinently revealed in the emergence of an historiography critical of many nationalist assumptions and in the natural sciences by the belated emergence of a modern science.

Both the 'processual' and 'output' side of the transformation of social spheres were sources and indicators of major change. In relation to process, the quantitative number of those working in new domains and their qualitatively different experience had profound implications for social structure and social interaction. On the output side, major social changes such as the 'technicisation' of social life that followed technologically complex economic development or new, modern curricula in education had complex, interconnnected repercussions that cannot be examined fully here but amounted to new circuits and networks of action that required modern, differentiated organisation with its concomitants of an appropriate institutional environment, a revisable relation to knowledge, activist cultures, and suitable structural configurations.

In line with these changes there were corresponding though less complete changes in the informally organised life-world spheres of family and community life. In the domain of the family, a slow but progressive activation of women's consciousness led to the flouting of church will on the crucial question of fertility with the gradual development of a contraception movement. The general, if very limited, sexual liberalisation that had been established by the mid-seventies was closely connected to the expansion of life opportunities that freed some young people from traditional household controls before marriage and, even more, to the expansion of the welfare state into the family domain. In general, the mainly symbolic power of the Church was beginning to lose its power as material factors such as changes in occupational structure, taxation regimes and welfare entitlements, and competing symbolic pressures carried in popular cultural forms, became more important determinants of the direction of family change. Finally, in the vital but elusive domain of the symbolic reproduction of community much of tradition-securing power was retained in both familial and non-familial networks, but major agencies of change emerged through the development of new social networks that were built around or included categorically defined group identities such as youth and women.

For most of the changes documented above, law was an important medium of change or retardation. The detailed constitutional provision for a Catholic form of life was a major impediment to independent statutory changes. However, in the more liberal climate of the 1960s and 1970s, constitutional provisions were interpreted in a more liberal manner in an era of judicial activism. This had significant implications in the area of the legal regulation of social life. The most celebrated example was the Magee case in 1973 where the denial of the right to contraception was interpreted as an infringement on privacy. The legal and statutory process had to increasingly recognise in the 1970s that citizens held different and incompatible values on social and moral questions (Brown, 1985, p. 305). The state, as already outlined, became a new pole of activism and the most dynamic early factor in propitiating rapid differentiation and disenchantment.

All of these changes together underpinned a reconstruction of both the public sphere and politics. The classical values of Irish political culture, emphasising authoritarianism, personalism, secrecy and limited examination of issues, had emerged from a national movement which had seen that which was external to itself as a threat. The definition of external included not only the British authorities but also its own population. In these circumstances, as explored in Chapter 6, the accountability of government to society was, by democratic standards, weakly articulated. The emergence of a secular intelligentsia and media power from the 1960s provided channels whereby a more autonomous civil society could demand greater responsibility from the political system. However, this was a very gradual process and a political culture that emphasised duties rather than rights was unable to address many pressing issues

for a considerable time. None the less, increased political pluralism even if not confidently asserted did follow the differentiation
of interests, preferences, beliefs and values, and none the less together with structural change, created the conditions for a more
deliberative form of democracy.

Enhanced deliberative capacities, in turn, signified the gradual
emergence of a democratic political identity that was substantially
uncoupled from national identity. In the quarter century after 1970,
Irish society has continuously struggled to separate the communitarian
considerations associated with a Catholic form of life and a single
communal identity from democratic political identity based on the
reciprocity and revisability of rights and duties. The use of Catholicism as a legitimating ideology in the Free State copperfastened
this substitutability of belief systems. Furthermore, little pride was
taken from a long history of democracy that was too easily equated
with claims of British domination and Protestant hegemony. The
numerical strength of minorities was never sufficient in itself to
compel a change of attitude and little account was taken of pluralism in the institutional order. The differentiation of religious and
political belief systems therefore progressed gradually, even tortu-
ously, and was highly correlated with the number of Catholics who
could afford to think different things in different contexts. This was
not achieved without a significant psychic toll for those concerned,
driven often by vague intuitions rather than self-confident beliefs.
It was accompanied by a feeling of continuous contradiction as dis-
regarding Church teaching in the name of political pluralism was
perceived as bringing uncertain benefits to the individual or to society.

The impetus towards a new relationship between cultural and
political identities was increased in the 1970s by two major issues
which were to dominate Irish politics in the last thirty years of the
century. These were the emergence of communal strife in Northern Ireland after 1969 and the decision to join the European Union,
then the European Common Market, in 1972. The Northern Ireland conflict, originally animated by Catholic grievances under the
Stormont government, escalated with the re-mobilisation of the IRA
in 1972 and proceeded thereafter as a constant process of sectarian
conflict with the IRA opposed by British soldiers and Protestant
paramilitaries.[8] A whole series of consociational attempts (O'Leary
and McGarry, 1993) to end the conflict by political means foundered
in the subsequent quarter century until a recent down-scaling of
paramilitary violence has opened new political possibilities (Delanty,

1995c). The effect of the conflict has been physically, culturally, and politically to separate the two communities rendering what Stewart (1977) has called 'the narrow ground' ever more narrow. However, the extent to which allegiances in Northern Ireland can be simply reduced to 'nationalist' and 'Unionist', a representation which is becoming more popular in the Republic, is questionable. Outside of the immediate sites of conflict in working-class and rural regions near the Irish border, and the existence of parties that articulate a confessional cleavage, many, especially among the middle-classes, cannot be so easily typecast. This applies in particular to the northern Catholic middle-class which is ambivalent about the nationalist desideratum of an united Ireland.

The impact of the Northern conflict on the Republic may be divided into three distinct periods. These are the initial period of response and political orientation; a second period in which the Northern conflict was like a background nightmare; and the third in which a new activism has emerged with an enhanced role for the southern government in partnership with the British government. In the first period, the outbreak of the conflict had a convulsive effect on southern politics with some talk of armed intervention by the then Fianna Fáil government and cabinet sackings over alleged arms supplies to Northern nationalists. As the seventies progressed, it became clear that no nationalist political consensus really existed in the south. Southern politics was on the whole hostile to northern nationalist violence and Northern Ireland dropped quite rapidly to a low priority on the political agenda. This period, in fact, marked a decisive, if understated, point in the separation of the political and cultural components of national identity. National identity as a basis for political identity had nowhere to go with the loss of legitimacy of irredentist claims to Northern Ireland territory.

The second period, which began after the failure of consociational attempts at power-sharing in 1975, lasted until the Anglo-Irish agreement of 1985. In this period, Northern Ireland dropped almost out of sight in southern politics, but it weighed on the collective unconsciousness of the society as an index of political failure and as a fear of becoming involved.[9] For the population of the south, the Northern conflict appeared to involve them but they could not work out exactly why or how. The answer which appeared in the Anglo-Irish agreement of 1985 pointed in a clear direction, even if southern public opinion did not fully recognise it. It involved a re-opening of the issue of nationalism, statehood and territoriality in which the Catholic nation-state of the Republic of Ireland was called upon to change substantially its political culture in the direction of liberal pluralism and public deliberation if it wished to forge new political relations between north, south and Great Britain.

However, the relationship between southern attitudes to Northern Ireland and the Irish national identity code continues to be ambivalent. Two distinct currents can be identified in present circumstances. One current is represented by those either indifferent or hostile to the expression of political nationalism by Catholics in Northern Ireland. These have successfully pressed for a recognition that Britain did not impose partition on Ireland but that partition must instead be attributed to historically long-run communal differences, re-elaborated in modern conditions. A smaller number amongst this current attribute significant responsibility for this situation to the primordial blindness of Irish Catholic nationalism. This is coupled with a long-run and understated commitment to a state patriotism in the Irish Republic which is indifferent to national unity. This first current, loosely associated with historiographical revisionism, has achieved some success in the institutional recognition by the Irish state that it has been the existence of two incompatible and legitimate traditions, not British imposition, that has created the violent stalemate in Northern Ireland. The other current is connected with recent developments in cultural nationalism and associated with new historical writing on Irish nationalism and identity such as that of Lee (1989b). This current is critical of aspects of Irish society but tends to base that criticism on a supposed betrayal of the cultural potential of nationalism. Within the second current, there is now a tendency to identify more closely with the concerns of Northern 'nationalists' and to include them into a pan-nationalist consensus that will newly legitimate Irish nationalism, albeit in a form that is more respectful of cultural pluralism. This current may be characterised as switching the external relations of Irish national identity from a predominantly primordial code based on the desirability of isolation and rejection to one of cultural expansionism based on a modified nation-code that has allegedly purified itself of its most doctrinaire elements.[10]

The second major issue to have a transformative impact on Irish identity was the decision, along with the United Kingdom, to join the European Community in 1972. This decision reversed a long half century in which isolationism was preferred. The referendum vote on the issue was a vote for assumed prosperity, especially the rural prosperity which at that time seemed more likely, and against peripherality. The manner in which the Irish became 'good Europeans' and the enthusiasm with which they have continued to embrace the successive phases of evolution of the Community highlights a state of affairs that was structurally apparent since the break with the UK in 1922: that a small, semi-peripheral, geographically isolated state needs to belong within a larger context unless it enjoys extraordinary levels of social mobilisation or good fortune in primary resources. Undoubtedly, for many, to opt for Europe was to consciously oppose continued poverty and failure. The interpretative power of nationalist explanatory constructs continue to obscure the relationship between the choices made for the world in 1972 and afterwards and against the world in the early part of the century. The significance of joining the European Community, together with the cultural and political implications of a far-reaching settlement of the Northern Ireland problem, are not widely perceived in relation to a fundamental re-thinking of historically legitimated identity patterns, that, even though they are losing legitimacy as pure constructs, still obscure the connections between related phenomena and deflect responsibility away from the sensitive core of reflecting on historical choices that did not deliver what was anticipated.[11] The inability to think through the full implications of European membership or Northern Ireland reveals a society still intoxicated by anticipations rather than sobered by reality, even if the latter is slowly gaining in force.

NATIONAL IDENTITY AND POLITICS IN CONTEMPORARY IRELAND

Irish politics, beginning in the 1970s, underwent a re-alignment. The era of Fianna Fáil hegemony, which had lasted for over forty years, came to a close as the other major conservative party,[12] Fine Gael, entered into a period of coalition formation with the small social democratic Labour Party. This coalition arrangement has alternated with exclusively Fianna Fáil, or Fianna Fáil-led, administrations ever since. There is sufficient evidence (Mair, 1987) to indicate that a rough cleavage of a somewhat more social democratic Fine Gael/Labour[13] coalition and a somewhat more conservative Fianna Fáil has emerged in a relatively stable form. The difference, relatively small in distributive and welfare issues, is more

marked on liberal issues with Fianna Fáil occupying a more conservative stance on the persistent social and moral questions which
had a major role in Irish politics from the late 1970s, including
contraception, abortion and divorce.

The new party political cleavage to some extent cut across a broader
social and cultural cleavage between traditionalists and modernisers that relatively weakly correlated with party allegiance. This
divide which expresses itself on moral and identity issues between
those who are reluctant to change basic socio-moral tenets and
forms of identification connected with the older national identity
code and those who, sometimes reluctantly, sometimes enthusiasti-
cally, are prepared to jettison some or most of it. This cleavage is,
of course, closely connected with structural change since the 1950s
with levels of urbanisation and professionalisation highly significant amongst those willing to embrace change and rurality and
property-holding prominent amongst those who resist it. But structural explanations will only go so far. A complex interplay of cultural factors has led to enhanced diversity in the social and culture
bases of Irish politics.

The perceived need for powerful national identity constructs in
Ireland has not disappeared. They have become less relevant it is
true in the functional sense of providing principles of social organisation, but they continue to be 'functional' in another sense,
the social psychological sense of collective belonging, we-feeling.
The contemporary form of institutionalisation of national identity
is not directly related to large elements of the material and symbolic reproduction of society. Instead, it functions more as a cultural good, an identification that provides a sense of belonging. In
a country where other forms of cultural engagement are limited
many social agents privilege a form of interaction that confirms
their sameness and their belonging to a common national habitus.

In Ireland from the late 1970s, new mechanisms for the articulation of national identity, or opposition to it, have become active.
While many social spheres have withdrawn from direct commitment to reproducing, or not significantly transgressing, national
identity, new cultural movements have stepped into the space. The
most significant of these movements is a right-wing Catholic movement that, propelled by a vision of saving traditional Ireland, has
consistently resisted the encroachment of modernisation. This is a
loose fusion of right-wing groups, Catholic secret associations, and
prominent social conservatives who command the core allegiance

of perhaps around one quarter of the population. Their value system emphasises Catholic primordialism and a traditional lifeworld and was considerably bolstered after the Pope's visit to Ireland in 1979. Opposed to them, is a movement of modernisers who are grouped around the media and other liberal constituencies, but who do not have anything like the same level of organisation. Many amongst these are suspicious of traditional, or neo-traditional, symbols of Irish identity. A third, and very diffuse movement, is composed of a growing number who identify with a neo-nationalism that compensates for the ennui of what they experience as a standardisation of cultural identities and who espouse a new commitment to national peculiarity. The combination of traditionalist national identity constructs, and neo-nationalist ones, ensure the continuing potency of inclusive, communitarian symbolisation in moral and political discourse. Communitarian symbolisation such as appeals to Irish tradition remains more powerful than liberal or social-democratic symbolisation as a resource for the symbolic 'packaging' of successful political messages.

The continuing power of communitarian symbolisation in social interaction, though substantially withdrawn from spheres of functional reproduction, continues in the evaluation by participants of the forms of life which they experience and in the symbolic bases of new movements carrying cultural innovation. In the first instance, communitarian symbolisation such as the association of the Irish with good fun (the 'craic'), hospitality, agreeableness, an ancient culture, distracts from critical reflections on how these constructs function as ideology, diverting attention from the sometimes oppressive intimacy and restricted range of acceptable values that characterises everyday life. In the second, even new cultural producers such as the environmental movement draw extensively from nationalist symbolism (O'Mahony and Mullally, 1995; Skillington 1993). This movement appears, in certain cases at least, to hold more nationalist positions than other political parties. The women's movement on the whole does not strongly relate a critique of patriarchy to Catholic nationalism, as distinct from Catholicism, and has not seriously raised the question of whether national independence benefited Irish women or inhibited them further. These tendencies are consistent with the generally nationalist orientation of leftist sub-cultures who somehow stay positive about national identity while criticising its effects. In another way, however, the very existence of manifestations of new politics marks a shift in the capacity for cultural innovation which today may go one way and tomorrow another. Certainly, the history of European environmental movements shows a tendency for these movements to embrace nationalist values at the beginning of a mobilisation phase while tempering them later (Eyerman et al., 1990). There are also some good arguments, on the one hand, for new political movements concentrating more of their attention at the national state level, where they are more organised and have more symbolic power at their disposal, and less on the supra-national European stage where they are not well-represented (Tarrow, 1995). On the other hand, new movements in Ireland owe much of their gains to the legislative context of the European Union which compels Irish governments to adopt changes they otherwise would evade. This especially applies to the issue of equality for women.

More generally, during the time when the country has been receptive to outside influences, and with ever more impetus, the globalisation process, interacting with an indigenous culture, is increasingly creating a hybrid culture with strong American and, latterly, European influences reshaping lifestyles and identities. This process has further added to the fragmentation of an homogenous cultural identity and to the sense of cultural uprooting experienced by many. For others, it has meant new opportunities for the expression of a distinctive lifestyle. Whatever the cultural options for the making of expressive identities, one phenomenon that has gathered increasing space since the 1960s is the privatisation of lifestyles. The technicisation of everyday life through the car, home entertainment and domestic technologies has been a major contributory factor to the erosion of solidary communities based on non-familial interaction networks.

The privatisation of lifestyles has ambivalent effects. It breaks the hold of the social over individuals while also inhibiting the creativity of the social. It is one facet of a contradictory modernisation in which the dominant notion of a single collectivity united against the world was replaced by a plurality of Gods and Demons. The decisive indicator of this process is that contemporary Irish culture can no longer be analysed through the category of national identity in the way it once could have been. Today, as national identity retreats to an uncertain space between politics and culture, it has to be sought amidst a plurality of cultural forms. That it remains powerful, in the absence of strong competing ideologies of political liberalism, social democracy, feminism, environmentalism and cultural modernism, is without doubt, but its power now either recedes to background consensus on an important part of cultural identity or is the product of specific mobilisation through unstable social networks or through the risky prism of public discourse. Its specific effects have shifted from the task of social mobilisation to one of cultural organisation. Today, it leads the resistance to cultural modernisation and to preventing the connection of ideas in a way that exposes the development path of the society, or its present configurations, to critique.

Notwithstanding the more risky and unstable mechanisms of its diffusion, nationalism is constantly being re-elaborated in a manner that never explicitly separates it from its historical role as the carrier of conservatism. On the contrary, Irish conservatism has proven adept at hiding between the we-feeling of nationalism. Because the historical memory of the Irish national movement continues to confer legitimacy on those who act in its name, Irish conservatism is never consistently and critically examined. A potent indication of a society still not able to face up to its past are recent sexual scandals in which a significant number of priests have been convicted of abusing young children. This has not yet, for example, issued in any sustained attempt to question the terms on which priests can gain access to young children. A second example is the internationally famous 'x-case' of the early 1990s in which a young girl was temporarily prevented from travelling to England to have an abortion after being made pregnant through rape. The issues raised by the x-case led to a referendum on the constitution to allow women the right to travel and to allow information on abortion in certain circumstances, but the results have never been legislated as successive governments refused to address the issue. A third example is the remarkably successful recent campaign against divorce,[14] spearheaded by right-wing Catholic groups, in which elected representatives of the major political parties conspicuously failed to actively campaign for divorce though all the major parties declared in favour of it. The issue caused psychic turmoil for many who hesitantly voted for divorce and against the precepts of a collective moral code binding on all. Furthermore, the arguments in favour of divorce tended to be not based on civil rights but on 'compassion for those in a difficult situation'.

It is in this dimension of the reluctance to abandon the possibility of a single, binding collective moral code that the relationship between nationalism and conservatism continues to show itself. The

desire to belong to the collectivity remains so potent as to continue to absorb alternative codes of identification. The examples
above indicate how alternative currents and oppositional voices
frequently remain beneath the surface with no secure foothold in
public culture.[15] Nationalism as a collective code of moral belonging therefore still prevents the articulation of difference, confers
continuing background social and political legitimacy on the Church,
underpins a political populism which is characterised by low levels
of political participation,[16] and resistance to ideological innovation.
The rhetoric of collective populism still holds sway over the language of rights and responsibilities in public culture. National identity
in contemporary Ireland throws a shroud of obscurity on the critical
reflective and innovating capacities of the society (Habermas, 1989b).

8 Conclusion: Nationalism in Contemporary Ireland

Nationalism in Ireland, once an anti-establishment discourse of civil society albeit one with an in-built conservative telos, has acted since the end of the Second World War as an annex to state-bureaucratic, economic and cultural power. At its post-war peak the cultural synthesis which it represented still directly legitimated and oriented the system of institutions though it has progressively since lost this central role and retreated to an indirect role of shaping social representations of what is culturally important and unimportant. In the latter role it could still have social consequences as the source of a new nationalist populism that acts against the diversification of cultural and political identities, spreading like a large weed to strangle discourses of rights and responsibilities about equality, participation, gender and nature that depend on the assertion of difference. The discourse of the nation in Ireland is admittedly caught in a bind. The ground on which it stood – the anti-modern values of a conservative social order – have declining salience, but the emotional substance of collective belonging which the older nationalism created lives on. This bind is accentuated, because the international return to a nation-oriented populism with the diminution of energies of collective solidarity also finds roots in Ireland and conflicts with the need to complete certain basic rights associated with modern citizenship, e.g., divorce, homosexuality, and recognition of the validity and rights of political Protestantism, which require the extension of solidarity and the recognition of difference. The power of nationalism is revealed, however, in the way in which issues of citizenship arise as inescapable societal problems of anomalies in marital status, civil strife in Northern Ireland, the denial of abortion to a 14-year-old pregnant girl, rather than as unequivocal, self-organising and creative mobilisations of civil society. This is not to deny that much ground has been travelled in order for these issues to be raised and minimally acted upon. It to raise the point that the legitimacy of genuine value difference and oppositional movements is still weak and these oppositional movements – including the far from successfully institutionalised social

181

democratic discourse of material equality – are still themselves divided over what importance to attach to identification with the nation.

This book has sought to explore the historical responsibility of the dominant conservative strand of Irish nationalism for creating an institutional order that, inter alia legitimated poor economic performance, inequality, low participation, the subjugation of women, and the denial or civil rights to homosexuals, and that continues to impede the exploration of values for enhanced citizenship and greater cultural pluralism. It has done so by attempting to place this nationalism in an historical context that shows how currents of social mobilisation that arose with the national movement were absorbed by it and how in this process, which produced a conservative hegemony, the radical values of the twentieth century were suppressed and distorted. The means to explore this process was to apply a sociological account of nationalism which firstly linked the mobilisation phase of the nationalist movement with the institutionalisation of a corresponding code of national identity in the subsequent nation-state, and subsequently analysed the fate of this national identity in the Irish nation-state.

Irish national identity emerged as a socially constructed collective identity in the late nineteenth century. It was a product of a multi-faceted nationalist mobilisation, that was in part also general of social mobilisation, that radically changed the trajectory of nationalist identity and goals. This identity and goals were dynamically created in the mobilisation phase drawing off longer-run confessional identities and structural contradictions emanating from the early-modern period. These structural contradictions and identities can be summed up in their nineteenth century legacy as a predominantly Protestant dominated state and class-system coming increasingly into conflict with growing Catholic power brought about by differentiation and democratisation and expressed in rising nationalist political consciousness. Religiously based social differences in the main tended to re-inforce political-cultural differences with Protestants, until the late nineteenth century, inclining towards a liberal social-contract view of political relations under the Union with Great Britain, and Catholic nationalist Ireland increasingly leaning to a republican political philosophy emphasising the supremacy of a collective national political will.

From the high point of Home Rule in the 1880s forwards, Irish national identity had already been formed to the point where the establishment of a separate, though not necessarily separatist, state was inevitable. What remained to be decided was the nature of the society that went with that state in the dimensions of, firstly, whether its relation to the external world would be one of cultural isolationism or international cultural 'contemporareity'; secondly, whether its constitutional order would be traditional-theocratic or secular-liberal; thirdly, whether its collective identity would be predominately based on solidarity before the nation or democratic identification located in rights of citizenship; and, finally, whether its social organisation would emphasise conservative de-differentiation or progressive differentiation. The key to understanding how these questions were answered is to be gained from examining competing identity codes, ethicised imaginary constructions of the future society, that were evolved in the process of struggling for the nation-state and applied after its foundation. These codes, mirroring the above questions, contained a relation to the outside, an understanding of constitutional and cultural bonds of identification and a strategy for an organisation of the social compatible with the code. The Irish national identity code that was institutionalised after the successful separatist movement, and which represented a particular synthesis of the different positions within the mobilisation phase of the movement, adopted a primordial relationship to the outside based on rejection of the culture of modernity; advocated a conventional relationship to cultural identification by subordinating the autonomy of citizens; ultimately produced a constitutional order that built in weak, liberal rights within a traditional-theocratic framework; and developed a conservative relationship to the social based on institutional de-differentiation and opposition to all forms of progressivism.[1] This identity code and its social programme was at one and the same time an ideology reflecting dominant propertied social interests but still supported by a majority, a cultural pattern that was functionally useful for the building of a conservative institutional order, and a restrictive determinant of capacities for agency and cognitive innovation within the society.

The mobilisation of the Irish national movement was simultaneously bound up with a struggle over material resources and a search for an identity that would provide both a legitimating framework for resource distribution and a moral and emotional world-relation in a period of intense dislocation. Grasping the dynamics of collective identity construction, the building of codes of inclusion and exclusion, is central to understanding the societal programme of the movement. The Irish national movement was mobilised through its different

wings. These wings formed several quasi-consensual alignments at
different historical junctures that allow us to speak of a consensus
movement. The key to understanding the movement, and the direction of its later institutionalisation, is to be found not in accepting consensus on collective identity as the 'natural' unfolding of a
seamless national will but as the product of differences within the
movement that were dynamically explored and conjecturally aligned
around two political cultural concepts, Home Rule and self-determination. These differences reflect the social and cultural situation
of a given wing, the identity project it mobilises to rationalise its
current situation and to project a future one, and its capacity to
realise that project in the prevailing political and cultural conditions.
The alignment of the various wings of Irish nationalism through
the construction of shared collective identity, and the foundations
of the successful push for independence, lay in the widespread
diffusion of a 'master-frame' of national self-determination on a
Catholic and conservative-communitarian basis.

The first wave of institutionalisation of this collective identity
occurring after the foundation of the state happened in circumstances in which a model of societal integration was built from
Catholic-conservative belief-systems and social goals. The process
of institutionalisation led to the primacy of a conception of ethical
life that imposed the values of a particular social stratum or class-
fraction, the propertied petit-bourgeoisie and associated professional
service providers and a supportive, dogmatic confessional code, on
the society as a whole. The institutionalisation of an ethical code
based on petit-bourgeois and Catholic cultural values, interpreted
against and elaborated through nationalist myths, was conducted
in a favourable climate created by the exclusion or minimisation of
those codes inside and outside the nationalist movement that might
have enforced difference. These included British and Protestant-
Irish cultural traditions and ethical codes of equality, gender rights,
and local political empowerment. The ethical code was built upon
a conservative, petit-bourgeois conception of appropriate moral and
evaluative standards, promulgating a narrow definition of national
identity, and dominant over differences in class and gendered interests
and over goals that might have sprung from the needs of a more
autonomous institutional order. The Irish national movement, while
absorbing goal elements connected with justice and modernisation,
ultimately produced a situation in which a conservative ethical code
dominated functional, class and gendered logics of innovation. In

these circumstances of the 'naturalisation' of Catholic-conservative cultural values, alternatives could not be deliberated upon and latent social cleavages within Ireland continued to be anaesthetised by restricting the creativity of the social, first in areas such as social services, economy, movements for justice, and cultural production, and, later, in new movement areas like the environment and second-wave feminism. The institutionalised code therefore was the expression of an ideologically successfully projection of a particular, male, propertied interest as a general one, of a Catholic-conservative 'packaging' of culture that restricted capacities for social and political mobilisation beyond those supportive of the code, and of a complex of institutionalised rule regimes that privileged traditional moral and evaluative standards over the autonomy of institutional spheres and the individual.

The success of this ethical code meant that contradictions could be kept latent and the developmental potential of the society artificially restricted. In the service of this goal, beginning in the late nineteenth century, organised class and cultural agency in the form of the Church and the propertied middle-class articulated, building on *existing structures*, a revised institutional and cultural order for the society. In this new order communitarian values emphasising the sanctity of the neo-traditions of Catholic social conservatism and nationality as a collective identification dominated both liberal values and the communicative exploration of innovation. The extent of the reliance on Catholicism as a legitimating ideology for the new state was in part enforced by divisions over the civil war that erupted after the effective winning of independence.

The society which resulted from this communitarian blueprint can be criticised from the observational standpoints of poor innovative capacities in a variety of social spheres, the moralisation of politics and law which led to a low estimation of reason and the triumph of conventional 'emotive' reasoning, the absence of social justice, the repression of personality through the diffusion of models that depended on low self-esteem, the denial of the need for cultural reflection and intellectual life, and the institutionalisation of patriarchy. At some level the majority of participants willingly lived through the consequences of the chosen cultural model. However, their views became apparent in the 1940s and 1950s in political reflection processes, in widespread perceptions of the failure of social programmes, in emigration, in increasing frustration at the inability to meet economic challenges. The view of significant failure is supported by later critique over the last twenty years of the society that was built to the 1950s and the millenarian significance attached to the sixties as a process of opening out. By the late 1940s, the functional and social order could no longer sustain the moral regulation ingrained in the dominant cultural model and change processes were set in motion.

The 'return of the social' in the late forties and fifties as a creative force took place within an environment constantly constrained by the continuing legitimacy and social power of the older cultural model. In the absence of real creative agency in civil society, the state itself took on the role of the primary force for social change. It adopted policies geared towards professional state-run welfare services and towards economic growth. These processes were later supported by a variety of other changes in civil society itself. These changes led to the expansion of social interests and to the power of new, non-propertied interest holders, to an elaboration of new cultural models that responded to differently defined needs and realities, and to expanded potentials for creative collective agency, in the first instance, ranging from bureaucrats, to entrepreneurial capitalists, to the labour movement, to media broadcasters and, in the second, to new kinds of agency represented in new movements, legal and citizens' activism, and new kinds of cultural production. These changes together signified that the relationship between conservative social interests, institutional de-differentiation and societal collective identity was weakened. Also weakened was the conservative order's power to suppress other identities reflecting a more autonomous civil society.

Notwithstanding its weakening hold, the conservative domination of national identity has continued importance in preserving the glaring contradictions between Catholic-conservative institutionalised norms and needs and values that are contrary to them from being comprehensively addressed. This has endured through the second half of the century and, in Marx's celebrated phrase, conditions the society to draw its poetry excessively from the past. 'Irishness' remains a key principle of identity even as national identity moves more over into culture and away from conventional politics. This interpretation current constantly seeks to renew itself. Over the last fifteen years there has seen both a backward-looking attempt to preserve the Catholic morality at the heart of the state's constitution and a 'forward-looking' attempt to revitalise a cultural neo-nationalism. The one draws sustenance from certain affinities with modern neoconservatism, the other from a revival of an international cultural nationalism which, like the earlier nationalism, is a response to wide-ranging cultural and structural changes. Today, however, these cultural currents no longer have the same level of domination of the cultural and political field as various alternatives to a single, nationalist communitarian ethic have become more prominent and, put another way, as the ethical code underpinning the identity is forced to spread itself more thinly and unevenly across a culturally differentiated society. But the ethic is some distance yet from withdrawing to a form of attachment to place and tradition that is compatible with pluralism towards others and with no longer usurping the space of democratic identification that could be expressed in the form of a 'constitutional patriotism' (Habermas, 1994; Delanty, 1996c, 1997a).[2] The tension inherent in attaching continuing legitimacy to a cultural model no longer consistent with many of the society's practices engenders a continuous conflict between the society's and individuals' needs and its institutional framework. Unless the adverse consequences of a monolithic identity code are named and addressed, it will continue to weaken and confuse the attempt to move beyond a contradictory and often hypocritical bind that obstructs the creation of modern cultural identities and of principles of democratic identification that stand on their own ground.

One key determinant of more self-confident democratic cultures and procedures, that have the capacity to explore and decide upon deep-lying issues and to initiate structural change, is whether proper responsibility is apportioned to the older model of national identity, and to the nationalist movement which mobilised and institutionalised it, for its social failures, inhibition of innovation and promotion of extensive inequalities. There is no clear evidence that this is happening. While the purpose of the nation as conceived by the national movement has been rejected in some of its more prominent dimensions, a deeper cultural 'matrix' has remained quite strong. The process of de-institutionalisation has in fact been ambivalent. The partial discrediting of the more overt and less sustainable ideological forms has facilitated the emergence of a more sophisticated defensive reasoning that wishes to go forward to the future without critical examination of the past. In academic parlance, much of the normative content of modernity remains unrealised while many are busy building new post-modern myths. De-institutionalisation has not in fact led as yet to fundamental cultural self-examination.

Nationalist symbolism is anchored deep in the lifeworld and offers continuing vitality to new forms of neo-nationalism that continue to have political significance and may gain more significance in time (Delanty, 1997b). This provides a continuing barrier to political pluralism in the island of Ireland and in the wider British and Irish context, to a growth in neo-racial intolerance towards travellers asylum-seekers and immigrants, to continuing confusion in the hard cultural realms of women and Catholic power, and to continuing difficulty in fully releasing the creativity of the social.[3]

Breaking with historical silences in late twentieth and early twenty first century Ireland involves the acceptance of differentiated perspectives arising from differentiated situations. Plurality requires a recognition of differences between situated cultures, not the assumption of their sameness, and the capacity of these cultures to rationalise their own concrete experiences and to engage in argumentation that presupposes the necessity of *rational* dissensus between groups with different identities and interests. A vital precondition for such an increase in deliberative power is to clarify how, historically, the fusion of conservative cultural and social power enforced a singular idea of an homogenous 'people' with 'traditional' needs and led the society into the long, shadowy night of unexamined contradictions and stagnation.

A crucial question for the future will be whether Irish society is capable of generating a 'post-national' identity, a collective identity that is no longer focused on the fiction of an 'homogenous people' and their alleged common, cultural attributes but on constitutional norms and cultural identifications that emphasise the right, but associated responsibilities, of being different (Delanty, 1996c, 1996e). Quite how the link between the nation-state, rights, responsibilities, and cultural identification, is going to evolve is hard to assess. In the Irish case, how three major challenges are addressed will prove crucial. These are the interconnected issues of, firstly, a deliberative-pluralistic solution to the Northern Ireland problem with its constitutional and social implications; secondly, the problem of adjusting institutionally to the society's growing contemporaneity with other democratic societies; and, thirdly, the economic, social and cultural dimensions of membership of the European Union. What appears clear in all of these cases is the urgency of Irish society beginning the task of establishing new forms of democratic identification and association that facilitate innovative currents and their institutionalisation. In pursuit of this, serious self-criticism will prove essential. In this process the conservatism of the nationalist tradition will have to be examined and its anachronistic, confusing, and populist tenets abandoned in the interests of establishing more solid ground to stand on to deal with the opportunities and problems of the new century.

Notes

1. The book is almost exclusively oriented to a consideration of national-ism in the territory that first had the name the Irish Free State after the Independence movement and later became the Republic of Ire-land. It therefore focuses on the 26 so-called southern counties of the island of Ireland. The six counties of Northern Ireland which were partitioned off from the Free State after 1922, remaining part of the United Kingdom, are considered only in so far as they are relevant to the development of nationalism within the Republic of Ireland.

2. It is now widely accepted in historical scholarship that most of what is believed to be the authentic long-run history of the nation was con-structed relatively recently to serve political purposes. There often remains a factual core to some beliefs about the nation but these are embedded in a wider context that is not reliable. The continuing con-troversy over the revision of Irish history shows how porous are the boundaries between fact and invention in the history of the nation. See Hobsbawm and Ranger (1983) for some revealing case studies.

3. Molony (1977) notes the crisis of the Vatican in the 1920s as it at-tempted to grapple with such modern phenomena as liberalism, anti-clericalism and socialism. The existence of such challenges, together with financial problems, led the Vatican to become more inward-looking and fundamentalist and led to Catholic movements in these countries becoming more hostile to the spirit and practice of democracy.

4. May 5, 1993. Kearney's (1997) more recent *Post Nationalist Ireland*, which while containing interesting ideas and suggestions to overcome historical divisions in the 'archipelago' of Britain and Ireland, seems to be of the view that the national identity of the nation-state of which he is a citizen does not require extensive criticism. There are many examples of this view throughout the book but one that is especially striking is the idea that, historically, the Gaelic League did not exhibit a strongly marked racism (p. 4) whereas in fact, as historians have argued, racial doctrines were intrinsic to it ever from Hyde's advocacy of the need to de-anglicise Ireland. See Boyce (1991b). See also Leerssen (1996) who shows how racial doctrines, both Anglo-Saxon and Celtic, reflected the contemporary climate of racial beliefs in the late nineteenth century. This view exemplifies Kearney's generally uncritical and over-consensualist stance towards the historical self-understanding of Irish nationalism which would precisely wish to project the impression that it is non-racialist and inclusive. This stance allows Kearney to go on to claim (pp. 5–6) that 'the Irish nation includes several different re-ligions – as Wolfe Tone's reference to Catholic, Protestant and Dis-senter recognised...' That this inclusive view of the composition of

the 'Irish nation' is highly contentious hardly needs saying.
5. The term 'as gaeilge' means 'in Irish'.
6. *Guardian*, 17/3/93; *Irish Times*, 19/3/93.
7. *Independent on Sunday*, 28/4/96.
8. See also Lee (1989b).
9. See also the collection of essays, *Revising the Rising* (Dhonnchadha and Dorgan, 1991), especially the contribution of Kiberd, Deane and Lee.
10. See also Kiberd (1995) and O'Ceallaigh (1994).
11. Joseph Lee claims, for example, that there is still 'enormous generosity of spirit in this country, which distinguishes us from several European states.' *Irish Times*, May 7, 1993
12. High ranking government and opposition spokespersons in the Irish Republic have in recent years routinely referred to 'nationalist Ireland' including under the term all the population of the Irish Republic and the Catholic population of Northern Ireland.
13. The epistemological divide between 'nationalists' and 'revisionists' in its classical form was closely related to the divisions in the Irish civil war between those who stood on the ground of the romantic will of the revolutionary elite and opposed the Anglo-Irish Treaty of 1921 and those who supported the Treaty with democracy on their side.
14. Above all, the dropping of Articles 2 and 3 in the Irish Constitution whereby the Irish Republic claims jurisdiction over the territory of the entire island.
15. The *Irish Times* editorial of 25/11/94 sums up well the extensively shared critical view of a society that evaded its own realities 'All around us, the old moulds are being broken, the old certainties challenged. Badly overdue legislation on contraception and homosexuality is on the statute books, a second divorce referendum is on the way [since passed in 1995]. After decades of turning a blind eye, there is an acceptance that this society must, at last, acknowledge its own realities.'
16. While assessing the responsibility of the coalition of forces that comprised the Irish national movement is the primary objective of this book, this responsibility has to be set in the context of other 'responsibilities', such as the centralist British constitutional framework and the nature of Unionist-Conservative opposition to Home Rule.
17. Such evasion was described in the *Irish Times* editorial of 16/3/96, referring to immediate, post-Independence Ireland, as the desire 'to shut reality out'; or as 'sweep-problems-under-the-carpet' values by Ferdia Mac Anna in the series on Irish identity in the same newspaper on 27/4/93.

CHAPTER 2

1. Gibbons (1996) is a good example.
2. Chapters 3, 4, 5 and 6 below will examine how this kind of political philosophy emerged and with what interests it was associated.
3. This theoretical point is important for addressing Irish nationalism. This nationalism has been explained symbolically as a long-run manifestation

of a self-evident national consciousness or materially as a response to immediate injustice. The two are usually fused in some fashion. The point here is that material injustice has to be constructed as a nationalist problem and that this construction may bear only indirect relation to the degree of material injustice actually suffered.

4. Skocpol (1994, pp. 7–9; 1979) emphasises the importance of the breakdown in the state as an essential element in social revolution. For her revolutionary leaderships are not master planners of revolutionary crises but marginal elites who emerge amid state break-downs. She thus criticises theorists for seeing revolution in terms of volunturistic collective wills and emphasises the crucial role of ascending elites in using popular political mobilisations for state-building purposes.

5. In our analysis below, the counter-movement is represented by Ulster Unionism and to a lesser extent by Southern Irish Unionism. While the Ulster movement in particular was an important overall contextual factor in shaping Irish nationalism we do not analyse it in detail due to limitations of space. However, its relationship to Irish nationalism does inform our analysis of critical junctures in the evolution of nationalist politics.

6. Rucht's comments described the populism of certain social movements but it can usefully be applied to a post-revolutionary nation-state order characterised by populism.

CHAPTER 3

1. See also Davies (1988), Kearney (1989), Morgan (1988) and Tilly (1993).

2. The older term 'British Isles' has become sensitive in some quarters. In the British press the term 'these islands' is often substituted. Here, we use a term taken from Kearney (1997) which does seem to have the benefit of neutrality.

3. There were many revolts against the extension of the central state in Tudor and Stuart times of which the Irish revolts can be seen as an expression. These included the Cornish Revolt (1497), the Pilgrimage of Grace (1536–7), rebellions of the south-east and East Anglia (1549–50), Wyatt's Rebellion (1553–4) and a revolt of the northern Catholic lords (1569) (Tilly, 1993, p. 115).

4. On the 'general crisis of the seventeenth century' see Aston (1965) and Parker and Smith (1985). On its application to Ireland see Clarke (1970). While arguments vary as to the nature of the general crisis, a central claim is that throughout Europe in this period, which saw the end of the medieval period, the newly established absolutist states entered a prolonged crisis as a result largely of social and economic changes but also because they had not fully discarded their medieval structures. The crisis eventually came to an end with the transformation of Renaissance absolutism into the Westphalian state system.

5. Bartlett (1993) thus sees the early extension of the Norman state to Ireland in the Middle Ages as an expression of the European-wide trend by which the core penetrated into the periphery. In his view, a

'colonial settlement in Munster would have a very strong resemblance to one in Brandenburg' (p. 21). This perspective is very different from the simple notion of state-driven colonialism in that it refers to a period prior to the age of the territorial nation-state when economic and social development was frequently brought about by large scale peasant colonisation spreading over most parts of Europe.

6. This is also reflected in Richter's (1985, p. 291) argument that the closest parallel to the Anglo-Norman invasion is provided by the German expansion into Western-Slav territories. In his view the medieval lordship can be viewed in the wider European context of demographic and economic growth.

7. This argument must be seen in light of the debate on whether Ireland's status as a colony was comparable to that of British colonies elsewhere in the world. See Canny (1988).

8. On the debate about the transition from feudalism to capitalism see Aston and Philbin (1985), Hilton (1976) and Holton (1985).

9. The estimated population of Ireland in 1500 was 800,000 people, in 1600 1 million, in 1687 2 million, in 1750 2.4, and 5 million in 1800 (Houston, 1992, p. 30).

10. Ford (1986) documents how the reception of the Reformation was more difficult in Ireland due, inter alia, to the absence of popular traditions to support Protestantism and the inability of the Tudor state to provide it with sufficient support. The latter was in part due to the incomplete extension of the state to cover the whole of the territory,

11. Wales became linked with England in 1301 when Edward I's son was given the title Prince of Wales. The last Welsh revival was put down in 1409 by Henry IV. See Williams (1982).

12. The nomenclature of Irish history is often confusing: the term Norman (sometimes 'Anglo-Norman' though the Normans who came to Ireland were in fact French speaking Welsh born settlers) is frequently replaced by the term 'English' or 'Old Catholic' in Tudor and Stuart times, with the distinction of 'New English' applied to the Protestant settlers and 'Anglo-Irish' for later centuries (See Richter, 1985, p. 292).

13. This is of course a simplification of a complex situation of constantly changing allegiances, for instance, the Catholic Confederation was for a time under the leadership of the Protestant Royalist, the Earl of Ormond. For a more detailed account of the complicated politics of the seventeenth century in Ireland see Fitzpatrick (1988). See also on Irish royalism O' Buachalla (1993). On the English Civil War see Hughes (1991) and on revolts in early modern Europe Goldstone (1991) .

14. The Stuarts were mostly Anglican but were led by James II who embraced Gallic Catholic absolutism.

15. The main concern of the pope was the restraint of French expansion in Europe which would have posed a threat to papal supremacy. Hence papal support for the Orange cause in England. Since the defeat of James was also a defeat for France, the Williamite victory at the Battle of the Boyne was celebrated by a Te Deum in Rome.

16. The Treaty of Limerick (1691) with which William made his peace with the Irish supporters of James was particularly favourable to

Catholics and continued to be an argument to undermine the Act of Union.

17. On the formation of British national identity see Colley (1992), Corrigan and Sayer (1985), Cunnigham (1981), Greenfeld (1992), Hirst (1994), Horsman (1976), Melman (1991).

18. Geographers such as Evans (1992) and Heslinga (1962) would argue that these cultural divisions have been reinforced by geographical variations, which in earlier centuries were more pronounced.

19. See MacDonagh's (1983, pp. 2–9) analysis of time in Irish historical consciousness.

20. On Scottish national identity see McCrone et al (1989) and Pittock (1991).

21. Dunne (1982) points out that Wolfe Tone, the leader of the United Irishmen, was not in fact as influenced by French revolutionary thought as is often thought and was essentially an independent Irish Whig whose radicalness was more domestic and reflected the old Protestant colonial tradition.

22. Whelan (1996) argues that the Union, even without Catholic Emancipation which was not to follow until 1829, immediately improved the political position of Catholics as it removed the pre-existing representative arrangements which were inherently discriminatory.

23. On other discrepancies see MacDonagh (1977, p. 34 and 1983, p. 53).

24. Norway, after its independence from Denmark in 1814 was possibly the most democratic country, with nearly half of the male population enfranchised in 1815, about 12%, in comparison to about 2% in Britain and 1% in France and Italy (Eckstein, 1966, p. 12).

25. On federalism see Bosco (1991), Burgess and Gagnon (1993), Friederich (1968), Forsyth (1981).

26. Whelan (1996, pp. 59–60) describes how the United Irishmen, a revolutionary organisation that rose in insurrection in 1798, sought to ignore the divisiveness of the Irish past and to play down inter-communal differences. The rhetoric of inclusion therefore became built into Irish nationalism from its Enlightenment origins and became a pivotal part of not just the ideology of the national movement but of the history of the Irish twentieth century as well.

27. Many Irish had successful careers as radicals in Britain where they had gone on a mass wave of emigration in the early nineteenth century. The most notable case is the Chartist leader, Fergus O'Connor.

28. The use of the term elite does not indicate a commitment to elite theory in preference to class-theory. We use these terms as appropriate to designate a stratum holding institutional power which may or may not be of similar class origins. In other words, the composition of the elite may be based substantially on those of lower-class origins as well as middle- and upper-class recruits. In the case of the term class, we understand a more embedded structural logic in which social position and not institutional or movement power is determining. However, elites may express a class divide as occurred within the national movement, and in the subsequent history of the nation-state in the distinction between the Irish Parliamentary Party and separatist

nationalism and between Cumann na nGaedheal and Fianna Fáil
29. Irish population fell by almost 50% between 1841 and 1911, from 8.2 million to less than 4.4 million. But the demographic experience of the farmers differed from the labours dramatically: while the numbers of labourers fell by two thirds, there was a drop of one quarter of farmers (Hoppen, 1989, pp. 85–6).
30. Even by the early nineteenth century Catholics owned about one-third of total middle-class wealth (Connolly, 1985 p. 5).
31. The domination carriers of modernisation in Ireland were as we have already remarked neither the bourgeois or working-classes in the classical understanding of these terms. In this sense, neither the universalistic ideas of individual rights stemming from the Enlightenment nor the generalisation of right which was the moral foundation of the nineteenth century workers movement were predominant. Instead, a lower-middle class, communitarian model of collectively asserted or denied rights were the basis of justice. The collective assertion of rights was of course shaped by social circuits of power that severely limited ideas of justice or legitimate dissensus. The model, therefore, from the early twentieth century had pronounced authoritarian implications.
32. This can be contrasted to Denmark where change occurred much more slowly but over a longer period of time. More than 30,000 bought their farms in the late eighteenth century and the rest followed over the next century (Ostegaard, 1992, p. 15).
33. Rural conflict and violence was rife in the society attesting to continuing social divisions over economic assets and conditions, which Paul Bew describes as an 'acute division of interests' in the countryside between landlords and tenants (Bew, 1978, p. 2; Jones, 1983). This finally erupted in the Land War of 1879–82 when tenants refused to pay rents that were legally due to landlords, thus beginning the long political and constitutional processes that were to see Irish farmers owners of the land they worked early in the twentieth century.
34. The extension of the franchise in 1885 led to antagonism between labourers and farmers (Vaughan, 1994, p. 228). Much earlier, the franchise act of 1850 benefited the middle to large farmers.
35. It is beyond the scope of this book to provide an analysis of class formation and mobility patterns. But a rudimentary glance at the social and political arrangements of twentieth century Ireland reveals the dominance of the lower middle-class whether one looks, inter alia, at the sphere of political representation, taxation policy, educational curricula, and religious recruitment. For those who were excluded, penetration to lower middle-class respectability became an obsession. This process was already well in train by the end of the nineteenth century. See Lee (1989a).

CHAPTER 4

1. The terms 'actors' and 'carrier groups' are sometimes used instead of 'wings', depending on context.

2. Garvin quotes the Bishop of Limerick testifying before the Commissioner on University Education in Ireland in 1902 as describing the corporation of Limerick as being composed of 'uneducated, unenlightened working men' and of acknowledging the need 'for educated laymen who are in sympathy with them [the people], and at the same time will control them and keep them within limits' (Garvin, 1987, p. 41).

3. Rumph and Hepburn (1977) make clear that the Church in spite of this populist ideology was anything but radical on social questions once the land issue was substantially solved in the early twentieth century. It consistently adopted a negative stance on urban radicalism.

4. This subsequently remained unchanged in that after Independence the Irish Catholic Church was not established. This owed something to the tradition of non-establishment under the Union but also because the Church felt it would lose as much as it would gain under establishment by conceding certain rights to the state.

5. Paseta (1994) correctly claims that the Church lost the battle for denominational Universities in 1908. But it did have substantial influence on the curriculum and it dominated the teaching of humanities and social sciences until quite late in the twentieth century.

6. The Church supported the replacement of Parnell as leader of the Irish Parliamentary Party when he was cited as co-respondent in a divorce suit against his wife brought by a Captain O'Shea. See Chapter 5 below, where the political implications of the Church's victory over Parnell are assessed.

7. See Leerssen (1996) for an account of the interplay of Christian and nationalist symbolism in mid-nineteenth century Ireland.

8. Alter's use of this typically German term is interesting when transferred into the Irish context. The *bildungsbürgertum*, literally the cultivated German professional middle-class, developed a resentment towards metropolitan elites and culture when located, for occupational reasons, in provincial settings for which they compensated by developing a strong romantic cult of the nation. It must however be pointed out that the German use of the term refers to a sharp cultural difference between the middle and upper middle class, on the one hand, and, on the other, the lower middle class. Moreover, the German *Bildungsbürgertum* were unpolitical.

9. For a classic survey of the political history of the Irish Parliamentary Party, see O'Brien (1957).

10. The second wave of Home Rule agitation began in the 1870s under the leadership of the conservative Protestant Isaac Butt. It was not, however, until it combined the social question concerning the land with the issue of political identity that Home Rule became a mass movement. The Land Question interacted with nationalist politics in complex ways from the late 1870s to the establishment of the Irish Free State in 1922. It evolved from a campaign for justice under the landlord system concerned with issues such as security of tenure and fair rent to an outright and successful campaign to replace landlordism altogether and take over the ownership of the land.

11. The general antipathy in lower middle-class Ireland for any form of

tax increase to pay for increased government expenditure was apparent as early as the 1890s with the emergence of a powerful movement dedicated to preventing increased taxation in Ireland. This agitation led to the establishment of a Royal Commission to investigate the alleged over-taxation of Ireland. The anti-taxation movement while striking many populist chords about greater Irish poverty was essentially a middle-class movement seeking to establish a taxation regime consistent with the political goal of Home Rule and in line with their own propertied interests. The essential arguments of nationalist opinion amongst the Commission's members, amongst witnesses called to give evidence, and in the wider societal debate which continued in the early twentieth century was that Irish self-government should be established on fiscally advantageous terms because Ireland had been historically over-taxed and that an Irish Home Rule government could be guaranteed to be more prudent in spending money raised in Ireland. A later Commission, the so-called Primrose Commission which reported in 1912, actually supported the view that the British Exchequer should meet the cost of Irish pensions. The over-taxation debate when investigated closely and set in the context of the financial policies of the later Free State governments in the twenties and the thirties supports the view that amongst middle-class nationalists the goal of fiscal conservatism was well-established in the mobilisation phase of the national movement.

12. For example Foster (1989) and MacDonagh (1977).
13. Foster (1993) in an interesting collection of essays argues that cultural nationalism up to World War One, neither in its own self-understanding where it lacked a well-developed theory of separatism nor in its popular impact which he estimates to be relatively small, did not really move far beyond existing political cultural representations based on Anglophobia and confessionalism. Some aspects of this argument have definite plausibility. Cultural nationalism did not become strongly fused with separatism until the militarisation of politics from 1913 onwards and its real separatist impact depended on the extension of the suffrage and the new political circumstances in 1917–18. However, interpretations of what Foster identifies as the critical symbolic currents of Anglophobia and confessionalism became more radical in the early twentieth century as new networks and mechanisms of diffusion turned nationalism from an elite to a mass political identification. This political identification was bound up with a distinctive innovation, a radical, offensive imaginary of the nation-to-be based on the legitimation of the situation interpretations of radical nationalism which was matched and given a sense of reality by the growing political power of Catholic nationalists. Thus, while Foster is right in his inference that something qualitatively new and unprecedented happened after 1913, he understates the impact of cultural nationalism in preparing the ground for these developments. The battle of two cultures, hesitant, anglophiliac modernism and romantic, anglophobic anti-modernism appears in the conflict between Gabriel and Miss Ivors in Joyce's *The Dead* set in early twentieth century Dublin. Joyce clearly

believed that the social psychological constructions of the new nationalism were stronger than those of its opponents.

14. Leerssen (1996, p. 143) notes the building up of tension between the historical facts and the historical imagination which he attributes to the discontinuity and fragmentation of Irish historical development 'caused by its oppression at the hands of the neighbouring isle'. He describes the consequences as 'facts lost in the ruins and ravages of the past, the imagination cut adrift on swells and currents of speculation and auto-exoticism.' He goes on: 'The result was the tendency, especially among nationalists, to look back to a golden primordial Gaeldom brutally ravaged by foreign incursions to cling to the more mythical or pseudohistorical embellishments concerning Gaelic antiquity and to perpetuate Milesianisms derived ultimately from Keating and the *Lebor Gabala*.' No better description could be found of what is implied when terms like 'transcendental' or 'primoridial' are used in this text in describing certain facets of the process of historically legitimating Irish national identity.

15. The influential editor of the nationalist newspaper *The Leader* founded in 1900.

16. A large number were educated at University College Dublin.

17. Women were attracted to cultural nationalism to some extent because it was a kind of politics in which they could participate in an era in which they did not have rights of suffrage.

18. Hobsbawm (1991) refers to the extraordinary volatility of nationalist politics where situations may change in a matter of weeks or even days. This suggests that until a close analysis of Sinn Fein's organisation, symbolic productions and popular resonance is conducted for the period 1917–18 it will not be possible to be confident on the precise basis of their overwhelming electoral support in the 1918 election.

19. Cairns and Richards (1988, pp. 38–9) document how Davis supported the secular tenets of the Universities Bill introduced in 1845 while O'Connell, following the lead of the Catholic hierarchy, condemned them as Godless. The writers conclude that Davis's non-sectarian conception of nationality could not prevail in the climate of increasing sectarian division.

20. The only political action it took was a farcical enactment of 1848 (Lyons, 1973, p. 110).

21. Boyce (1991b, pp. 280–3) describes the growing intransigence of both Protestant and Catholic Ireland after the passing of the Government of Ireland Bill in 1912 which granted limited Home Rule to Ireland. Protestant Ireland refused to accept the Home Rule settlement, a refusal that soon led to an armed Volunteer Force determined to preserve Protestant Ulster from a Home Rule Ireland. This armed force led in turn to the formation of a nationalist Volunteer Force in late 1913. In the face of this growing militarisation of the political divide in Ireland, the British government was uncertain as to how to proceed. Special treatment of the mainly Protestant Ulster counties was proposed but it was unclear how this could be achieved given large Catholic minorities in these counties. In both the nature of the problem, and in

the respective intransigence of the responses to it on both sides the pattern of Irish constitutional politics in the twentieth century was formed.

22. A commitment which was fatefully reversed all over Europe in the build-up to the First World War.

23. O'Connor Lysaght (1991) describes the early years of the Free State as one of 'social counter-revolution'.

24. The legislation in 1918 confined the vote to women of thirty years of age or older.

25. These issues are taken up again in the next chapter.

CHAPTER 5

1. The literature on nationalism, in common with the literature on social movements, has tended to focus on issues of success or failure rather than effects. This reflects a concern with mobilisation rather than institutionalisation.

2. The cultural nationalist wing is not considered in this first phase as it had not achieved mature political expression. The separatist Irish Republican Brotherhood is covered in passing in the section on the Parliamentary Party. In the case of radical politics, for similar reasons, only the agrarian radicals are considered.

3. This alignment goes back to 1868 when the Church declined to condemn the Manchester Martyrs, who were members of the IRB (MacDonagh, 1983, p. 99).

4. The Church had provided an organisational basis for the other major movement for the repeal of the Union, O'Connell's mass Repeal Movement in the 1840s.

5. This was manifested relatively clearly within the long debate on the finances of Home Rule Ireland which lasted for the entire duration of the period under question. The constitutional movement, dominated by the Parliamentary Party, was hostile to the expansion of the welfare-state because of its financial implications for a Home Rule Ireland. One should note, however, that these positions were conditioned by the political exigency of demonstrating that Ireland had the financial capacity to discharge its governing responsibilities without major support from the imperial exchequer. But the link between the fiscal conservatism of the party and its social conservatism was demonstrated clearly in the continuation of the party's traditions in the first Free-State government of Cumman na nGaedheal. The most notable expression of this tradition in that government was the cut in old-age pensions.

6. According to Hutchinson (1987, p. 184) large sections of the Church were alienated by the Gaelic League's campaign against the Catholic hierarchy on the subject of compulsory Irish.

7. This pedagogical activity took place both in the schools and in the activities of the Gaelic Athletic Association (Hutchinson, 1987, p. 161).

8. Lyons (1982, p. 77) points out that the Church threw its weight against

Larkin's movement when it prevented children of starving slum children from being sent to England where their faith might be endangered.

9. The hunger strikes in Northern Ireland in the early 1980s led to a similar rise in support for the latest version of Sinn Fein.

10. The lack of support given to the strikers by the British labour movement to which they were affiliated was also important in turning the Irish labour movement to a strong pro-nationalist position.

11. The manner in the term 'communitarianism' is utilised in this book is in close association with exclusive and conventional identifications. Exclusive in the sense that only some can belong, in this case Catholic, and conventional in the sense that belonging means accepting highly codified community-specific rules. The use of the term also signifies that the republican general will that has been a feature of Irish political culture has been refracted in a Catholic nationalist direction.

12. O'Connor Lysaght (1991, p. 41) observes that the Free State's counter-revolution was a holding operation in the interests of some who had benefited from the revolutionary change in state power. As evidence, he notes how the Free State army was used to smash the Irish Transport and General Workers Union organisation of Irish workers. Hutton (1991) notes how the army and police were used against strikes organised at wage cuts in 1923 and documents the decline in the number of the Irish Transport and General Workers Union from 100,000 members in 1921 to a membership of 15,453 in 1929.

13. The very name, Sinn Fein, which means 'Us' or 'We Ourselves', encapsulated the idea of an essentialistic national Self embodying itself in political institutions and framing the new society that was emerging in its image. Sinn Fein was above all a consensus movement which succeeded in absorbing through selective assimilation the nationalist ideologies espoused by the other wings of the broader nationalist movement. It was a movement whose secret was comprehensiveness: language and culture, local government, economy and politics were all drawn together (MacDonagh, 1983, p. 65).

14. In the next chapter we will analyse how the core conservatism was associated with the first institutional wave dominated by the Church and Cumann na nGaedheal while the second under Fianna Fáil in the thirties and forties built in a small-scale corrective while heavily employing the rhetoric of equality.

CHAPTER 6

1. This is not to argue that a solution could have been found to the problem of different political cultural traditions in the context of Home Rule for Ireland. Ulster Unionists in 1912 and 1913 were themselves quite prepared to abandon constitutional politics to avoid being included in a Home Rule settlement for all Ireland. This does not alter the fact that for whatever reason the turn to violence in Irish nationalism involved an escalation that made a less polarised settlement more unlikely. Violence as a political tactic may have served the needs of

southern nationalism – much of the violence of what is called the 'War of Independence' was conducted in the extreme south of the island – but it was not likely to lead to a satisfactory outcome to the Ulster Question. This applied not just to Northern Protestants but the large Catholic population who were excluded from the new southern state under partition. The plight of fellow Catholics under partition was not a significant factor in subsequent southern politics which attests to a significant aspect of Irish nationalism, its localised differences.

2. Fanning (1983) argues for instance the question of the sovereignty of the Free State was more important than the Ulster Question, which was effectively regarded as being practically irredeemable.

3. Lee (1989b, p. 77) points out that Ireland was extremely homogeneous when compared to other relatively new states in eastern and central Europe: Romanians constituted only 72% of the country bearing their name and similarly, Poles 70%, Czechs 50%, and Serbs 43%.

4. T. W. Cosgrove, the Prime Minister, was a devout Catholic and friend of the Archbishop of Dublin, who got special permission from the Holy See to have an Alter built in his house where mass could be said (Keogh, 1994, p. 28).

5. Garvin (1996, pp. 180–1) comments that 'The Legitimacy of the state remained uncertain for a considerable time. The Free State dealt with this in several ways. Firstly, it drew upon the superabundant reserves of political legitimacy enjoyed by the Catholic Church in that period' and goes on to observe: 'The Alliance between the authoritarian, Counter-Reformation Catholic Church with the populist and egalitarian traditions of Irish nationalist democracy might seem paradoxical at first glance but was actually a new expression of an old alliance, originated by Daniel O'Connell and exported to Catholic Europe in the nineteenth century as one of the central ideas of the tradition of Christian Democracy.' While Garvin's contribution to the study of this period in this and other texts has been a major one, we take issue with his characterisation of 'populist and egalitarian traditions of Irish nationalist democracy'. Irish nationalism, as we have argued above, was certainly associated with democratisation and social mobilisation but only to a limited degree. When the major social goals of the newly propertied lower middle-class had been satisfied, Irish nationalism, while containing elements committed to social justice, became on the whole conservative. Nothing else can satisfactorily explain the construction of an unequal and authoritarian society in the period since the foundation of a separate state. In addition, we also differ from Garvin (1996) and from Prager (1986) in the extent to which we perceive Cumann na nGaedheal in the 1920s as carriers of enlightenment values. Their utilisation of confessional belonging as a principle of legitimation, their lack of respect for either the autonomy of the individual or freedom of thought, their uncertainty about the value of public debate, are examples of a compromised adherence to these values.

6. De-differentiation has been at the core of a variety of major twentieth century movements including various communist movements and contemporary religious fundamentalism (Alexander & Colomy, 1988).

7. There is extensive recent evidence of sexual abuse by clergy of young people entrusted to their care.

8. This assumed that the Free State was unhappy with partition. On the whole it was not unhappy since partition excluded the only minority large enough to require accommodation.

9. The humanities and literary criticism were to some extent exceptions.

10. An organisation promoting Irish rural community development.

11. This was especially pronounced in the post-war period. Coleman (1992, p. 74) notes than only 7.5% of married women in Ireland were in the workforce compared to 40% in most Western countries.

12. Rumph and Hepburn (1977, p. 74) describe the government's situation. The expansion of tillage might not prove as profitable as cattle-farming and the imposition of industrial tariffs was not internationally normal in the 1920s. Both measures in any case were opposed by farmers who comprised the government's main supporters in a situation where agriculture supported 70% of the population. More generally, Cumann na nGaedheal never seriously considered mass industrialisation as a strategy. This was in substantial part due to the romantic rejection of industrial society that had been at the heart of much of the Irish nationalist movement.

13. The Army Mutiny was an attempt to reorganise the IRA with the Free State's army, but was defused by Kevin O'Higgins, the Minister for Justice and a leading member of the new government. O'Higgins was assassinated in 1927. The Boundary Commission, set up to review the question of the boundary with Northern Ireland, was abandoned by 1925, when the government finally accepted the *status quo*. The abandonment of this effectively marked the official recognition of the southern state's recognition of Northern Ireland (see Prager, 1986).

14. Dunphy (1995, p. 50) notes that Cumann na nGaedheal never developed policies that would satisfy the hunger of the lower echelons of the petit-bourgeois stratum for increased prosperity and therefore handed them over to Fianna Fáil.

15. Personalism and clientelism as features of Irish political culture had emerged with the Parliamentary Party in the nineteenth century which in turn had borrowed from the patronage model of nineteenth century conservative politics.

16. In this respect too Irish conservatism borrowed from British conservatism which had increasingly turned against the state as it increased in scale and became associated with progressive social reform from the turn of the century onwards. An argument for an Irish legislature in the 1890s and the early twentieth century had been that an independent Ireland would contain the growth in total expenditure and hence preclude any necessity for rising taxation.

17. The Blueshirt Movement was the principal fascist movement (see Manning, 1987; Cronin, 1994).

18. Eamon de Valera the most significant political figure in twentieth century Ireland took part in the Easter Rising of 1916, led the first Dail established from 1918 to 1921, rejected the Anglo-Irish Treaty and fought on the Republican side in the Civil War of 1922–3. He re-entered the

Dail at the head of a newly formed party, Fianna Fáil in 1927, and became Taoiseach (Prime Minister) in 1932 with the electoral success of Fianna Fáil and remained in office for sixteen years before returning to office again in the 1950s. In contemporary retrospection de Valera is seen as the epitome of conservative Ireland and his conservative rural vision for the development of the society is much quoted as exemplifying a by now questioned identity.

19. In 1938 de Valera secured the return of the ports specified in the 1921 treaty to be occupied by the Royal Navy, thus ensuring Irish military neutrality in the Second World War.
20. O'Drisceoil (1996, p. 296) observes that war-time censorship was used to suppress dissident socially critical opinion.

CHAPTER 7

1. The Catholic presence was either dominating or strong in a whole range of voluntary associations which beyond specifically religious and political associations included associations for the provision of welfare, youth associations of all kinds, sporting associations and international charity associations.
2. The meaning of the Irish term Sinn Fein is 'ourselves alone'.
3. The term 'disenchantment' is used in the Weberian sense to signify the loss of a unified world-view as society is differentiated into systems and cultures which have different functions and different ideas of valid meaning. The term disenchantment in this text signifies the loss of religious authority over social spheres such as art, science, law, the economy, education, health, sexuality and everyday life conduct.
4. The authors of this valuable book on the whole operate with a state-centred theory in which state elites are the pivotal actors. We combine this with an additional theoretical orientations stressing the centrality of the interest projections of classes in civil society, in particular, property based interests, and also by an account of the importance of culture that is both constructivist and functionalist. See Chapter 2 for a fuller development.
5. A modernising minister in the Fianna Fáil administrations from the 1930s through to the 1950s who was a key figure in the modernisation movement of the state as Taoiseach (Prime Minister) in the 1950s and 1960s.
6. Noel Browne was a left-wing Minister of Health in the Inter-Party government that replaced Fianna Fáil in 1948 who sought to introduce, by Irish standards, radical welfare reform in the form of a Children's Allowance system but was trenchantly opposed and deposed by the Church on the grounds that his proposed reform threatened the integrity of the family.
7. Whelan et al. (1992, pp. 125–6) note the high barriers to upward mobility into the service class from origins in the industrial working class. They note that 'these barriers are of a scale sufficient to mark out Ireland as an exceptional case'.

8. The situation in Northern Ireland of the early 1970s where evident discrimination against the Catholic minority led to manifest civil strife was certainly a propadeutic to the re-emergence of the Irish 'physical force tradition'. However, beyond circumstances and legitimate grievances as political motivations for a politics of civil rights, the descent into organised violence on the Catholic side reveals traditions of militarist elitism that drew sustenance from the institutionalisation of Republican violence in the collective memory and rituals of the Irish Republic. Notable in this regard was the embarrassing over-the-top nature of the coverage of the 50th anniversary of the Easter Rising in 1966.

9. O'Halloran (1987, p. 56) argues southern views of Northern Ireland continued to express the contradiction that Northern Ireland was a British colonial garrison which properly belongs within an all-Ireland republic: 'Nationalists in effect created an artificial northern landscape peopled by stereotypes in an effort to minimise the unpalatable realities of the situation which were in conflict with their ideology'. This depiction of Northern Ireland as a British colony allowed Irish nationalists to preserve the illusion of national unity and the view that partition was a British imposition and not the result of the internal divisions of the island.

10. The tendency towards 'exporting' Irish culture is associated with the new importance attached to portraying the national heritage within the Irish Tourist industry (Brett, 1996).

11. It is widely assumed in Ireland that the opening to Europe involves a move beyond an obsessive relationship with Britain. The European path to modernity is taken to have more promise. This is certainly an arguable proposition given the current state of British society and its own ambivalence about Europe. What should not, however, be excluded from this process of reflection is whether the degree of Irish rejection of the British path to modernity was in itself justified.

12. Fine Gael by most criteria was a conservative party in the early 1970s though it liberalised substantially, but uncomfortably in relation to its electoral base, thereafter. How far remains a matter of debate though now the outlines of a more conservative and a more liberal wing can be clearly discerned.

13. This coalition in its most recent form has included the small left-wing party, Democratic Left.

14. The proposed amendment to the constitutional prohibition on divorce, the subject of the country's second divorce referendum in 1995, was only carried by a few thousand votes in spite of being supported by all the major political parties.

15. Environmental discourse is one example. The debate and politicisation of environmental issues tends to be highly contingent. High mobilisation potentials on certain emotive and immediate issues do not translate into active involvement in environmental politics.

16. This applies in particular to local politics which is dominated by the centre and has little power.

CHAPTER 8

1. Reaction to progressivism is one of the two mechanisms that Freeden (1996) identifies as central to the way in which political conservatism preserves its core values. See Chapter 5, above.
2. Habermas's idea of constitutional patriotism is a patriotism not based on ethnic origins or on community but rather one based on attachment to universalistic principles reflected in an appropriate constitutional order. The latter point is important as some in contemporary Ireland call for a new beginning with a new constitution.
3. It should be said that not only the unexplored and uncriticised potency of Irish nationalism but the equally potent and unreflective symbology of much of Northern loyalism present barriers to this political pluralism. The political rigidities and anti-federalism of the Westminster model, institutionally ingrained in the Republic as well as the UK, also acts as a barrier.

Bibliography

Alexander, J. and P. Colomy (eds) (1988) *Differentiation Theory and Social Change: Historical and Comparative Approaches* (New York: Columbia University Press).

Alter, P. (1971) *Die irische Nationalbewegnung zwischen Parlament und Revolution: Der konstitutionelle Nationalismus in Irland, 1880–1918* (Munich: Oldenburg).

Anderson, B. (1991) (Rev. edn) *Imagined Communities: Reflections on the Origin and Spread of Nationalism* (London: Verso).

Anderson, P. (1974) *Lineages of the Absolute State* (London: NLB).

Archer, M. (1988) *Culture and Agency* (Cambridge: Cambridge University Press).

Armstrong, J. (1982) *Nations before Nationalism* (Chapel Hill: University of North Carolina Press).

Aston, T. (ed.) (1965) *The Crisis in Europe, 1560–1660* (New York: Basic Books).

Aston, T. and C. Philpin (eds) (1985) *The Brenner Debate: Agrarian Class Structure in Preindustrial Europe* (Cambridge: Cambridge University Press).

Banard, T. (1990) 'Crises of Identity Among Irish Protestants, 1641–1685', *Past and Present*, 127, 39–83.

Barraclough, G. (ed.) (1992) *The Times Concise Atlas of World History* (London: Times Books).

Bartlett, R. (1993) *The Making of Europe: Conquest, Colonization and Cultural Change, 930–1350* (London: Allen Lane).

Benton, S. (1995) 'Women Disarmed: The Militarisation of Politics in Ireland, 1913–23', *Feminist Review*, 50, 148–52.

Berresford, Ellis, P. (1985) *A History of the Irish Working Class* (London: Pluto Press).

Bew, P. (1978) *Land and the National Question in Ireland, 1858–82* (Dublin: Gill & Macmillan).

Bew, P. (1987) *Conflict and Conciliation in Ireland, 1890–1910* (Oxford: Clarendon).

Bew, P. (1991) 'The Dynamics of Irish Nationalism: Review Article', *Social History*, 16, 89–94.

Bew, P. (1994) *Ideology and th Irish Question: Ulster Unionism and Irish Nationalism, 1912–1916* (Oxford: Clarendon).

Bielenberg, A. and P. O'Mahony (1998) 'An Expenditure Estimate of Irish GNP in 1907' Working Paper (Economic and Social Research Institute, Dublin).

Birnbaum, P. (1991) 'Catholic Identity and Universal Suffrage: the French Experience', *International Social Science Journal*, 43, 571–82.

Bosco, A. (ed.) (1991) *The Federal Idea: The History of Federalism from the Enlightenment*, Vol. 1 (London: Lothian Foundation Press).

Bourdieu, P. (1991) *Language and Symbolic Power* (Cambridge: Polity).

Boyce, D. (1987) 'Brahmins and Carnivores: the Irish Historian in Great Britain', *Irish Historical Studies* 25.

Boyce, D. (ed.) (1988) *The Revolution in Ireland, 1879–1923* (London: Macmillan).

Boyce, G. (1990) *Nineteenth-Century Ireland: The Search for Stability* (Dublin: Gill & Macmillan).

Boyce, G. (1991a) 'Federalism and the Irish Question', in Bosco (1991).

Boyce, G. (1991b) (2nd edn) *Nationalism in Ireland* (London: Routledge).

Boyce, G. et al. (eds) (1993) *Political Thought in Ireland since the Seventeenth Century* (London: Routledge).

Bradshaw, B. (1994) 'Nationalism and Historical Scholarship in Modern Ireland', in C. Brady (1994a).

Brady, C. and R. Gillespie (eds) (1986) *Natives and Newcomers: The Making of Irish Colonial Society, 1534–1641* (Dublin: Irish Academic Press).

Brady, C. (1991) 'The Decline of the Irish Kingdom', in M. Greengrass (ed.) *Conquest and Coalescence: The Shaping of the State in Early Modern Europe* (London: Edward Arnold).

Brady, C. (ed.) (1994a) *Interpreting Irish History: The Debate on Historical Revisionism* (Dublin: Irish Academic Press).

Brady, C. (1994b) 'Introduction' in Brady (1994a).

Brady, C. (1994c) '"Constructive and Instrumental": The Dilemma of Ireland's First "New Historians"', in Brady (1994a).

Brand, K.-W. (1992) 'Zur Neustrukturierung kollektiver Identitäten: Nationalistische Bewegungen in west- und Osteuropa', in B. Schäfers (ed.) *Lebensverhältnisse und soziale Konflikte im neuen Europa* (Frankfurt: Campus).

Breen, R., Hannan, D. F., Rottman, D. B., Whelen, C. T. (1990) *Understanding Contemporary Ireland: State, Class and Development in the Republic of Ireland* (Dublin: Gill & Macmillan).

Brett, D. (1996) *The Construction of Heritage* (Cork: Cork University Press).

Brown, T. (1985) *Ireland: A Social and Cultural History, 1922–1985* (London: Fontana Press).

Bull, P. (1988a) 'The United Irish League and the Reunion of the Irish Parliamentary Party, 1898–1900', *Irish Historical Studies*, 26, 51–78.

Bull, P. (1988b) 'Land and Politics, 1870–1903', in Boyce (1988).

Bull, P. (1993) 'The Significance of the Nationalist Response to the Irish Land Act of 1903', *Irish Historical Studies*, 28, 283–305.

Burgess, M. and A.-G. Gagnon (eds) (1993) *Comparative Federalism and Federation* (London: Harvester Wheatsheaf).

Burns, T. and Dietz, T. (1992) 'Institutionelle Dynamik: Ein evolutionarer Ansatz', *Journal für Soziale Forschung*, 32, 3/4, 283–306.

Cairns, D. and S. Richards (1988) *Writing Ireland: Colonialism, Nationalism and Culture* (Manchester: Manchester University Press).

Calhoun, C. (1982) *The Question of Class Struggle* (Oxford: Oxford University Press).

Calhoun, C. (1983) 'The Radicalness of Tradition', *American Journal of Sociology*, 88, 886–914.

Callanan, F. (1992) *The Parnell Split, 1890–91* (Cork: Cork Universty Press).

Canny, N. (1987) 'The Formation of the Irish Mind: Religion, Politics and Gaelic Irish Literature, 1580–1750' in Philipin op cit. (1987).

Canny, N. (1988) *Kingdom and Colony: Ireland in the Atlantic World, 1560–1800* (Baltimore: Johns Hopkins University Press).

Carty, R. K. (1981) *Party and Parish Pump: Electoral Politics in Ireland* (Waterloo, Canada: Wilfred Laurier University Press).

Chadwick, O. (1985) *The Secularization of the European Mind in the 19th Century* (Cambridge: Cambridge University Press).

Clark, S. (1978) 'The Importance of Agrarian Classes: Agrarian Class structure and Collective Action in Nineteenth-Century Ireland', *British Journal of Sociology*, 29, 1, 22–40.

Clark, J. C. D. (1985) *English Society 1688–1832* (Cambridge: Cambridge University Press).

Clark, S. (1971) 'The Social Composition of the Land League', *Irish Historical Studies*, 15, 447–69.

Clark, S. (1975) 'The Political Mobilisation of Irish Farmers', *Canadian Review of Sociology*, 22, 483–99.

Clark, S. (1979) *Social Origins of the Land War* (Princeton: Princeton Univeristy Press).

Clark, S. and J. Donnelly (eds) (1983) *Irish Peasants: Violence and Political Unrest, 1790–1914* (Dublin: Gill and Macmillan).

Clarke, A. (1970) 'Ireland and the General Crisis', *Past and Present*, 48, 79–99.

Clarke, D. (1985) *Church and State* (Cork: Cork University Press).

Clifford, J. (1988) *The Predicament of Culture* (Cambridge, MA: Harvard University Press).

Coleman, D. A. (1992) 'The Demographic Transition in Ireland in International Context' in Goldthorpe, J. H. and Whelan, C. T. (eds) *The Development of Industrial Society In Ireland* (Oxford: Oxford University Press).

Cohen, J. and Arato, A. (1992) *Civil Society and Political Theory* (Cambridge, MA: MIT Press).

Colley, L. (1992) *Britons: Forging the Nation, 1707–1837* (New Haven:Yale University Press).

Connolly, S. (1985) *Religion and Society in Nineteenth-Century Ireland* (Dublin: Economic and Social History Society of Ireland).

Constitution of Ireland (1937) (Dublin: Government Publications).

Corrigan, P. and D. Sayer (1985) *The Great Arch: English State Formation as Cultural Formation* (Oxford: Blackwell).

Cronin, M. (1994) 'The Socio-Economic Background and Membership of the Blueshirt Movement, 1932–5', *Irish Historical Studies*, 29, 234–9.

Crotty, R. D. (1966) *Irish Agricultural Production: Its Volume and Structure* (Cork: Cork University Press).

Cullen, L. (1976) *An Economic History of Ireland since 1600* (London: Batsford).

Cullen, L. (1983) *The Emergence of Modern Ireland: 1600–1900* (Dublin: Gill and Macmillan).

Cullen, L. (1988) *The Hidden Ireland: Reassessment of a Concept* (Dublin: Lilliput Press).

Cunnigham, H. (1981) 'The Language of Patriotism', *History Workshop*, 12, 8–33.

Curtin, N. (1985) 'The Transformation of the Society of United Irishmen into a Mass-Based Revolutionary Organization, 1794–6', *Irish Historical Studies*, 24, 463–92.

Daly, M. E. (1992) *Industrial Development and Irish National Identity, 1922–1939* (Dublin: Gill and Macmillan).

Daly, M. and D. Dickson (eds) (1990) *The Origins of Popular Literacy: Language Change and Educational Development, 1700–1920* (Dublin: Trinity College).

Davis, R. (1987) *The Young Ireland Movement* (Dublin: Gill and Macmillan).

Davis, R. R. (1988) *The British Isles, 1100–1500: Comparsions, Contrasts and Connections* (Edinburgh).

Delanty, G. (1995a) *Inventing Europe: Idea, Identity, Reality* (London: Macmillan).

Delanty, G. (1995b) The Limits and Possibility of a European Identity: A Critique of Cultural Essentialism', *Philosophy and Social Criticism*, 21, 4, 15–36.

Delanty, G. (1995c) 'Negotiating the Peace in Northern Ireland', *Journal of Peace Research*, 32, 3, 257–64.

Delanty, G. (1995d) The Revolutions in Eastern Europe: a New Social Contract?', *Contemporary Politics*, 1, 1, 74–91.

Delanty, G. (1996a) 'The Frontier and Identities of Exclusion in European History', *History of European Ideas*, 22, 2, 93–104.

Delanty, G. (1996b) 'Northern Ireland in A Europe of Regions', *The Political Quarterly*, 67, 2, 127–134.

Delanty, G. (1996c) 'Habermas and Postnational Identity: Theoretical Perspectives on the Conflict in Northern Ireland', *Irish Political Studies*, 11, 20–32.

Delanty, G. (1996d) 'The Resonance of Mitteleuropa: A Habsburg Myth or Antipolitics? *Theory, Culture and Society*, 14, 4, 93–108.

Delanty, G. (1996e) 'Beyond the Nation-State: National Identity and Citizenship in a Multicultural Society', *Sociological Research Online*, 1, 3.

Delanty, G. (1997a) 'Habermas and Occidental Rationalism: The Politics of Identity, Social Learning and the Cultural Limits of Moral Universalism', *Sociological Theory*, 15, 1, 30–59.

Delanty, G. (1997b) 'Social Exclusion and the New Nationalism: European Trends and their Implications for Ireland', *Innovation*, 10, 2.

Delanty, G. (1997c) 'Models of Citizenship: Defining European Identity and Citizenship', *Citizenship Studies*, 1, 3, 285–303.

Devine, T. and D. Dickson (1983) *Ireland and Scotland, 1600–1850* (Edinburgh: John Donald).

Dhonnchadha, M. and Dorgan, T. (1991) *Revising the Rising* (Derry: Field Day).

Donnolly, J. (1989) 'The Land Question in Nationalist Politics', in T. Hachey et al. (eds) *Perspectives on Irish Nationalism* (Lexington: University Press of Kentucky).

Dudley Edwards, R. (1977) *Patrick Pearce: The Triumph of Failure* (London: Gallanz).

Dudley Edwards, R. (1981) (2nd edn) *An Atlas of Irish History* (London: Routledge).

Dunne, T. (1982) *Theobald Wolfe Tone, Colonial Outsider* (Cork: Tower Books).

Dunne, T. (1992) 'New Histories: Beyond "Revisionism"', *Irish Review*, 12, 1–12.

Dunphy, R. (1995) *The Making of Fianna Fail: Power in Ireland, 1923–1948* (Oxford: Clarendon Press).

Eckstein, H. (1966) *Division and Cohesion in Democracy: A Study of Norway* (Princeton: Princeton University Press).

Eder, K. (1985) *Geschichte als Lernprozess?: Zur Pathogenese politischer Modernität in Deutschland* (Frankfurt: Suhrkamp).

Eder, K. (1993) *The New Politics of Class: Social Movements and Cultural Dynamics in Advanced Societies* (London: Sage).

Eisenstadt, S. N. and B. Giesen (1995) 'The Construction of Collective Identity', *European Journal of Sociology*, 26, 1, 72–102.

Ellis, S. (1985) *Tudor Ireland: Crown, Community and the Conflict of Cultures, 1470–1603* (London: Longman).

Ellis, S. (1991) 'Historical Debate: Representations of the Past in Ireland: Whose Past and Whose Present', *Irish Historical Studies*, 27, 289–308.

Ellis, S. (1994) 'Nationalist Historiography and the English and Gaelic Worlds in the Late Middle Ages', in Brady (1994a).

English, R. (1993) '"Paying no Heed to Public Clamor": Irish Republican Solipsism in the 1930s', *Irish Historical Studies*, 28, 426–39.

Evans, E. (1992) *The Personality of Ireland: Habitat, Heritage and History* (Dublin: Lilliput Press).

Eyerman, R., Jamison, A., Cramer, J. (1990) *The Making of the New Environmental Consciousness: A Comparative Study of Environmental Movements in Sweden, Denmark and the Netherlands* (Edinburgh: Edinburgh University Press).

Fanning, R. (1983) *Independent Ireland* (Dublin: Helicon).

Faughnan, S. (1988) 'The Jesuits and the Drafting of the Irish Constitution of 1937', *Irish Historical Studies*, 26, 79–102.

Fennell, D. (1989) *The Revision of Irish Nationalism* (Dublin: Open Air).

Fitzpatrick, B. (1988) *Seventeenth-Century Ireland: The Wars of Religion* (Dublin: Gill & Macmillan).

Fitzpatrick, D. (1977) *Politics and Irish Life, 1913–21: Provincial Experience of War and Revolution* (Dublin: Gill & Macmillan).

Fitzpatrick, D. (1987) 'The Geography of Irish Nationalism, 1910– 1921', in Philipin (1987) op cit.

Fizpatrick, D. (1988) *Ireland and the First World War* (Dublin: Lilliput Press).

Fitzpatrick, D. (1989) 'Ireland since 1870', in Foster (1989).

Ford, A. (1986) 'The Protestant Reformation in Ireland' in Brady, C. and Gillespie, R. (eds) *Natives and Newcomers* (Dublin: Irish Academic Press).

Forsyth, M. (1981) *Union of States: The Theory and Practice of Confederation* (New York: Holmes and Meier).

Foster, R. (1988) *Modern Ireland: 1600–1972* (London: Penguin).

Foster, R. (ed.) (1989) *The Oxford History of Ireland* (Oxford: Oxford University Press).

Foster, R. (1993) *Paddy and Mr Punch: Connections in Irish and English History* (London: Allen Lane).

Foughan, S. (1988) 'The Jesuits and the Drafting of the Irish Constitution of 1937', *Irish Historical Studies*, 26, 79–102.

Freeden, M. (1996) *Ideologies and Political Theory: A Conceptual Approach* (Oxford: Oxford University Press).

Friederich, C. (1968) *Trends of Federalism in Theory and Practice* (London: Pall Mall Press).

Gailey, A. (1987) *Ireland and the Death of Kindness: The Experience of Constructive Unionism, 1890–1905* (Cork: Cork University Press).

Galtung, J. (1990) 'Cultural Violence', *Journal of Peace Research*, 27, 291–305.

Garvin, T. (1986) 'Priests and Patriots: Irish Separatism and Fear of the Modern, 1890–1914', *Irish Historical Studies*, 25, 67–81.

Garvin, T. (1987) *Nationalist Revolutionaries in Ireland, 1858–1928* (Oxford: Clarendon).

Garvin, T. (1988) 'Great Hatred, Little Room: Social Background and Political Sentiment among Revolutionary Activists in Ireland, 1890–1922', in Boyce (1988).

Garvin, T. (1993) 'Unenthusiastic Democrats: The Emergence of Irish Democracy' in Hill, R. J. and Marsh, M. (eds) *Modern Irish Democracy* (Dublin: Irish Academic Press).

Garvin, T. (1996) *1922: The Birth of Irish Democracy* (Dublin: Gill and Macmillan).

Gellner, E. (1964) *Thought and Change* (London: Weidenfeld and Nicolson).

Gellner, E. (1983) *Nations and Nationalism* (Oxford: Blackwell).

Gerson, G. (1995) 'Cultural Subversion and the Background of the "Easter Poets"', *Journal of Contemporary History*, 30, 33–47.

Gibbons, L. (1991) '"A Shadowy Narrator": History, Art and Romantic Nationalism in Ireland, 1750–1850', in C. Brady (ed.) *Ideology and the Historians* (Dublin: Lilliput Press).

Gibbons, L. (1996) *Transformations in Irish Culture* (Cork: Cork University Press).

Giddens, A. (1985) *The Nation State and Violence* (Berkeley: University of California Press).

Giesen, B. (1993) *Die Intellektuellen und die Nation* (Frankfurt: Suhrkamp).

Gillespie, R. (1991) *The Transformation of the Irish Economy, 1550–1700* (Dublin: Economic and Social History of Ireland).

Goldring, M. (1993) *Pleasant the Scholar's Life: Irish Intellectuals and the Construction of the Nation State* (London: Serif).

Goldstein, R. (1983) *Political Repression in 19th Century Europe* (London: Croom Helm).

Goldstone, J. (1991) *Revolution and Rebellion in the Early Modern World* (Berkeley: University of California Press).

Graham, B. and S. Wood. (1994) 'Town Tenant Protest in Late Nineteenth- and Early Twentieth-Century Ireland', *Irish Economic and Social History*, 21, 39–57.

Greenfeld, L. (1992) *Nationalism: Five Roads to Modernity* (Cambridge, MA: Harvard University Press).

Habermas, J. (1984) *The Theory of Communicative Action*, Vol. 1, *Reason and the Rationalization of Society* (London: Heinemann).

Habermas, J. (1987) *The Theory of Communicative Action,* Vol. 2, *Lifeworld and System: A Critique of Functionalist Reason* (Cambridge: Polity Press).

Habermas, J. (1989a) *The Structural Transformation of the Public Sphere* (Cambridge, MA.: MIT Press).

Habermas, J. (1989b) *The New Conservatism: Cultural Criticism and the Historians' Debate* (Cambridge, MA: MIT Press).

Habermas, J. (1994) 'Struggle for Recognition in the Democratic Constitutional State', in *Multiculturalism*, edited by A. Gutmann (Princeton: Princeton University Press).

Habermas, J. (1996) 'Citizenship and National Identity', in *Between Facts and Norms* (Cambridge: Polity).

Hechter, M. (1975) *Internal Colonialism: The Celtic Fringe in British National Development, 1536–1966* (London: Routledge, Kegan and Paul).

Heslinga, M. W. (1962) *The Irish Border as a Cultural Divide* (Assen: Van Goran).

Heyck, T. (1974) *The Dimensions of British Radicalness: The Case of Ireland, 1874–95* (Urbana: University of Illnois Press).

Hill, C. (1967) *Society and Puritanism in Prerevolutionary England* (London: Weidenfeld and Nicolson).

Hill, C. (1969) *From Reformation to Industrial Society* (London: Penguin).

Hill, J. (1980) 'The Intelligentsia and Irish Nationalism in the 1840s', *Studia Hibernia*, 20, 73–109.

Hill, J. (1988) 'Popery and Protestantism, Civil and Religious Liberty: The Disputed Lessons of Irish History, 1690–1812', *Past and Present*, 118, 96–129.

Hilton, R. (ed.) (1976) *The Transition from Feudalism to Capitalism* (London: NLB).

Hirst, D. (1994) 'The English Republic and the Meaning of Britain', *Journal of Modern History*, 66, 451–86.

Hobsbawm, E. and T. Ranger (eds) (1983) *The Invention of Tradition* (Cambridge: Cambridge University Press).

Hobsbawm, E. (1991) *Nations and Nationalism since 1789* (Cambridge: Cambridge University Press).

Holton, R. L. (1985) *The Transition from Feudalism to Capitalism* (London: Macmillan).

Hooghe, L. (1992) 'Nationalist Movements and Social Factors: a Theoretial Perspective', in Coakley, J. (ed.) *The Social Origins of Nationalist Movements: The Contemporary West European Perspective* (London: Sage).

Hopkinson, M. (1988) *Green Against Green: The Irish Civil War* (Dublin: Gill and Macmillan).

Hoppen, R. H. (1984) *Elections, Politics and Society in Ireland, 1832–85* (Oxford: Clarendon).

Hoppen, T. (1989) *Ireland Since 1800: Conflict and Conformity* (London: Longman).

Horsman, R. (1976) 'Origins of Racial Anglo-Saxonism in Great Britain Before 1850', *Journal of the History of Ideas*, 27, 3, 387–410.

Houston, R. (1992) *The Population History of Britain and Ireland* (London: Macmillan).

Hroch, M. (1985) *Social Preconditions of Nationalist Revival in Europe: A*

Comparative Analysis of the Social Composition of Patriotic Groups among the Smaller European Nations (Cambridge: Cambridge University Press).

Hroch, M. (1993) 'From National Movement to the Fully-Formed Nation: the Nation-building Process in Europe', *New Left Review*, 198, 1–20.

Hughes, A. (1991) *The Causes of the English Civil War* (London: Macmillan).

Hume, J. (1988) 'Europe of the Regions', in Kearney (1988).

Hutchinson, J. (1987) *The Dynamics of Cultural Nationalism: The Gaelic Revival and the Creation of the Irish Nation State* (London: Allen & Unwin).

Hutchinson, J. (1994) *Modern Nationalism* (London: Fontana).

Hutchinson, J. (1996) 'Irish Nationalism', in G. Boyce and A. O'Day (eds) *The Making of Irish History: Revisionism and the Revisionist Controversy* (London: Routledge).

Hutton, S. (1991) 'Labour in the Post-Independence Irish State: An Overview', in Hutton, S. and Stewart, P. (eds) *Ireland's Histories: Aspects of State, Society and Ideology* (London: Routledge).

Inglis, T. (1987) *Moral Monopoly: The Catholic Church in Modern Irish Society* (Dublin: Gill and Macmillan).

Jacobsen J. K. (1994) *Chasing Progress in the Irish Republic: Ideology, Democracy and Dependent Development* (Cambridge: Cambridge University Press).

Jay, R. (1989) 'Nationalism, Federalism and Ireland', in M. Forsyth (ed.) *Federalism and Nationalism* (Leicester: Leicester University Press).

Jones, D. (1983) 'The Cleavage between Graziers and Peasants in the Land Struggle, 1890–1910', in S. Clark and Donnelly (1983).

Kearney, H. (1989) *The British Isles: a History of Four Nations* (Cambridge: Cambridge University Press).

Kearney, R. (ed.) (1988) *The Irish Mind* (Dublin: Wolfhound Press).

Kearney, R. (1997) *Post-Nationalist Ireland*: *Politics, Culture, Philosophy* (London: Routledge).

Keating, P. (1992) 'Cultural Values and Entrpreneurial Action: The case of the Irish Republic', in J. Melling and J. Barry (eds) *Culture in History: Production, Consumption and Values in Historical Perspective* (Exeter: University of Exeter).

Keating, P. and D. Desmond. (1993) *Culture and Capitalism in Contemporary Ireland* (Aldershot: Avebury).

Keenan, D. (1983) *The Catholic Church in Nineteenth-Century Ireland* (Dublin: Gill and Macmillan).

Kendle, J. (1989) *Ireland and the Federal Solution: The Debate over the United Kingdom Constitution, 1870–1921* (Montreal: McGill University Press).

Kennedy, F. (1975) *Public Social Expenditure in Ireland* (Dublin: Economic and Social Research Institute) Broadsheet No. 11.

Kennedy, L. (1983) 'Farmers, Traders and Agricultural Politics in Pre-Independence Ireland', in S. Clark and Donnelly (1983).

Keogh, D. (1994) *Twentieth-Century Ireland: Nation and State* (Dublin: Gill and Macmillan).

Kiberd, D. (1991) 'The Elephant of Revolutionary Forgetfulness', in Dhonnchadha and Dorgan (1991).

Kiberd, D. (1995) *Inventing Ireland* (London: Cape).

Kitschelt, H. (1986) 'Political Opportunity Structures and Political Protest:

Anti-Nuclear Movements in Four Democracies', *British Journal of Sociology*, 16, 57–85.

Kramnick, I. (1990) *Republicanism and Bourgeois Radicalness* (Ithaca: Cornell University Press).

Lahiff, E. (1988) *Industry and Labour in Cork, 1890–1921* (M.A. Thesis: University College, Cork).

Larkin, E. (1972) 'The Devotional Revolution in Ireland', *American History Review*, 77, 3, 625–52.

Larkin, E. (1975) *The Roman Catholic Church and the Creation of the Modern Irish State, 1878–86* (Philadelphia: American Philosophical Society).

Larkin, E. (1978) *The Roman Catholic Church and the Plan of Campaign in Ireland, 1886–1988* (Cork: Cork University Press).

Larkin, E. (1987) *The Consolidation of the Roman Catholic Church in Ireland, 1860–1870* (Chapel Hill: University of North Carolina Press).

Lee, J. (1989a) *The Modernisation of Irish Society, 1848–1918* (Dublin: Gill and Macmillan).

Lee, L. (1989b) *Ireland, 1912–1985* (Cambridge: Cambridge University Press).

Leerssen, J. (1996) *Rememberance and Imagination: Patterns in the Historical and Literary Representation of Ireland in the Nineteenth Century* (Cork: Cork University Press).

Leighton, C. (1994) *Catholicism in a Protestant State: A Study of the Irish Ancien Régime* (London: Macmillan).

Lennon, C. (1994) *Sixteenth-Century Ireland: The Incomplete Conquest* (Dublin: Gill & Macmillan).

Luhmann (1982) *The Differentiation of Society* (New York: Columbia University Press).

Lyons, F. S. L. (1973) *Ireland since the Famine* (London: Fontana).

Lyons, F. S. L. (1979) 'The Minority Problem in the 26 Counties', in F. MacManus (ed.) *The Years of the Great Test, 1926–39* (Cork: Mercier Press).

Lyons, F. S. L. (1982) *Culture and Anarchy in Ireland, 1890–1939* (Oxford: Oxford University Press).

McBride, I, (1993) 'The School of Virtue: Francis Hutcheson, Irish Presbyterians and the Scottish Enlightenment', in Boyce et al. (1993).

McCrone, D. et al. (eds) (1989) *The Making of Scotland: Nation, Culture and Social Change* (Edinburgh: Edinburgh University Press).

MacDonagh, O. (1977) *Ireland: The Union and its Aftermath* (London: Allen and Unwin).

MacDonagh, O. (1983) *States of Mind: A Study of Anglo-Irish Conflict, 1780–1980* (London: Allen and Unwin).

Macfarlane, A. (1978) *The Origins of English Individualism* (Oxford: Blackwell).

McFarland, E. (1994) *Ireland and Scotland in the Age of Revolution* (Edinburgh: Edinburgh University Press).

Macmillan, G. (1993) *State and Authority in Ireland: The Foundations of the Modern Irish State* (London: Macmillan).

McMinn, R. (1981) 'Presbyterianism and Politics in Ulster, 1871–1906', *Studia Hibernia*, 21, 127–46.

Maier, C. (1988) *The Unmasterable Past: History, the Holocaust, and German National Identity* (Cambridge, MA: Havard University Press).

Mair, P. (1987) *The Changing Irish Party System* (London: Pinter).

Mandle, W. (1987) *The Gaelic Athletic Association and Irish Nationalist Politics* (London: Christopher Helm).

Manning, M. (1987) *The Blueshirts* (Dublin: Gill & Macmillan).

Manseragh, N. (1968) *The Irish Question* (London: Unwin).

Mayer, A. (1981) *The Persistance of the Old Regime* (London: Croom Helm).

Marshall, T. H. (1992) *Citizenship and Social Class* (London: Pluto).

Melman, B. (1991) 'Claiming the Nation's Past: The Invention of an Anglo-Saxon Tradition', *Journal of Contemporary History*, 26, 575–95.

Molony, J. N. (1977) *The Emergence of Political Catholicism in Italy* (London: Croom Helm).

Morgan, A. (1988) *James Connolly: a Political Biography* (Manchester: Manchester University Press).

Morgan, K. (ed.) (1988) *The Oxford History of Britain* (Oxford: Oxford University Press).

Morris, A. and C. McClurg Mueller (eds) (1992) *Frontiers in Social Movement Theory* (New Haven: Yale University Press).

Mosse, G. (1975) *The Nationalization of the Masses* (New York: Fertig).

Mosse, G. (1985) *Nationalism and Sexuality* (Madison: University of Wisconsin Press).

Murphy, C (1989) *The Women's Suffrage Movement and Irish Society in the Early Twentieth Century* (London: Harvester).

Murphy, C. (1993) 'Suffragists and Nationalism in early Twentieth Century Ireland', *History of European Ideas*, 16, 4, 1009–15.

Murray, P. (1993) 'Irish Cultural Nationalism in the United Kingdom State: Politics and the Gaelic League, 1900–18', *Irish Political Studies*, 8, 55–72.

Newsinger, J. (1995) 'The Catholic Church in Nineteenth-Century Ireland', *European History Quarterly*, 25, 247–67.

Nolan, M. (1975) 'The Influence of Catholic Nationalism on the Legislature of the Irish Free State', *Irish Jurist*, 10, 128–69.

O'Buachalla, B. (1993) 'James our True King: The Ideology of Irish Royalism in the Seventeenth Century', in Boyce et al. (1993).

O'Brien, C. C. (1957) *Parnell and His Party* (Oxford: Clarendon Press).

O'Brien, C. C. (1972) *States of Ireland* (London: Hutchinson).

O'Brien, C. C. (1994) *Ancestral Voices: Religion and Nationalism in Ireland* (Dublin: Poolbeg).

O'Callaghan, M. (1984) 'Language, Nationality and Cultural Identity in the Irish Free State, 1922–7', *Irish Historical Studies*, 24, 226–45.

O'Cathain, D, (1993) 'An Irish Scholar Abroad: Bishop John O'Brien of Cloyne and the Macpherson Controversy' in O'Flanagan, P. and Buttimer, C. G. (eds), *Cork History and Society: Interdisciplinary Essays on the History of an Irish County* (Dublin).

O'Ceallaigh, D. (1994) *Reconsiderations of Irish History and Culture* (Dublin: Leirmheas).

O'Connor-Lysaght D. R. (1991) 'A Saorstat is born', in Hutton, S. and Stewart, P. (eds) *Ireland's Histories: Aspects of State, Society and Ideology* (London: Routledge).

O'Connor, E. (1992) *A Labour History of Ireland, 1824–1960* (Dublin: Gill and Macmillan).

O'Drisceoil, D. (1996) *Censorship in Ireland; 1913–1945: Neutrality, Politics and Society* (Cork: Cork University Press).

O'Halloran, C. (1987) *Partition and the Limits of Irish Nationalism* (Dublin: Gill and Macmillan).

O'Leary, B. and McGarry, J. (1993) *The Politics of Antagonism: Understanding Northern Ireland* (London: Athlone Press).

O'Mahony, P. and Mullally, G. (1995) 'Ecological Communication in Ireland', in *Final Report of Project Framing and Communicating Environmental Problems: Public Discourse and the Dynamics of Environmental Conflict in Europe*, co-ordinated by K. Eder (Brussels: CEC).

O'Mahony, P. (1996) 'European Identity and European Society'. (Unpublished manuscript).

O'Neil, P. (1976) 'The Reception of German Literature in Ireland, 1750–1850', *Studia Hibernia*, 16, 122–39.

O'Neil, P. (1977) 'The Reception of German Literature in Ireland, 1750–1850', *Studia Hibernia*, 17, 91–106.

O'Tuathaigh, M. A. G. (1994) 'Irish Historical "Revisionism": State of the Art or Ideological Project?', in C. Brady (1994a).

Ostergaard, A. (1992) 'Peasants and Danes: The Danish National Identity and Political Culture', *Comparative Studies in Society and History*, 34, 3–27.

Paseta, S. (1994) *Education, Opportunity and Social Change: The Development of a Catholic University Elite in Ireland, 1879–1922* (Unpublished Ph.D. dissertation, Australian National University).

Parker, G. and L. Smith. (eds) (1985) *The General Crisis of the Seventeenth Century* (London: Routledge and Kegan Paul).

Peillon, M. (1992) *Contemporary Irish Society* (Dublin: Gill & Macmillan).

Perkin, H. (1989) *The Rise of Professional Society: England since 1880* (London: Routledge and Kegan Paul).

Petler, D. (1985) 'Ireland and France in 1848', *Irish Historical Studies*, 24, 493–505.

Philipin, C. (ed.) (1987) *Nationalism and Popular Protest in Ireland* (Cambridge: Cambridge University Press).

Pimley, A. (1988) 'The Working Class Movement and the Irish Revolution, 1896–1923', in Boyce (1988).

Pittock, M. (1991) *The Invention of Scotland: The Stuart Myth and the Scottish Identity, 1638 to Present* (London: Routledge).

Pocock, J. (1982) 'The Limits and Divisions of British History: In Search of the Unknown Subject', *American Historical Review*, 87, 2, 311–36.

Prager, J. (1986) *Building Democracy in Ireland: Politcal Order and Cultural Integration in a Newly Independent Nation* (Cambridge: Cambridge University Press).

Richter, M. (1985) 'The Interpretation of Medieval Irish History', *Irish Historical Studies*, 24, 289–98.

Richter, M. (1988) *Medieval Ireland: The Enduring Tradition* (Dublin: Gill and Macmillan).

Rogowski, R. (1985) 'Causes and Varieties of Nationalism: A Rationalist Account', in Tiryakin, E. and Rogowski, R. (eds) *New Nationalisms of the Developed West* (London: Allen & Unwin).

Rucht, D. (1982) 'Neue soziale Bewegungen oder Die Grenzen burokrakischer Modernisierung', *Politisches Vierteljahresschrift*, 13, 272–92.

Rumpf, E. and A. Hepburn (1977) *Nationalism and Socialism in Twentieth-Century Ireland* (Liverpool: Liverpool University Press).

Ryan, L. (1994) 'Women without Votes: the Political Strategies of the Irish Suffrage Movement', *Irish Political Studies*, 9, 119–139.

Schmitt, D. E. (1973) *The Irony of Irish Democracy: The Impact of Political Culture on Administrative and Democratic Political Development in Ireland* (Lexington: Lexington Books).

Skillington, T. G. (1993) *Contextual Considerations in Accounting for the Robustness of the Irish (and more generally) British and German Environmental Movements* (M.A. thesis: University College, Cork).

Skillington, T. (1997) 'Politics and the Struggle to Define. A Discourse Analysis of the Framing Strategies of Competing Actors in a "New" Participatory Forum', *British Journal of Sociology* 48, 3.

Skocpol, T. (1994) *Social Revolution in the Modern World* (Cambridge: Cambridge University Press).

Smith, J. (1992) *The Men of No Property: Irish Radicals and Popular Politics in the Late Eighteenth Century* (Dublin: Gill and Macmillan).

Snow, D. et al. (1986) 'Frame Alignment Processes, Micromobilisation, and Movement Participation', *American Sociological Review*, 51, 464–81.

Snow, D. and R. Benford. (1988) 'Ideology, Frame Resonance, and Participant Mobilisation' in Klandermans, B., Kriesi, H. and Tarrow, S. (eds) *International Social Movement Research*, vol. 1, *From Structure to Action* (London: JAI Press).

Snow, D and R. Benford. (1992) 'Master Frames and Cycles of Protest', in Morris and McClurg (1992).

Spring, D. (ed.) (1977) *European Landed Elites in the 19th Century* (Baltimore: Johns Hopkins University Press).

Strauss, E. (1941) *Irish Nationalism and British Democracy* (London: Methuen).

Stewart, A. T. Q. (1977) *The Narrow Ground: Aspects of Ulster, 1609–1969* (London: Faber and Faber).

Swart, W. (1995) 'The League of Nations and the Irish Question: Master Frames, Cycles of Protest, and Master Frame Alignment', *The Sociological Quarterly*, 36, 3, 465–81.

Tambini, D. (1996) 'Convenient Cultures: Nationalism as Political Action in Ireland (1890–1920) and Northern Italy (1980–1994)' (Ph.D. dissertation, European University Institute).

Tarrow, S. (1992) 'Mentalities, Political Cultures, and Collective Frames: Constructing Meanings through Action', in Morris and McClurg (1992).

Tarrow, S. (1994) *Power in Movement: Social Movements, Collective Action and Politics* (Cambridge: Cambridge University Press).

Tarrow, S. (1995) 'Cycles of Collective Action: Between Moments of Madness and the Repertoire of Contention', in M. Tragott (ed.) *Repertoires and Cycles of Collective Action* (Durham: Duke University Press).

Thompson, E. P. (1991) *The Making of the English Working Class* (London: Penguin).

Thompson, W. I. (1982) *The Imagination of an Insurrection: Dublin, Easter 1916* (West Stockbridge, MA: Lindisfarne Press).

Thompson, J. B. (1984) *Ideology and Modern Culture* (Cambridge: Polity).

Thuente, M. (1994) *The Harp Re-Strung: The United Irishmen and the Rise of Irish Literary Nationalism* (New York: Syracuse University Press).

Tilly, C. (1993) *European Revolutions, 1492–1992* (Oxford: Blackwell).

Tilly, C. (1993/94) 'Social Movements as Historically Specific Clusters of Political Performances', *Berkeley Journal of Sociology*, 38, 1–30.

Tipton, L. (ed.) (1972) *Nationalism in the Middle Ages* (New York: Holt, Rinehart and Winston).

Tiryakian, E. and Nevitte, N. (eds) (1985) *New Nationalisms of the Developed West* (London: Allen and Unwin).

Townshend, C. (1981) 'Modernisation and Nationalism: Perspectives in Recent Irish History', *History*, 66, 233–43.

Townshend, C. (1989) 'The Making of Modern Irish Public Culture', *Journal of Modern History*, 61, 535–54.

Travers, P. (1988) *Settlements and Divisions: Ireland 1870–1922* (Dublin: Criterion Press).

Vaughan, W. E. (1984) *Landlords and Tenants in Ireland, 1848–1904* (Dublin: Economic and Social History Society of Ireland).

Vaughan, W. E. (1994) *Landlords and Tenants in Mid-Victorian Ireland* (Oxford: Clarendon).

Walker, B. (1972/3) 'The Irish Electorate', *Irish Historical Studies*, 27, 359–71.

Walker, G. (1990) 'Irish Nationalism and the Uses of History', *Past and Present*, 126, 203–14.

Ward. A. (1994) *The Irish Constitutional Tradition: Responsible Government and Modern Ireland, 1782–1992* (Dublin: Irish Academic Press).

Watkins, S. (1991) *From Provinces into Nations: Demographic Integration in Western Europe, 1870–1960* (Princeton: Princeton University Press).

Weber, E. (1979) *Peasants into Frenchmen: The Modernisation of Rural France, 1870–1914* (London: Chatto and Windus).

Whelan, K. (1996) *The Tree of Liberty: Radicalism, Catholicism and the Construction of Irish Identity 1760–1830* (Cork: Cork University Press).

Whelan, C. T., Breen, R., Whelan, B. J. (1992) 'Industrialisation, Class Formation and Social Mobility in Ireland', in Goldthorpe, J. H. and Whelan, C. T. (eds) *The Development of Industrial Society in Ireland* (Oxford: Oxford University Press).

Whyte, J. (1980) *Church and State in Modern Ireland, 1923–1979* (Dublin: Gill & Macmillan).

Williams, G. (1982) *When was Wales?* (London: Croom Helm).

Winstanley, M. (1984) *Ireland: The Land Question, 1800–1922* (London: Methuen).

Wuthnow, R. (1992) 'Cultural Change and Sociological Theory', in Haferkamp, H. and Smelser, N. J. (eds) *Social Change and Modernity* (Berkeley: University of California Press).

Index